INCLUSIVE BUSINESS MODELS

Inclusive Business Models talks about organizations that employ principles of business to address the needs of the poor. It takes an analytical approach to derive insights about business models by comparing with other inclusive models seen within the same sector and through comparisons with models from a different sector. This cross-sector comparison, especially with a number of case studies, would enable readers to cumulate their learning, and act as a guide to management students, practising managers and entrepreneurs for understanding and analysing any business model that intends or claims to be inclusive. This book is beneficial for students of entrepreneurship, social enterprises and human resource management. Sections of this book would be relevant for courses on social enterprises, developmental economics and inclusive business models taught globally, given that India today has emerged as a hotbed of experiments and innovations to deal with the problems of poverty and inequality.

Sourav Mukherji is Professor of Organizational Behaviour and IIMB Chair Professor of Excellence at the Indian Institute of Management, Bangalore. His research interest is inclusivity and social enterprises – businesses that address the needs of the poor in a financially sustainable manner. In this domain, he has published several case studies and papers in academic and practitioner-oriented journals.

INCLUSIVE BUSINESS MODELS

Transforming Lives and Creating Livelihoods

SOURAV MUKHERJI

CAMBRIDGE
UNIVERSITY PRESS

CAMBRIDGE
UNIVERSITY PRESS

University Printing House, Cambridge CB2 8BS, United Kingdom

One Liberty Plaza, 20th Floor, New York, NY 10006, USA

477 Williamstown Road, Port Melbourne, VIC 3207, Australia

314 to 321, 3rd Floor, Plot No.3, Splendor Forum, Jasola District Centre, New Delhi 110025, India

103 Penang Road, #05–06/07, Visioncrest Commercial, Singapore 238467

Cambridge University Press is part of the University of Cambridge.

It furthers the University's mission by disseminating knowledge in the pursuit of education, learning and research at the highest international levels of excellence.

www.cambridge.org Information on this title: www.cambridge.org/9781108491082

© Sourav Mukherji 2021

This publication is in copyright. Subject to statutory exception and to the provisions of relevant collective licensing agreements, no reproduction of any part may take place without the written permission of Cambridge University Press.

First published 2021

Printed in India by Thomson Press India Ltd.

A catalogue record for this publication is available from the British Library

Library of Congress Cataloging-in-Publication Data
Names: Mukherji, Sourav, author.
Title: Inclusive business models : touching lives, creating livelihoods / Sourav Mukherji.
Description: Cambridge, United Kingdom ; New York, NY : Cambridge
    University Press, 2021. | Includes bibliographical references and index.
Identifiers: LCCN 2021005341 (print) | LCCN 2021005342 (ebook) | ISBN 9781108491082
    (hardback) | ISBN 9781108811316 (paperback) | ISBN 9781108867399 (ebook)
Subjects: LCSH: Social responsibility of business--India. | Social entrepreneurship--India. |
    Poverty--India. | Public-private sector cooperation--India. | Sustainable development--India.
Classification: LCC HD60.5.I4 M85 2021 (print) | LCC HD60.5.I4 (ebook) | DDC 658.4/08--dc23
LC record available at https://lccn.loc.gov/2021005341
LC ebook record available at https://lccn.loc.gov/2021005342

ISBN 978-1-108-49108-2 Hardback
ISBN 978-1-108-81131-6 Paperback

Cambridge University Press has no responsibility for the persistence or accuracy of URLs for external or third-party internet websites referred to in this publication, and does not guarantee that any content on such websites is, or will remain, accurate or appropriate.

To all my students who inspire me to be a better teacher.

CONTENTS

TABLES

FIGURES

PREFACE

Harish Hande, the founder of SELCO, was my senior at Indian Institute of Technology (IIT) Kharagpur. Our paths crossed a decade later when I learnt that Harish, having completed his PhD, was building an organization that would provide solar lights to poor villagers in his home state of Karnataka. I travelled with him in upcountry Karnataka and saw first-hand how the lack of access to energy created challenges in the lives of villagers and how the work that Harish was planning to do was a lifesaver for them. Having grown up in a town and later staying in a city, I had little familiarity with the life in villages. I had never seen as much darkness in my life as I witnessed in those villages at night. Harish was lighting up their lives. I came back awestruck and inspired. But I did not fully comprehend what Harish meant when he said he would create a business where he would sell solar lights to the villagers. Looking at their economic conditions, I could not imagine how the villagers were going to pay Harish. Should he not raise funds from charitable institutions and just donate these lights, I wondered.

After I joined Indian Institute of Management (IIM) Bangalore as a faculty member, I focused on researching about Indian multinationals competing in international markets. While I continued to follow Harish's and SELCO's journey with admiration, it was quite distant from what I was teaching and researching as an academician. Around 2007, at an international conference in Bratislava, I met Sahba Sobhani from the United Nations Development Programme (UNDP) who explained to me the concept of inclusive markets and gave the example of SELCO. Sahba was looking for academics who could write case studies on organizations that created inclusive business models. Suddenly, I remembered what Harish had tried to explain to me almost a decade ago – how it was possible to address the needs of the poor by building a financially sustainable business – and things started to make sense.

I told Sahba that I would write a case on SELCO and I started my research in this domain. As I learnt about many inclusive businesses, I got further motivated to know more about them. I was keen to make inclusive business models central to my academic pursuits and decided that the best way to do it was to offer an elective on the topic in the MBA curriculum at IIM Bangalore. The plan was to develop several case studies that would provide me with deeper insights as well as first-hand familiarity with social enterprises and entrepreneurs. I named the elective 'Inclusive Business Models' to make it distinctive from a few other courses like 'Social Entrepreneurship' and 'Economics and Development' that were already being offered by my colleagues. I wanted to focus on business models that address the needs of the poor, quite similar to what SELCO was doing, as were others who I came to know about during my work for UNDP. I planned my course to be entirely based on case studies about inclusive businesses from various domains, such as healthcare, education and energy access. The teaching objective was to educate students about how to apply management principles to solve problems of poverty. But a deeper intention was also to sensitize them about the sad reality of poverty and inequality in our country, and how some inspirational individuals were applying their knowledge to alleviate the situation. I hoped that the course would open the minds of the students to new possibilities and motivate them to apply their knowledge and use their privileges to solve societal problems.

As I started developing the cases, I found useful allies among my colleagues, notably Professor P. D. Jose, who co-authored several of the cases, and Professor Gita Sen, an economist who kindly agreed to co-teach the elective with me and provide inputs in developmental economics since I had no academic background in the domain.

I have been teaching this elective at IIM Bangalore since 2010 and writing case studies on organizations pursuing inclusive business models. Despite IIM Bangalore being perceived as a business school and its students keen to join the for-profit sector, I have received encouraging response from the students year after year, who have subscribed to this course in large numbers and given me enthusiastic feedback. My understanding about this domain has also evolved during this period. While I was a strong advocate of inclusive business models to solve problems of the poor in the initial years, I have now also realized the models' limitations and how other forms of organizations, such as the not-for-profit or the government, have complementary roles to play. Meanwhile, even SELCO's model has evolved where, apart from the private limited entity about which I have written in the first case, they have started a foundation through which Harish and his team do some fascinating work.

This book, coming after a decade of my teaching and doing research, is an important milestone. It has helped me crystallize many thoughts that crossed my mind while teaching and discussing the cases with students. The case studies that we publish are accompanied by teaching notes, which are only shared with faculty members. Teaching notes provide answers to questions raised in the cases as well as provide insights. However, if one is not a student in a class where the case is being taught, one will never get to know about these answers and insights. Therefore, I have written this book as a reading companion, where the journey of ten organizations that have adopted inclusive business models have been described in a semi-formal story form, followed by some of the insights and learning that can be derived from their journey. The stories are not substitutes for the actual case studies, many of which I have published through the Harvard Business Publishing Education portal. Therefore, faculty members who teach using cases should use the actual case studies and provide this book as additional reading. Faculty members who do not use case method of teaching can directly use this book to structure their lectures and discussions in class.

However, this book is not only for faculty members but intended for a larger audience, anyone who is interested in the domain of inclusive businesses or social entrepreneurship but does not have the time or intention to sit through a postgraduate-level class. This book will inform the readers about the experiments and innovations that are happening in this domain. For such readers, the analysis towards the end of the chapters or the framework developed towards the end of the book may not be of much interest. But this book should give them a reasonable idea about how inclusive businesses are different from not-for-profits or corporate social responsibility.

This book will also be useful to entrepreneurs, especially those who are working in the developmental or social sector. Based on my experience of teaching them in executive education programmes at IIM Bangalore and elsewhere, I have realized that many of them are not sure about the organization form they should adopt – whether it should be a for-profit, inclusive business or a non-profit model. The cases that I discuss should provide them with substantial information and examples on the trade-offs involved in choosing one organizational form over other as well as the challenges of maintaining the duality of creating social impact and being financially sustainable. In almost all the cases, I have written about how the idea of the organization came to the founders and how they gave shape to it through their entrepreneurial venture and how it evolved into a social enterprise. This, I hope, will provide budding social entrepreneurs with a realistic idea of what it takes to bring an idea of doing good to society to its fruition. While each of these organizations, their founders, leaders and employees continue to inspire me, I do not present any of them as success stories. In fact, some of them are likely to fail. But that should not take away from them the sincerity they had devoted in creating and sustaining these organizations and the innovations they came up with to solve tough problems. Any entrepreneurial venture has a high chance of failure; social entrepreneurship possibly more so. I agree with Harish when he says that any model of an inclusive business, even if that is considered a success, cannot be copied by someone else. They can only teach about the failures that preceded such success, so that others do not repeat the same mistakes and enhance their learning curve. I would go one step further and add that such models show possible pathways to overcome a seemingly intractable problem. However, above all, they inspire.

I hope that is what it does to every reader who picks up this book.

ACKNOWLEDGEMENTS

This book would not have been possible if my employer, IIM Bangalore, had not provided me with the academic freedom to experiment by doing research about and offering a course on inclusive business models. There were doubts whether such a course would have any relevance in an MBA programme and whether there would be enough interest among the students to subscribe to it. However, IIM Bangalore believes that *we will not know unless we try*, and successive Directors and Deans have lived up to this entrepreneurial spirit of the institute. Therefore, I am grateful to the academic leaders of IIM Bangalore who have encouraged me and provided me with the necessary support.

Six chapters of this book are based on case studies that I had written with my co-authors. The cases and their authorship have been provided on the next page. I thank all of them – P. D. Jose, Bringi Dev, Kunal Basu, Sridhar Pabbisetty, Caren Rodriguez and Milena Muller – for helping me write the cases, sharing with me the pleasures and travails of case-writing and for giving me their consent to use the cases as basis for the chapters in this book.

No creative endeavour can come to its fruition without the support of family members. Therefore, I owe it to the two ladies in my life, my mother Indrani Mukherjee and my wife Suparna Bhattacharya, who in their own spoken and unspoken ways teach me to be sensitive to society, to give my best to any initiative that I undertake and who, by taking care of me, ensure that I can begin every day in my life with high energy and positivity.

Finally, I thank the team at Cambridge University Press (CUP) for helping me convert the idea of this book into a finished product, especially Anwesha Rana for giving me the courage to start and Jinia Dasgupta and Aniruddha De for guiding me at every step towards the finish line. Working with the CUP team has been a delightful experience.

Chapter Reference	Name of Case	Authors
2	Vaatsalya Healthcare: Affordable Healthcare in Proximity	S. Mukherji and P. D. Jose
5	LaborNet: Empowering Informal Sector Laborers	S. Mukherji, C. Rodriguez and S. Pabbisetty
6	SELCO: Harnessing sunlight to Create Livelihood	S. Mukherji and P. D. Jose
8	Reliance Retail: Creating Social Value through Banana Supply Chain	S. Mukherji, K. Basu and M. Muller
9	IDE Nepal: Creating and Ecosystem for Development	S. Mukherji and P. D. Jose
11	GNFC's Neem Project: Creating a Blueprint for Social Business	S. Mukherji and B. Dev

1

INTRODUCTION

This book is about organizations that positively impact the lives of the poor through their businesses. Therefore, I call their business models *inclusive.*[1] Normally, businesses are not supposed to worry about poverty. The raison d'être of businesses, by which I imply for-profit commercial enterprises, is to maximize shareholders' wealth. We assume that it is the responsibility of the government and some not-for-profit organizations to address the needs of the poor. Therefore, the organizations that are the subject matter of the book are a relatively new breed and somewhat paradoxical – they want to solve one of mankind's toughest problems, poverty, by deploying business principles. They want to create a positive social impact without depending on grants or charities; they want to maintain financial sustainability without maximizing profitability. What is the need for such organizations, how they can achieve, if at all, this dual objective and what have been the challenges in their journeys so far are worth knowing, debating and disseminating because this innovative organization form might just be an answer to many of the open questions that the world faces today in its battle with growing economic inequality despite rising global prosperity.

This book is mostly written in the context of India with one case study from Nepal and a few references to Bangladesh. However, I have discussed the subject matter of this book with several international audiences and most of them could derive insights from these that could be translated to their own

---

[1] I do not claim any originality here. I was introduced to the idea that businesses can be inclusive through a chance assignment that I had received from the United Nations Development Programme (UNDP).

contexts, such as Connecticut, Johannesburg, Sao Paolo or Seville. Therefore, I am hopeful that the inclusive business models that I describe and analyse in this book will have important lessons for anyone who wants to engage with the problem of poverty, irrespective of their geographic location.

INDIA TODAY: POISED FOR A DEMOGRAPHIC DIVIDEND OR A DEMOGRAPHIC DISASTER?

India has made rapid economic progress during the last 25 years, post the liberalization of its economy. However, one problem that remains intractable is that of poverty. While estimates vary, there are still a significant number of people in India who are below or live perilously close to the poverty line. It was assumed that with the economic progress of the country, levels of poverty would reduce through the *trickle-down effect*.[2] During the past 25 years, poverty in India has reduced in absolute terms, but it has not reduced enough.[3] India is home to nearly half of the world's malnourished children, with 1.7 million of them dying even before reaching the age of one. Our primary education system is derelict, resulting in India having the largest number of illiterate adults in the world,[4] since less than 40 per cent of Indian children complete school education and only 75 per cent reach middle school (standard V). Moreover, data from recent studies indicate that even students who attend

---

[2] Loosely stated, this implies that when the economically privileged gain in an economy, their increased income and wealth eventually filter down to all sections of the society, benefitting even the economically underprivileged.

[3] According to the International Labour Organization's *India Wage Report 2018*, during the period 1993–2014, India's gross domestic product (GDP) increased four times but the average daily wage adjusted for inflation increased only twice (Das 2019).

[4] Given India's population, it is not too difficult to become 'world leading' in any of these parameters. However, it points to the fact that India is the worst performing among nations of comparable characteristics, notably China (size) and the United States (form of government – democracy).

school develop proficiencies in reading, writing and mathematics that are far below students from other comparable Asian countries. While 65 per cent of India's population lives in villages, contribution of agriculture to the gross domestic product (GDP) has declined to 17 per cent, indicating a high degree of explicit and disguised unemployment in rural India. This results in millions migrating from villages to cities every year in search of odd jobs, contributing to India's large pool of informal labour, who do not have any social security, are often at the receiving end of the law and, being exploited by opportunistic contractors, have little chance of breaking through the vicious cycle of poverty. In the absence of weather forecasting tools or risk hedging mechanisms, Indian farmers need to depend on the vagaries of nature to grow their crops. Even when they are lucky to have a good harvest, inefficient supply chains, characterized by multiple intermediation and wastages, result in the farmers receiving a very small percentage of the price paid by the consumer.

Historically, India viewed its large population to be a disadvantage, given its limited resource position. However, towards the latter part of the last century, the narrative about India's population took a positive turn. India realized that a large portion of the population was young, comprising people who would earn a living to support not only themselves, but also the children and the elderly. While a large population can be a burden, a young population can be an advantage in driving the economic growth of a nation. Therefore, India started talking about 'demographic dividend' and it was estimated that by 2030, India would be the only country in the world to have a favourable demographic ratio, where the working age population would outnumber those that it needed to support. However, what got lost in this narrative was the fact that a large young population does not get automatically translated into a productive workforce. Enough opportunities need to be created in the economy and the young population needs to be healthy, educated and skilled to take advantage of such opportunities before the demography can start paying dividends in terms of economic growth. The employment and livelihood generation scenario in India at present is far from encouraging, with a growing gap between the number of jobs being created in the economy and number of people joining the labour force. With healthcare and education systems that fail to effectively reach a large section of the population, the potential demographic advantage can turn into a demographic disaster.

INCLUSIVE BUSINESSES FILL
INSTITUTIONAL VOID

What is the way out of this potential disaster? Surely, there is no silver bullet, no single solution. Many institutions will need to work assiduously and collaboratively for India to deal with these myriad challenges. Traditionally, markets, the domain of for-profit organizations, fail to address the needs of the poor because of a combination of factors, such as their objective of profit maximization and the limited ability of the poor to pay. Thus, it is the government who is expected to serve the needs of the poor, for example, by running free schools and hospitals or by giving highly subsidized fertilizers. But the government is not able to meet all the needs of the poor, and charitable institutions or not-for-profits step in those areas, either on their own or in collaboration with the government. The charitable institutions have their own methods of raising money and many such institutions have been doing commendable work in India, serving various economic and social needs of the poor, during the past several decades. However, even they are not enough to serve the needs of the poor in a large country like India. Apart from a growing demand for their services, charitable organizations are also feeling pressure from their traditional sources of funding – the donors. Donors are increasingly raising questions about the way their funds are being deployed by the not-for-profits and about the kind of impact that is being created. International donors and foundations are also wondering whether India is the best country for them to deploy funds, given India's economic progress during the past decades. Is their money better deserved by a country like India that boasts a USD 3 trillion economy and has 11 of world's 50 richest people, or should they donate money to charitable organizations working for the poor in nations such as Ethiopia, Nepal and Haiti?

In his book *The White Man's Burden*, the author William Easterly (2007), a fierce critic of foreign aid to Third World countries, comes up with an interesting comparison. He writes that the developed world has spent trillions of dollars in foreign aid over several decades trying to eradicate malaria, which essentially involves reaching medicine worth 12 cents to the mother of a newborn. Yet they have not been able to win the war over malaria.[5] On the other hand, on a single day of 16 July 2005, the publisher of *Harry Potter* books delivered 9 million copies of the sixth edition to eager fans in the United States of America (USA) and the United Kingdom (UK). At some level, this comparison seems preposterous. The developed markets are geographically concentrated, have easier accessibility and the *Harry Potter* fans had access to information so that they could be at the right place at the right time. The mothers in sub-Saharan Africa, where most of the malarial deaths persist, are much more difficult to reach and might even need a fair bit of convincing to get those medicines. Such differences notwithstanding, both of these – delivery of 9 million copies of books on a single day across the world and supplying medicines for malaria to mothers – are complex supply chain problems that involve multiple handoffs and coordination between different organizations. While the for-profit commercial organization seems to be doing it well, the results are mixed for the development sector. And the problem is not the lack of financial resources. At least in this case, there seems to be enough donor money being spent to solve the problem.

What then is the real problem? It may be that of accountability. The hierarchy of for-profit organizations makes every individual accountable for a measurable aspect of work and there are financial incentives for achieving their assigned tasks. One can assume that in managing the supply chain of malaria medicines, accountability might be diffused and while there are several individuals who are highly motivated to eradicate malaria, in the absence of financial incentives and penalties, it is difficult to control the behaviour of those who are not so motivated or those who are prone to being opportunistic. This is not to suggest that everything that is done by the for-profit commercial enterprises achieves success, and complex coordination can always be achieved through hierarchies and financial incentives. However, there are *certain aspects* of the for-profit enterprises, especially those pertaining to efficiency and

---

[5] About 200 million cases of malaria are reported every year resulting in 500,000 deaths (Desmon 2018). About 70 per cent malarial deaths occur in children below 5 years of age (WHO 2019).

complex coordination, that the development sector can learn from and deploy to achieve their objectives. To a large extent, inclusive business models intend to do that. By imposing on themselves the discipline of financial sustainability akin to for-profit enterprises, they intend to adopt those aspects of business that can make them more efficient in leveraging their resources and more effective in achieving their objectives.

One may argue that it is impossible to selectively adopt some of the business principles of for-profits and yet maximize social impact instead of maximizing shareholders' wealth. Such half-way houses eventually get stuck in the middle! The examples that we will be talking about in this book will show that, at least in some cases, it is possible. Is it difficult? Of course it is, possibly more difficult than running either a for-profit or a not-for-profit organization? That is the reason why accounts of these organizations must be told. They are innovative, they have taken the untrodden path and their difficult journeys are inspirations in themselves, irrespective of where they are able to reach. But that alone is not the purpose of this book. The insights that we will derive from these cases should be useful for anyone interested in or engaged with the social sector to understand both the usefulness and limitations of applying business principles in solving problems of the poor. Such insights and learning should also be useful for students of management and business practitioners to understand the role of various institutions and economic agents in the larger ecosystem comprising businesses, government and society. To employ management terminology, the only difference between an inclusive business model and a for-profit commercial model is a reversal of objective functions. While the objective function of the for-profit is to maximize financial profitability without doing any harm to society, the objective function of inclusive business is to maximize social welfare without making financial losses.

BOTTOM OF THE PYRAMID: OPPORTUNITIES AND CONTROVERSIES

Dr M. Yunus and Dr C. K. Prahlad are among the pioneers of the idea of addressing the needs of the poor in a financially sustainable manner. Yunus, whose contribution we will discuss in detail in a later chapter on inclusive finance, created Grameen Bank in Bangladesh that adopted an innovative model for lending to the poor, mostly women (Yunus and Jolis 1998). Traditionally, the poor were viewed as highly risky to lend to and, therefore, no bank would like to have them as their customers. Through Grameen Bank, Yunus showed the world that not only were the poor bankable, but they were often better in paying back their loans than the traditional well-off customers of the banks. More interestingly, Grameen Bank was a financially sustainable bank that received no grants or donor money after 1998, proving the point that one can run a micro-lending organization addressing the financial needs of the poor in a business-like for-profit mode. Inspired by their success, Grameen and Yunus went on to create many other social businesses in domains as diverse as telecommunication and dairy, some of which succeeded while others failed. However, Yunus became a firm believer and an evangelist of the inclusive business model, which, he believed, addressed many of the shortcomings of grant-based and philanthropic organizations.

According to Yunus, grants and philanthropies create a relationship of dependency between the giver and the receiver, and thus reduce the sense of responsibility and ownership. People who receive charity spend a lot of time chasing things that were given for free rather than spending their energy and skill on doing things on their own. Such relationships also encourage corruption, suppress voice, accountability and transparency, and make the poor vulnerable to exploitation. On the other hand, inclusive businesses make better use of resources at their disposal. He also saw a lot of value in motivating for-profit enterprises to pursue social objectives by structuring such initiatives in a business-like manner, rather than asking them for grants and donations. In the book *Creating a World Without Poverty*, Yunus (2007) described how the French multinational Danone got motivated to create nutrition fortified yogurt that would be sold to the poor in Bangladesh. Because making yogurt was well aligned with Danone's main line of business, they took it as a business challenge rather than doing charity and were able to tap into the wealth of talent and knowledge that existed within Danone for the project. The initiative also created a powerful meaning of work for the employees of Danone when they realized how their work was going to address a larger societal problem of nutrition and hunger in a country like Bangladesh. Such experiments made

7

Yunus conclude that inclusive business models, when applied within the context of for-profit organizations, can be a powerful way of leveraging their talent and keeping their employees motivated. In Chapter 11, I describe a similar initiative undertaken by an Indian public sector company, Gujarat Narmada Valley Fertilizers & Chemicals (GNFC), which has been able to create a small inclusive business within itself that is creating livelihood opportunity for half a million men and women who are economically underprivileged.

Prahlad was a Professor of Strategy at Ross School of Business at the University of Michigan when he wrote an influential book titled *The Fortune at the Bottom of the Pyramid: Eradicating Poverty through Profits* (Prahlad 2004). CK, as he was fondly called, became globally renowned for his *Harvard Business Review* paper written with G. Hamel, 'The Core Competency of the Organization', and subsequently was an advisor to several multinational corporations in the USA. Towards the end of the last century, these corporations realized that their traditional customer bases in North America and Western Europe were no longer growing and they needed to look for new markets in nations such as Brazil, India and China. CK, having grown up in India and travelled extensively in these countries, understood that while these markets were indeed large, they presented a very different kind of opportunity because a significant number of people in these countries were poor. His calculations indicated that there were about 4 billion people in these markets who earned less than USD 1,500 annually, which he called the 'bottom of the (economic) pyramid'. He hypothesized that if for-profit enterprises could create products and services suitable for these people, it would present them with a huge opportunity. Even if consumers at the bottom of the pyramid could not individually pay high prices for the products and services, they represented a 'fortune' because by their sheer numbers, they would enable organizations to make enough profit. And in the process, such consumers, who until then were underserved, would get the benefit of having products and services of high quality.

CK's thesis caught the imagination of the for-profit organizations because he was able to talk their language, such as markets and profitability, even while he argued that their products would serve the needs of the poor and thus eradicate poverty. He cited examples of Aravind Eye Hospital (we will discuss the Aravind model in the chapter on inclusive healthcare) doing thousands of cataract surgeries free of cost for the poor even while being financially profitable and organizations creating one-rupee shampoo sachets that enabled a village girl to use it for a single wash of her hair. Very often, the poor have a cash-flow problem and are, therefore, unable to afford a full bottle of shampoo. But, CK argued, if organizations are innovative in creating single-serve products like the shampoo sachet, many consumers at the bottom of the pyramid will be able to afford it. CK was careful to tell the organizations that accessing such markets would not be easy because these markets were characterized by poor infrastructure, information asymmetry and absence of enabling institutions, such as banks and financial institutions. Therefore, over and above customizing their products, organizations planning to address these markets will need to worry about improving access, influencing aspirations and catalysing buying power. Despite such investments, he argued, organizations will be able to make profits as the numerous examples that he cited in his book proved.

While the for-profit organizations became excited by CK's dream of eradicating poverty through profits, CK received a fair share of criticism for being unrealistic. His colleague Professor Anil Karnani (2007) described CK's hypothesis as a combination of 'harmless illusion and dangerous delusion'. He argued that for none of the businesses that CK cited was there evidence that they were profitable on their own. Many of CK's examples, such as that of single-serve, increased convenience and not affordability and CK failed to consider their real costs, such as environmental damage caused by small plastic pouches. Moreover, unleashing the sleek marketing machinery of for-profit enterprises on an economically vulnerable population might unnecessarily increase their desire for products that they do not need, resulting in them making poor choices. Thus, while there should be no objection to for-profit enterprises trying to be innovative in addressing the markets at the bottom of the pyramid, it was wrong to say that such activities would help to eradicate poverty. Though it is difficult to discount Professor Karnani's well-researched and analytically rooted criticisms, CK must be credited for his ability to make poverty a board room discussion topic for for-profit enterprises, which motivated many of them to seriously look at these markets in a more realistic manner.

PLAN FOR THIS BOOK

Where do we stand now, almost two decades after Yunus and CK laid before the world a blueprint for addressing the needs of the poor in a financially sustainable manner? We have not found a universally effective model, neither have we found any easy solutions. However, there have been innumerable experiments by organizations and entrepreneurs to marry these two seemingly disparate objectives of creating social impact and achieving financial sustainability, which have refined our understanding of what is possible and what is not. The case studies in this book are testimony to that. I have personally written most of the case studies that I discuss in this book, which involved in-depth interviews with the founders, employees and other stakeholders. I had known some, such as Harish Hande of SELCO, even before I had heard of and started to understand inclusive business models, while others, such as Ram and Smita of Rang De, have become good friends. This has enabled me to see their organizations evolve, from social start-ups to social enterprises, and has given me the opportunity to know about their challenges, struggles and triumphs from close quarters. I have tried to bring all of that to you so that you appreciate the complexities of creating and managing businesses with such hybrid objectives even while you get inspired by the journeys of these extraordinary men and women who created businesses not with the objective of making money but with the sole desire and passion for making this world a better place for its most vulnerable and neglected population, the poor.

As I do in my course of a similar name, I devote each of the chapters to a specific sector, such as healthcare, education and informal labour, and describe the challenges of creating an inclusive business model in that sector through an anchor case study. An introductory section provides some macro-level information about the sector, which is followed by a detailed case study. Most of the cases are written such that the readers are able to understand the evolution of the organization, the various decisions that it took along its journey, the challenges that it faced and how it was able to overcome those challenges, if at all. I end each of the chapters with some discussion about how the organization added value, what the key drivers of its success were and what might be some of its challenges in the future. In some cases, I compare the anchor organization with some other inclusive businesses.

In the following chapter, I discuss inclusive healthcare through the case study of Vaatsalya Hospitals, which planned to deliver low-cost primary healthcare in semi-urban and rural locations. By establishing a chain of low-cost hospitals, Vaatsalya intended to bring healthcare close to patients in semi-urban and rural India, thereby reducing their total cost of healthcare. While initially successful, Vaatsalya faced challenges of scaling up its business model, which was essential to make it financially viable. I end the chapter by comparing Vaatsalya's model with that of Aravind Eye Hospitals and Narayana Health to explain the three pillars of inclusive healthcare, namely availability, affordability and accessibility.

In Chapter 3, I talk about inclusive models in education through the case study of Gyan Shala. Gyan Shala's innovation comprises making fundamental changes in the delivery of education that reduces costs and makes education accessible to children from very poor households. Their model, having parallels with that of Aravind and Narayana hospitals, provides important insights about how to achieve good quality in delivering a service despite reducing the cost of operations. I end the chapter by discussing the reasons why it is far more difficult to create inclusive business models in education than it is in healthcare. Chapter 4 talks about the importance of microfinance in alleviating poverty through the anchor case of Rang De, an Indian pioneer in peer-to-peer lending. A lot of controversies in microfinance exist because of the high interest rates that are charged to the poor. Rang De leveraged their information technology platform to reduce transaction costs and to reach out to social investors that reduced their borrowing costs. As a consequence, they could lend to the poor at possibly one of the lowest interest rates charged anywhere across the world.

More than 90 per cent of India's labour force works in the informal sector, a significant part of which comprises migrant labourers. They are poor, underpaid and exploited, work under inhospitable conditions and are often at the receiving end of law enforcement agencies. The anchor case of Chapter 5 is LaborNet, an organization that helps informal sector labourers by providing them skills that enhance their livelihood opportunities. They also provide the labourers with identity proofs and access to financial services. Finally, their technology platform connects the labourers to potential employers. While LaborNet's services were adding considerable value to the lives of the labourers, as an organization LaborNet struggled to become financially viable, largely because of demand–supply conditions in the labour market. Their struggles thus provide us with insights about the trade-offs between value creation and financial viability that inclusive business models have to face.

The anchor case in Chapter 6 is that of SELCO, an organization that provides solar lights to the poor. The poor in India do not have access to affordable and non-polluting sources of energy and SELCO customizes its products to address their needs pertaining to livelihood and day-to-day living. SELCO's case highlights the challenges of selling a product to the poor. Not only should the product be customized to the specific needs, but the organization also needs to arrange for suitable financing mechanisms and back their sales with a responsive service network. SELCO's case is an ideal example of a business model that simultaneously addresses the challenges of poverty and environmental sustainability, even while itself being financially sustainable, an objective termed as the triple bottom line of being able to serve the needs of people, planet and profitability (Elkington 2018).

Chapter 7 describes the work of Hasiru Dala Innovations (HDI), an organization that is working to create sustainable livelihood opportunities for waste pickers. Most big cities in India face the problem of processing its waste and Hasiru Dala has created a business model that can solve this problem by delivering high quality service to bulk waste generators even while enhancing the income of the waste pickers. The case reveals that waste management is a difficult and complex sector for any inclusive business to operate in, largely because it falls at the intersection of various stakeholders, including the government, and HDI presents a good example of how to maintain a fine balance among the various interest groups even while maintaining focus on the welfare of the waste picker who is at the bottom of the economic and social pyramid. I discuss in this chapter briefly about HDI's sister organization, Hasiru Dala Trust, that focuses on providing social justice to waste pickers through policy advocacy. This discussion gives us an opportunity to understand the complimentary role that an inclusive business and a not-for-profit can play in creating a positive impact on the lives of the poor.

The next three chapters talk of business models that solve problems of the poor that are endemic in rural settings, such as inefficient supply chain of farm products, inadequate physical resources and other enabling mechanisms that are essential to increase farm income and lack of employment opportunities. Chapter 8 describes the efforts of Reliance Retail in establishing an efficient procurement process of fruits from rural India that resulted in greater income for the farmers as well as delivered better quality of fruit to the urban customers. The case exemplifies the role that a large for-profit corporation can play in creating an inclusive business model if they are prepared to make the necessary investment to overcome the inherent problems of supply chain, such as inefficiency and wastage. Reliance's case is interesting because their investment in supply chain was directly relevant for their main line of business, which ensured that they could devote enough time and attention to design the supply chain and achieve the results that they desired.

Chapter 9 talks of the work of a not-for-profit, International Development Enterprises (IDE), that provides a variety of agricultural extension services to small-holder farmers of Nepal which improves farmers' income. Starting with low-cost technology for irrigation, IDE evolved into an ecosystem builder by making impactful interventions in the input and output markets as well as enabling marginal farmer communities to become self-sufficient. IDE Nepal serves as an example of how a developmental organization can create financial sustainability among marginalized communities, even while it is structured as a not-for-profit.

RuralShores, the anchor case of Chapter 10, has taken business process outsourcing operations to rural India. It is an example of involving the poor in delivering service, a task more challenging than involving them in product supply chain. By creating service centres in rural India, RuralShores promises to address a fundamental problem of the Indian economy – lack of employment opportunities in Indian villages, home to more than 800 million people. The case shows that enhanced employment opportunities in villages have resulted in empowering women, who are able to support their families financially and thus able to resist pressures of getting married off at a young age.

The final case in the book talks of another inclusive business that is incubated by a commercial enterprise. GNFC, a public sector chemicals and fertilizer organization, created livelihood opportunities for thousands in rural Gujarat by creating a business out of neem seed collection, extraction and using neem oil to manufacture soaps and other consumer goods. The promises and challenges of this model, termed as social business by Yunus, is the focus of this chapter. In contrast to Reliance Retail as discussed in Chapter 8, production and selling of neem-oil-based consumer goods was not the main line of business for GNFC. Therefore, even if their business was inclusive in nature, I discuss how not being their main line of business could create some serious challenges in scaling up the business as well as being sustainable in the long run.

In Chapter 12, the concluding chapter, I summarize our learning from the various cases and develop a schematic to represent the role played by inclusive business models in society. Our ideas about addressing the needs of the poor have evolved over the years, from considering the poor as recipients of charity (we did not discuss this much in the book) to considering the poor as potential customers (several cases, such as Gyanshala, Vaatsalya and SELCO, discussed in the book) to creating livelihood for them by involving them in the production of goods and services (as exemplified in the cases of RuralShores, Reliance, GNFC and Hasiru Dala) and finally providing the poor with capabilities that enable them to make choices. Many inclusive business models may not address this dimension of capability building as their focus, though elements of it are found in models that work towards empowering marginalized communities, as in the case of IDE Nepal, or providing them skills, such as with LaborNet. I next summarize, based on learning from the cases, the various measures that organizations have taken to address the 'life' (for example, education, healthcare, energy access) and 'livelihood' needs (skills, credit, market access) of the poor, what the key questions are that need to be answered by a business model if it wants to sell products or services to the poor and what the key challenges are that need to be overcome if one intends to create an inclusive model that involves the poor in the value chain. In the end, I present a schematic that explains the role of different kinds of organizational forms in addressing the needs of the poor – the not-for-profits, the for-profits, the governments and inclusive business models. Apart from explaining the unique position of inclusive business models, the schematic makes the larger point that all these organizations have an important part to play if we want to solve the problem of poverty and inequality, possibly mankind's toughest challenge till date.

2

VAATSALYA HOSPITALS

Affordable Healthcare in Proximity

This case describes the evolution of Vaatsalya Hospitals – a network of hospitals, set up in small towns and cities in the southern Indian state of Karnataka. In India, good quality healthcare services are mostly provided by private hospitals that are located in large cities and focus on tertiary care. Nearly 800 million Indians living in semi-urban and rural India have little or no access to high quality healthcare services at affordable prices. Vaatsalya was founded by two doctors, Dr Ashwin Naik and Dr Veerendra Hiremath, in 2004 to fill this gap. They decided to provide good quality primary and secondary healthcare to semi-urban and rural India by setting up a network of low-frills and low-price hospitals. In their four-and-a-half years of operation, Vaatsalya established nine hospitals across seven districts in Karnataka, created a capacity of more than 450 beds and treated close to 175,000 patients, making it the largest chain of its kind. The case describes the various challenges that Vaatsalya faced and the different ways in which it overcame them in the process of establishing a financially sustainable business model.

STATE OF HEALTHCARE IN INDIA

The inadequacies of the Indian healthcare system cause 1 million Indians to die every year and leave 700 million without any access to specialized care. While more than three quarters of the Indian population lives in villages and small towns, 80 per cent of specialist doctors are located in urban areas.[1] As a result, patients from semi-urban and rural India are forced to choose, more often than not, between the local unqualified practitioner and the free treatment provided at the nearest government-run hospitals that are characterized by poor quality equipment, unhygienic conditions and perennial absence of appointed doctors and hospital staff. A survey of government-run healthcare centres revealed that there was a high rate of absenteeism among doctors (43 per cent), nurses (40 per cent) and pharmacists (30 per cent) (Muralidharan, Chaudhury and Hammer 2011). Likewise, researchers found the infrastructure in Indian healthcare facilities to be more deficient than that of many countries in sub-Saharan Africa, which are poorer than India (Bajpai 2014).

As and when patients realize that neither of these two options – the local quack or the government hospital – is going to provide them with the necessary cure, they undertake long journeys to reach hospitals in big cities. Sometimes, the delay in getting proper medical attention can result in irreversible damage to their conditions. Even when they are lucky to be cured, the total time and resources that they spend in the process leave them economically impaired. Ill health and high healthcare cost have been found to be one of the key reasons of poverty in rural India. An incidence of a major illness is often enough to obliterate an entire life's savings or to condemn an individual to a lifetime of indebtedness. A World Bank report on Indian healthcare in 2002 noted that

> one episode of hospitalization is estimated to account for 58 per cent of per capita annual expenditure, pushing 2.2 per cent of the population below the poverty line. 40 per cent of those hospitalized have to borrow money or sell assets.

The Indian healthcare system is largely driven by the private sector. India ranks 171 in the world for public healthcare spending. While 5.2 per cent of its GDP is spent on healthcare, the government only spends 0.9 per cent

---

[1]   'Emerging Markets Report: Health in India', PricewaterhouseCoopers, 2007; ISI Analytics, Healthcare Industry, 1H 2010. According to the Economic Survey of 2009–10, only 13 per cent of the rural population has access to a primary healthcare centre.

and the private sector accounts for the remaining 4.3 per cent. A majority of the private sector focuses on the most profitable tertiary segments, leaving a large unmet demand in the primary and secondary segment. This demand–supply mismatch is depicted in Figure 2.1. Dr Zachariah, a former professor at Christian Medical College, Vellore, one of the leading hospitals in India, echoed a similar philosophy when he wrote,

> The Indian medical system is like an iceberg. The part that gets most recognition is the relatively small tertiary care segment with advanced technology and highly specialized medical personnel. But in truth, this narrow apex of the profession makes little difference to whether every pregnant mother will deliver safely, whether every child will grow into a healthy adult or how long that adult will live without morbidity. The foremost prerequisite is the availability of physicians with multiple competencies within easy reach of one's home and one's purse, and capable of resolving most of the common needs and emergencies. (Zachariah 2009)

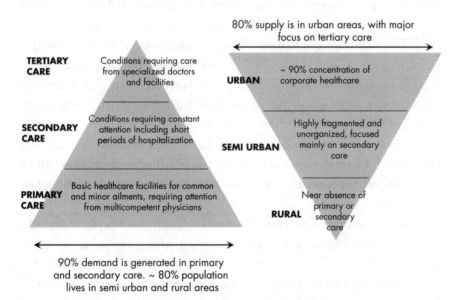

Figure 2.1 Demand–Supply Mismatch in India's Healthcare System

Source: Representative diagram created by the author based on descriptions and data commonly available from secondary sources such as KPMG report (2015).

Ashwin and Veerendra wanted Vaatsalya Hospitals to address this need of providing high quality primary and secondary healthcare services within easy reach of rural and semi-urban population at affordable prices.

EVOLUTION

Ashwin and Veerendra were roommates at Karnataka Medical College in Hubli.[2] After completing his bachelor's course in medicine, Ashwin spent six years in the USA, initially studying and later working for Celera Genomics, decoding human genome. In 2002, he came back to India, where he joined the founding team of Triesta Sciences in Bengaluru, a clinical research organization that conducted advanced genomic research in the field of oncology. While Triesta initially started collecting data from large urban hospitals, it soon moved to hospitals in smaller cities and towns. It was during his visits to the smaller cities that Ashwin became aware of the acute shortage of basic healthcare facilities there, driven largely by unavailability of medical practitioners. He was intrigued by the fact that despite a large unmet demand for quality healthcare in these small towns and cities, doctors, even those that belonged to these cities, migrated to larger cities and metros for employment. On enquiring with his friends, Ashwin learnt that doctors faced great difficulties in establishing their practices in smaller towns and cities because those places lacked the basic infrastructure and technology[3] that they would need to deliver their services. If they wanted to practise what they had learnt in medical colleges, they needed to build the healthcare infrastructure from the ground up, as well as attract other doctors to build a team that was necessary to address the basic healthcare needs of the target population.

It was around this time that Ashwin once again met his old roommate, Veerendra, who, having specialized in hospital administration from ASCI,

---

[2] Hubbali or Hubli is a city in the state of Karnataka.

[3] Infrastructure and technology refer to facilities such as emergency room, operation theatre and medical equipment necessary for delivering primary and secondary care.

Hyderabad, was working in Malaysia. The duo started discussing the idea of setting up a hospital that could address the unmet demand of healthcare in Indian hinterlands. Ashwin recalled,

> We realized that there was not only an opportunity to do good, but also to have a financially sustainable business, because there was capacity and willingness to pay if we offered the right services at the right price.

In 2004, they both quit their jobs and started off with a pilot project. Their idea was to select a small town, build a large hospital and attract good doctors. However, they soon realized that given the size of the problem, one hospital in a town will not have much impact – they needed to have a model that could be replicated across several towns and small cities, so that they were able to cater to a larger spectrum of the underserved population. They also decided to focus on primary and secondary healthcare and not on tertiary healthcare. Even though tertiary healthcare was the most profitable segment, it accounted for only 10 per cent of the total volume in India, with primary and secondary healthcare accounting for 60 per cent and 30 per cent respectively. Ashwin and Veerendra reasoned that availability of physicians at the primary and secondary care levels could make the maximum impact on the state of healthcare, and a well-functioning primary and secondary care system would reduce the demand on the tertiary care system, thereby reducing the overall cost of healthcare. Moreover, by not catering to tertiary care they were able to de-risk their employment model, since the availability of specialist doctors needed for running a tertiary care hospital was far less compared to doctors needed for primary and secondary care.

They, however, found it difficult to raise money for their healthcare venture. While investors and venture capitalists in India were willing to fund business ventures related to information technology, start-up hospitals were not considered worthwhile. Therefore, Ashwin and Veerendra made emotional appeals to friends and relatives, many of whom were from small towns and villages, for funding their venture. They were able to raise about USD 150,000 from such angel investors and Vaatsalya was set up as a private limited company in November 2004. In February 2005, the first of the Vaatsalya Hospitals was opened in Hubli.

Table 2.1 Vaatsalya's Source of Funds

EQUITY		INR Million
	Oasis Capital	190
	Seedfund	50
	Avishkar	27.2
	Angel Investors	7.6
DEBIT		
	State Bank of India	69

Source: Data was provided by Vaatsalya.

Subsequently, by the middle of 2005, Aavishkaar India Micro Venture Capital Fund decided to invest an additional USD 150,000 for two more facilities in Gadag and Karwar. As Vineet Rai, CEO of Aavishkaar India, pointed out,

> We've been investing in rural businesses for 8–9 years and Vaatsalya offered a compelling business proposition. It was a real initiative and I don't think very many initiatives like this exist in India.

In April 2008, Vaatsalya obtained its second round of funding, USD 1.5 million, from Avishkaar and Seedfund, another venture fund, to roll out 10 more hospitals within a year. Anand Lunia, CFO of Seedfund, said,

> They were not profitable when they came to us. But we liked the price point that they were addressing and decided to fund them to test the model.[4]

In May 2009, Vaatsalya obtained a funding of USD 4.2 million from Luxemburg-based Oasis Fund. Table 2.1 provides Vaatsalya's source of funds. Forty per cent of Vaatsalya's equity was owned by institutional investors who expected financial returns from their investments in the long run. Therefore, almost since its inception, the founders of Vaatsalya had been focused on

---

[4] Quoted in *Outlook*, 11 July 2009, 'Low Cost Cures', available at http://business.outlookindia.com|Low-Cost Cures (accessed 2 September 2009).

Table 2.2 Vaatsalya's Financial Performance (2005–08)

	2005–06	2006–07	2007–08
Outreach (number of patients)	9,361	17,270	42,300
Revenue (in INR million)	2.4	4.5	20
Operating Expenses (in INR million)	5.1	7.4	40
Profits (in INR million)	-3.4	-4.3	-20

Source: Data was provided by Vaatsalya.

Note: According to a report in 2013, Vaatsalya served approximately 100,000 patients per quarter in their outpatient departments and 3,500 patients per month in their inpatient departments, across its 17 hospitals. Vaatsalya had 1,500 employees and approximately 1,200 beds, including 100 intensive care unit beds, neonatal intensive care unit beds and surgical intensive care unit beds.

making their venture commercially viable and profitable, even though the purpose of Vaatsalya's existence had been to address the unmet healthcare needs of a largely impoverished population. Vaatsalya' s hospitals in Gadag and Hubli soon turned profitable and the founders acknowledged that support from strategic investors such as Aavishkaar and Oasis was instrumental in reorienting Vaatsalya from a social organization to a social enterprise that could balance social objective with financial viability. Table 2.2 gives Vaatsalya's financial performance.

HOSPITAL OPERATIONS

Vaatsalya is a Sanskrit word that signifies the unconditional love that a mother has for her child. Vaatsalya Hospitals started by focusing on healthcare for mother and child. Thus, most of their hospitals catered to the basic specialization of gynaecology and paediatrics, which were complemented by general surgery and general medicine. This enabled them to address about 70 per cent of the needs of the local community.[5] Table 2.3 and its note explain the various specialties addressed by Vaatsalya Hospitals.

---

[5] Approximately 90 per cent of healthcare needs are in the primary and secondary segments, out of which most major ailments are addressed by

Table 2.3 Details about Vaatsalya Hospitals as on October 2009

Hospital	Hubli	Gadag	Bijapur	Mandya	Raichur	Hassan	Mysore	Gulbarga	Shimoga
Launched in	Feb 05	Jun 05	Sep 08	Feb 09	Apr 09	Apr 09	Jul 09	Aug 09	Sep 09
No. of full-time doctors	3	2	7	4	1	4	4	4	4
No. of external doctors	12	5	14	20	11	10	64	0	0
Total no. of employees	42	48	120	73	27	58	112	58	54
No. of beds	15	25	43	72	18	48	58	63	84
No. of Star Specialties	10	3	2	3	1	3	5		3
No. of other services	3	3	7	5	4	1	15		2

Source: Data was provided by Vaatsalya.

Note: Star Specialties comprise gynaecology, paediatrics, general surgery, general medicine, nephrology, paediatric surgery, neonatology, anesthesia, urology and orthopedics. Other services comprise some of the above and ENT, plastic surgery, physiotherapy, urosurgery, oncology and angiography. Star Specialties and other services together contribute 80 per cent of the hospital revenue.

The exact model of Vaatsalya Hospitals in terms of its size, location and type of doctors was not apparent to Veerendra and Ashwin at the outset. They, therefore, experimented with three different models at Gadag, Hubli and Karwar.[6] The hospital at Gadag had 20 beds and offered a comprehensive range of healthcare services in the primary and secondary segments; Karwar was a 'Clinic' where patients were provided treatment without any provision for admissions[7] and Hubli was designed as a 'Day Care' with additional facilities for minor surgeries and admission of patients for observation. While the hospital at Hubli had 10 beds, patients could be admitted only during the day and there was no provision for admitting them overnight. The initial plan was to create a 'hub and spoke' model, where a full-service hospital, such as the one at Gadag, would act as a hub to the smaller units, such as those at Karwar and Hubli, which could provide primary care and shift patients to the hub when there was need for secondary care. The 'hubs' would not only be larger, but would also provide additional specialized services, such as dialysis, intensive care units, diabetology and neurosurgery. Services that were provided at the hubs were essential but not viable to be provided at the spokes because of low demand. These services needed to be pooled.

Dr Renganathan, Vice President Alliances, of Vaatsalya said,

Most healthcare outfits have a hub and spoke model in one form or another. (The) hub will be a central, large hospital with facilities for providing advanced medical care and the spoke will be either smaller hospitals or clinics mainly considered as feeder units. Our earlier plan was to create several spokes for each of our hub hospitals, thereby creating one small network of 'hub and spoke' at a time. However, through experience we found it is much easier to build the hubs. Hence, we decided to build them first.

After experimenting with several sizes, Vaatsalya settled on a 50-bed hospital as the most suitable size for the kind of places they operated from.

Vaatsalya Hospitals.

[6] Gadag and Karwar are cities in the Indian state of Karnataka.

[7] A clinic is like an outpatient department (OPD) of a regular hospital.

Larger hospitals needed to have super specialties, which was unsuitable for Vaatsalya, given the dearth of such doctors in small towns and cities. A hospital with less than 50 beds was found to be inadequate to differentiate the hospital from small clinics and government health centres that already existed in such localities. Moreover, it was usually difficult to attract good doctors at a lower scale and scope of operations.

A typical Vaatsalya Hospital had three or four full-time specialists and a total staff strength ranging between 60 and 100, including nurses, matrons, administrator and social workers. Vaatsalya Hospitals also used the services of a large number of external doctors, depending on local demand and supply conditions. Table 2.3 provides details of Vaatsalya Hospitals in terms of staff composition and other physical parameters. Apart from a surgical suite, a basic diagnostic laboratory and intensive care facility, each of the hospitals had a pharmacy attached to it. Vaatsalya charged INR 100–300 per bed per night, while consultancy fees ranged from INR 25 to 100. These prices were 15–20 per cent of what an average urban hospital would be charging its patients. The medicines, however, were sold at market price, since Vaatsalya had no control over the price of medicines. Vaatsalya's doctors preferred to prescribe branded generic medicine to avoid any chance of exposing their patients to spurious or adulterated medicines that were very common in small cities and towns in India.

Vaatsalya Hospitals were set up and run to minimize non-core expenditure and provide 'no-frills' service. Vaatsalya minimized capital expenditure by leasing its hospitals rather than buying real estate, thus taking advantage of lower prevailing rents in semi-urban locations. The hospitals did not own or operate ambulances and equipment purchase was kept to the essentials, such as X-ray and ultrasound machines and ventilators. Bed categories were designed to accommodate an equal number of general, private and critical care beds. For example, a typical 50-bed hospital had 20 beds in the general ward, 20 in the semi-private and private categories and the rest in critical care (general, paediatric, surgical and neonatal intensive care units [ICUs]). The interiors and furniture were spartan and most of the rooms did not have air conditioning. Operational expenses were minimized by not having complementary facilities, such as a cafeteria. A common kitchen was provided to the patients' families to cook their food. Vaatsalya also saved on wages for non-clinical or support staff, who were hired locally. Moreover, Vaatsalya had centralized all its procurement, which resulted in cost savings of more than 20 per cent. Bulk procurement increased Vaatsalya's bargaining power vis-à-vis its suppliers, who provided Vaatsalya with favourable terms since they perceived that Vaatsalya had a large potential for growth and it would be beneficial for them to be associated with Vaatsalya.

Adopting the no-frills approach, Vaatsalya Hospitals did not invest in diagnostics and completely outsourced pharmacy. However, over the course of time, Vaatsalya realized certain advantages of owning the pharmacy themselves, especially in terms of having control over availability and quality of medicines. They, therefore, integrated pharmacy within their fold of operations. For diagnostics, they decided to get into revenue-sharing arrangements with local partners who would make the capital investment to set up diagnostic facilities on the premises of Vaatsalya Hospitals.

At a steady state, with a capacity utilization of 80 per cent, it was estimated that Vaatsalya Hospitals earned annual revenues of INR 2.5 million. Close to 40 per cent of their expenses were accounted for by compensation given to doctors; another 20 per cent was for staff salaries. Vaatsalya Hospitals spent 10 per cent of their expenses on rent and another 10 per cent on utilities, such as electricity and water. After meeting all these expenses, Vaatsalya, on average, earned about 15–18 per cent earnings before interest, taxes, depreciation and amortization (EBIDTA).[8]

MANAGING HEALTHCARE PROFESSIONALS

One of the critical challenges for Vaatsalya was to attract doctors to their hospitals in semi-urban locations. Veerendra said,

---

[8] Vaatsalya Hospitals did not disclose revenue or profitability figures either for the entire venture or for the individual hospitals. The figures quoted are from secondary sources, such as newspapers and business magazines, and are therefore, at best, indicative. Vaatsalya had an operating expense of INR 150 million per annum. However, the operating expense per hospital varied, depending on its size, specialties offered and stage of operations.

We realized that it was only those doctors who have a deep connection with rural or semi-urban India who would be willing to establish their practices in these locations. It is unrealistic to expect that someone who has been born and brought up in urban India will be willing to establish his practice in a small town – he might do it for a while, but it is unlikely that he will like to build his career there.

Therefore, Ashwin and Veerendra started to scout for doctors who originally belonged to small towns and villages, still had their roots there, but had gone to big cities and towns for their medical education. A few among them, they found out, were willing to go back to their places of origin because they liked the idea of settling down within their community. Since there is an adequate supply of medical practitioners in urban India, it takes a long time for a doctor to establish oneself or one's independent practice. Contrasted to that, a doctor can establish oneself and earn a reputation a lot faster in a small town that is devoid of qualified medical practitioners. To attract such doctors, Ashwin and Veerendra decided to offer them a compensation that was 20–25 per cent higher than the market rates prevailing in urban hospitals.[9] The fact that the cost of living in small towns was comparatively lower made the compensation even more attractive.

At Vaatsalya, doctors were also offered higher designations and positions of responsibility than what they would have had in urban hospitals. For example, while a doctor might become a consultant after about 10 years of service in a private urban hospital, some of Vaatsalya's doctors became consultants after 5 years of professional experience. At Vaatsalya Hospitals, doctors also shared greater managerial responsibilities and had significant autonomy in decision-making. Vaatsalya made a conscious effort to maintain a flat hierarchy in the organization and retained the entrepreneurial spirit in each of their hospitals by keeping formalization to a minimum and allowing the doctors to be in charge of all operational matters. Strategic decisions, especially those that were going to impact the individual hospitals, were taken consensually and

---

[9] At Vaatsalya Hospitals, the starting salary for doctors who had recently graduated with specializations was approximately INR 40,000 per month, which in large cities was typically in the range of INR 25,000-40,000.

senior management made a conscious effort to be in constant touch with every doctor to understand the challenges they faced and to have a first-hand feel of their aspirations.

Vaatsalya Hospitals were located in areas where there was a significant unmet demand for healthcare. Prior to setting up any hospital, a dedicated project team made a thorough analysis of potential locations to understand the quantity and quality of demand that existed in that region. They refined their start-up operations over the years such that a new Vaatsalya Hospital could break even within a period of 12–18 months and had more than 80 per cent capacity utilization in its steady state of operations. Such high demand implied that the average doctor at Vaatsalya Hospitals got to treat a lot more patients and conducted many more procedures than what they would have done in an urban, private hospital. That not only helped the doctors to develop their expertise rapidly but also gave them the satisfaction of being able to heal a greater number of patients, thereby creating greater impact through their profession.

Since the operating model of Vaatsalya could not support a large number of full-time resident doctors, Vaatsalya got into a variety of partnerships with local medical practitioners. Thus, every Vaatsalya Hospital had specialist doctors who were full-time employees and were paid a fixed salary and incentive. Resident medical officers were the duty doctors in charge of running hospital operations. They were usually fresh graduates who gained experience at the hospitals before they went for specialization. The third category of doctors were full-time consultants whose primary place of practice was Vaatsalya and who worked on a revenue-sharing basis with the hospitals. Finally, Vaatsalya had visiting doctors, such as an ophthalmologist, whose specialist services were usually not needed on a full-time basis. Such a variety of relationships with local doctors not only gave Vaatsalya Hospitals flexibility in adjusting to local demand-and-supply conditions, but also enabled Vaatsalya to maintain a collaborative relationship with other healthcare service providers of the local community.

Vaatsalya realized that it might be a challenge to retain some of their doctors within their fold in the long run. Once the doctors made a name for themselves, there might be the temptation of establishing their independent practice. Ashwin reasoned out that one way of reducing this problem was to make their hospitals so good that it would create a barrier for any individual doctor to enter the market. If their hospital was superior in terms of its infrastructure and was able to attract a good team of medical practitioners, nursing and support staff, all their doctors would see greater value in being part of a Vaatsalya Hospital, rather than venturing out on their own. Vaatsalya also explored the idea of offering doctors some stake in the organization by means of stock options.

Vaatsalya recruited nursing and other support staff locally. Even after paying them market rates,[10] Vaatsalya saved considerably in the wage bill, compared to an average hospital in urban India. Since there were several nursing colleges in the state of Karnataka, there was usually no dearth of supply. However, retaining support staff sometimes became a challenge because some of them got attracted to corporate hospitals in urban areas. Moreover, since most of the fresh nursing recruits were young, unmarried women, they sometimes moved on to different towns and cities after marriage. However, even among the support staff, there was a tendency to settle down in towns and communities where they belonged and given that Vaatsalya was the biggest name in such towns, attracting and retaining them was not a major challenge.

DEVELOPING LOCAL RELATIONSHIPS

Vaatsalya encouraged its doctors to develop long-term relationships with their patients. It focused on chronic diseases and chronic care, and such patients preferred to stay with one doctor. In its initial days of operation, Vaatsalya found that patients were hesitant to visit its hospitals. This was partly because of their perception that a private hospital like Vaatsalya would be expensive. Patients were also concerned that if they started getting treated at Vaatsalya, their relationship with local doctors, very often an unqualified practitioner, would be adversely impacted. They might not have the option of going back to local doctors in case Vaatsalya closed down after some time. Therefore, it was important for Vaatsalya to gain the confidence of the local

---

[10] An entry-level support or nursing staff was paid INR 3,400 per month and provided additional benefits, such as insurance and education for children.

community and they achieved this by creating an environment of trust and care in its hospitals.

Closely associated with such an environment was the transparency that Vaatsalya ensured in every aspect of its operations. Anecdotal evidence suggested that patients in private corporate hospitals sometimes had the feeling that they were unduly charged for certain procedures or medicines, which they were unable to verify because of the lack of transparency in billing. Ninety-nine per cent of Vaatsalya's customers were uninsured[11] and, therefore, needed to pay for their treatment in cash. Vaatsalya made every element of the bill transparent such that there was no misapprehension on that count. Results of internal customer surveys[12] indicated that patients appreciated the care that doctors and nurses took of them at Vaatsalya. The caring nature of doctors and nurses, as identified by the patients, was particularly a matter of joy for Vaatsalya, since that was a differentiator that they intended to develop vis-à-vis their competitors, especially other private corporate hospitals, which, despite their impressive infrastructure and richness of resources, appeared to be impersonal, often lacking the human touch.

Healthcare in rural and semi-urban India is often characterized by an unholy nexus that exists between local practitioners, diagnostic laboratories and pharmacists. Local doctors have a stranglehold over the patients because of the relationships they develop over long periods. Many of them receive commissions for referrals to city hospitals and diagnostic laboratories, which can range between 20–25 per cent of the bill value. The patients have little idea of such payback arrangements and often end up spending a lot of money in the process. However, because of the dependency they develop over the local

---

[11] In 2013–14, 76 per cent of India's population did not have any health insurance. This number was significantly high among the poor. Source: Indian Life and Health Insurance Sectors, Milliman Consulting Report (2018).

[12] Vaatsalya Hospitals conducted telephonic surveys with all patients who were admitted and 10 per cent of patients who were treated at its hospitals. Patients were asked questions on various dimensions, such as efficiency, competence, care and price as well as their propensity to visit Vaatsalya Hospitals again or refer Vaatsalya to their friends and relatives.

doctor, it is difficult for them to realize how they are being exploited. Vaatsalya Hospitals did not pay any referral fees and ensured that none of its doctors had any such arrangement with urban hospitals or diagnostic laboratories where they sometimes referred their patients. Close to 70 per cent of local doctors refused to get associated with Vaatsalya once such a zero-tolerance policy was articulated. Local administrators at Vaatsalya Hospitals closely monitored hospital operations to ensure that all their practices were above board. Apart from meeting its objective of being ethical in all practices, this policy had the benefit of significantly reducing the overall price of the healthcare services that Vaatsalya provided.

SETTING UP NEW HOSPITALS

During the first four years of its operation, Vaatsalya set up nine hospitals, with seven of them between September 2008 and September 2009. Like every aspect of their operations, Vaatsalya arrived at a nearly standardized model of setting up a new hospital. Based on their experience, Vaatsalya learnt that for financial viability, it needed to open hospitals in cities that had at least a population of 200,000 to 300,000 and an additional catchment population of 150,000 from nearby villages and towns. While there was an expectation of rapid scaling from most of Vaatsalya's investors, it preferred to be conservative in its approach. Vaatsalya's new project division, which was in charge of setting up hospitals in new locations, reported directly to Ashwin. This group was internally specialized into business development, infrastructure management and project management. Usually, the business development team searched for and located suitable doctors and signed agreements with them, while the infrastructure team identified suitable facilities and equipment. Once the physical and human resources were identified, the task of project planning and execution was passed on to the project management team. Vaatsalya had put in place a launch plan for all its hospitals, whereby several stakeholders were engaged with Vaatsalya from a month before the launch. Thus, the business development team invited every doctor from the local community for a dinner where they were taken on a tour of the facility, explained the various services that the new hospital was planning to offer and how the local medical practitioners could collaborate with Vaatsalya. During the same period, Vaatsalya organized a screening camp for the local population with the purpose of introducing Vaatsalya doctors and facilities to the local community. All these events were given due publicity through local press and radio shows.

Vaatsalya Hospitals were either built from the scratch (greenfield) or acquired. Acquired hospitals took about 45 days to start operations and about eight months to break even, since customers and doctors were already available. Most of the employees in acquired hospitals were retained and trained, and Vaatsalya ensured that the price of treatment did not increase post acquisition, which was often an apprehension among their patients. Typically, hospitals that had space and opportunity to grow were suitable for acquisitions. This enabled Vaatsalya to introduce more specialties that gave it a competitive edge. Greenfield hospitals took 90 days to get commissioned and subsequently 12–15 months to break even, the larger time accounting for identifying and recruiting doctors, support staff as well as earning the confidence of local communities. These offered at least one exclusive service in order to differentiate themselves from the rest of the hospitals in the area. The choice of location was determined by the willingness of doctors to relocate to such places and its connectivity to surrounding areas. Proximity to medical colleges that could offer complementary services, such as availability of a blood bank, was also an important determinant. While relocating, doctors considered the possibilities of admitting their children to good schools as well as whether their spouses could be employed. Therefore, small towns that had a high growth potential, such as Gadag, were better suited for locating greenfield hospitals. Vaatsalya also considered the possibility of partnering with some government hospitals, which were usually situated in prime locations, even though other resources in government hospitals needed to be improved significantly to be at par with Vaatsalya's quality standards.

Doctors at Vaatsalya were recruited through different methods that included advertisements, referrals and employment databases. The business development team also evaluated local practitioners to understand their suitability. While referrals were the most effective method, over time there was a gradual increase in direct applications from doctors seeking opportunities in Vaatsalya.

While Vaatsalya seemed to have understood the physical aspects of growth well, the sociological dimension of growth remained a critical challenge.

Good quality doctors needed to be recruited and acculturated with the values of Vaatsalya, which was difficult when scaling happened fast and in a decentralized manner. Acculturation was achieved by ensuring that the new recruits spent enough time with the core team members to understand, appreciate and imbibe their philosophy. Veerendra said,

> Our hospital network is proud to have attracted highly inspired doctors from across India, who has shown a keen desire and passion to work in our hospitals, particularly doctors who were born and who grew up in semi-urban India. Our strategy is to tap into the entrepreneurial spirit of such doctors and work with them on expanding our network.

One of the challenges of building and running an organization with a young set of doctors was a relatively lower level of professional maturity. To compensate for that, Veerendra, who was in charge of overall operations, kept in touch with the new recruits personally and ensured that there was enough handholding taking place at the individual locations. New recruits were sent for conferences and attended training programmes, so that they got adequate exposure to professional events that helped them to build confidence. Vaatsalya held meetings, once a month, among all their doctors for exchange of ideas and best practices that also served as an orientation platform for the newly recruited doctors.

CHALLENGES OF GROWTH

Nearly five years and nine hospitals later, Ashwin and his team at Vaatsalya were ever more convinced about the viability of their model that balanced social inclusion with financial sustainability. Their next step was to figure out what could be the best way of extending and scaling their business model. While there were various options, the leadership team at Vaatsalya was looking at the following three, each of which had its unique challenges.

Vaatsalya's first option was to extend its portfolio. Realizing that many of their patients had to travel hundreds of kilometres twice a month for dialysis, some Vaatsalya Hospitals added facilities for dialysis. Dialysis equipment was expensive to set up. A reverse osmosis plant for four dialysis beds cost INR 600,000. Vaatsalya charged INR 900 per dialysis of which INR 450 was spent on reagents and equipment allocation costs, while INR 450 accounted for operational costs. Additionally, some Vaatsalya Hospitals needed to buy water worth INR 5,000 per day because they operated in very arid zones of Karnataka where water supply was scarce. Such contingent costs could not be passed on to its patients, especially given their economic status. However, even at INR 900, its price point was beyond what could be afforded by poor patients. Sooner or later, Vaatsalya expected the costs for dialysis to come down, partly because of technological advancement and partly because of scale economies that they would get from higher volumes. However, price was not the only constraint when it came to dialysis – there was an acute shortage of nephrologists all over the country. Vaatsalya estimated that the whole of India possibly had about 600 nephrologists and only three of them were available in the cities where Vaatsalya operated, all of whom were employed by Vaatsalya. Likewise, there was shortage of dialysis technicians. This put a constraint on the total volume that each hospital could handle.

Vaatsalya's second growth option was to extend the reach of the individual hospitals deeper into the hinterland. In Gadag, a small town in northwest Karnataka, Vaatsalya established four outreach centres linked to the main hospital. However, the outreach centres could not be sustained because the sole gynaecologist in the main hospital could not handle all the cases that were brought as reference. Moreover, Vaatsalya found it difficult to retain qualified practitioners at the outreach centres because most of them wanted to be a part of the main hospital, rather than work at the outreach centre. Subsequently, Vaatsalya explored the option of partnering with local practitioners in order to extend the reach of their hospitals. However, finding local partners who were willing to accept Vaatsalya's values in terms of transparency and honesty was difficult.

Vaatsalya's third and possibly the most challenging option lay in extending healthcare to patients at the lowest economic strata – the bottom 30 per cent. A study by an external agency indicated that Vaatsalya catered typically to a population whose monthly income ranged from INR 5,000 to INR 15,000 (USD 100–300). Those that were below this level were unable to afford Vaatsalya's services, even if it operated at cost. Among these patients, there were those that could afford Vaatsalya prices, but had difficulty paying by cash for their treatment, given the incremental nature of their income. Therefore, there was need for a financing model that could effectively bridge the gap between their income-led cash inflows and one-time lumpy cash outflow that was typical in case of healthcare expenses. Microfinance institutions usually provided finance for income generating activities but not for healthcare. Models of micro health insurance were still evolving and were mostly unavailable in the areas where Vaatsalya operated. As a result, there were not many options available before Vaatsalya to cater to the healthcare needs of the bottom 30 per cent.

It was possible for Vaatsalya to get into a partnership with government hospitals and healthcare programmes. For example, the Indian government had introduced the Rashtriya Swastha Bima Yojana (RSBY), a national health insurance scheme for below-poverty-line (BPL) citizens where, for a small registration fee of less than USD 1, families were entitled to INR 30,000 worth of hospital care per year. The scheme was implemented by leveraging technology, where families were provided smart cards that could be used to reimburse their expenses at the hospitals. The hospitals were paid in tranches of INR 300,000 in advance by the government. The scheme was intended to involve private hospitals as well as private insurance companies to deliver healthcare to BPL citizens. The Indian government also spent money in providing subsidized healthcare to the poor through other programmes, such as INR 3,000 given to poor pregnant women for delivery. However, such schemes had a high degree of leakage and were largely ineffective because they were delivered through public hospitals. If the government provided the same kind of subsidies to hospitals like Vaatsalya, they would be able to implement such government-aided healthcare programmes much more effectively. The Government of India introduced a scheme of providing unique identification numbers to each of its citizens. Lack of identity proof often resulted in harassment and denial of services to the poor and marginalized. It was envisaged that a unique identity number would improve the delivery mechanism of the government's pro-poor schemes and programmes, by ensuring enhanced access to government services for every intended beneficiary and by preventing leakages. It would also facilitate the implementation of private–public partnership in services such as RSBY by taking away the burden of identity verification from service providers such as Vaatsalya, who could then focus only on their expertise of delivering healthcare.

Another way in which Vaatsalya planned to address the healthcare needs of the economically impoverished, who could not afford their services, was by launching programmes aimed at preventive healthcare. Since such programmes would not be commercially viable, Vaatsalya intended to raise money from charitable trusts or find other means of finance, such as renting out spaces for advertisements. Renganathan said,

A significant cause of many ailments among the poor is lack of knowledge. For example, lack of awareness about right nutrition makes them vulnerable to diseases such as diabetes and anaemia. In many villages, pregnant women are discouraged from taking multivitamin tablets, so that their babies do not grow big because they think big babies would make their delivery difficult.

Vaatsalya planned to create content that would teach people in these towns and villages about preventive healthcare and when to seek the help of doctors. They intended to disseminate such information by using mobile vans. The total expense of such operations was expected to be funded by advertisements that could be displayed on the mobile vans. Ashwin said,

Anytime we notice a repeated pattern of ailment, we try to ascertain the cause. For example, there is a high incidence of cerebral palsy in Gadag. When we investigated the cause, we found that there is a high incidence of anaemia among the population, which leads to difficult childbirth. All of this can be traced to the lack of or poor anti-natal care available in these areas. Therefore, Dr Renganathan wrote a proposal and we got our initiative funded through the Deshpande Foundation.[13]

---

[13] Deshpande Foundation was a not-for-profit that focused on creating enterprises having significant social and economic impact. It largely operated from Boston in the USA and Hubli in India.

With the funding, Vaatsalya launched a pilot programme in four regions where, in collaboration with local general practitioners (GPs), they planned to set up rural birth centres. These birth centres would screen cases of pregnancy from an early stage and decide on the next course of treatment whenever there was a necessity. The local GPs would provide treatment to cases that were not complicated but needed medical attention, while those that were complicated would be referred to Vaatsalya Hospitals.

Vaatsalya planned to set up a testing laboratory to check the fluoride content in water in areas where there was a high incidence of fluorosis, characterized by blackening, cracking and pitting of the teeth of patients. Likewise, they explored means of creating a database of blood banks by leveraging technology such as Google Maps. By means of such database and a toll-free number, blood could be located quickly from the nearest blood bank. This was very important in situations of post-delivery haemorrhage. Ashwin continued,

> These activities are unlikely to generate revenues or be profitable. Therefore, we will fund them through our foundation or take grants from other foundations. Since we understand the context, we are in the best position to address these needs. These are our corporate social responsibility (CSR) activities, ways of giving back to the society.

In many ways, Vaatsalya was a pioneer in the Indian healthcare sector. By means of innovations on multiple fronts, it was able to bring quality and affordable healthcare to semi-urban and rural Karnataka. Vaatsalya established a model that was financially viable and scalable. The founders believed that if they were able to attract a dedicated set of medical practitioners, as they had done so far, they would be able to set up 50 more hospitals in the next few years that would span across several Indian states and reach out to more than a million patients a year, which would, in turn, benefit 4 to 5 million of the Indian population living in semi-urban and rural India. However, their services were still outside the reach of the poor (earning less than USD 1 per day) and the vulnerable (earning between USD 1–2 per day), comprising 300–400 million of the Indian population. From Vaatsalya's experience, there seemed to be no way of addressing their healthcare needs through a business model that was financially viable. While Vaatsalya was addressing this segment at present through charitable funds, the founders were hopeful that partnership with the government or with other private institutions providing complementary services, such as health insurance, would very soon enable Vaatsalya to bridge this gap.

DISCUSSION: THE CHALLENGES OF DELIVERING INCLUSIVE HEALTHCARE

In the following sections, we discuss the need that Vaatsalya was addressing through their social enterprise, the key drivers of their business model, explore the feasibility of their scaling options and compare Vaatsalya's operating model with two other inclusive healthcare models that are highly reputed in India. This should enable us to understand the relevance of Vaatsalya's model of decentralized – small – low-cost hospitals and its challenge of scalability and sustainability.

THE NEED VAATSALYA IS FULFILLING

Why does semi-urban and rural India need socially inclusive healthcare and why do market forces not operate there given the high demand? The majority of people living in these areas have a limited capacity to pay. Moreover, they have little or no health insurance. Thus, it is not attractive for any commercially motivated private enterprise to offer healthcare services in these areas, given the dispersed nature of clientele and their low paying capacities. This is a typical situation where the government should have stepped in and filled the supply gap, which is unlikely to be addressed by the markets. Unfortunately, government's spending on healthcare is abysmally low at 0.9–1.4 per cent of the GDP. While the government has established health centres in small towns and villages, these are characterized by inadequate infrastructure, poor maintenance and a perennial absence of qualified medical practitioners. Even where medical practitioners are available, they often indulge in seeking rents through private practice and referrals to private hospitals because of inadequacies in their salary and compensation.

Thus, a vast majority of patients in semi-urban and rural India, many of whom are poor, pay a 'poverty penalty' for healthcare services. Either they are reconciled to having poor quality treatment from local unqualified practitioners (quacks) and government hospitals or they have to undertake long journeys to urban centres where most of the good hospitals and qualified practitioners are located. Apart from the delay involved in travelling, private urban hospitals are expensive, both for treatment of the patient and for the accompanying family members or friends who confront an alien or unfamiliar environment. Such travels also result in loss of livelihood for both the patient and the companion. Scholars have pointed out that health related expenses were found to be the largest cause of poverty in rural India (Krishna 2006).

Therefore, when it comes to healthcare for the rural poor in India, it is necessary to consider the 'total cost of healthcare' (TCH), which comprise not only the direct cost of treatment but the associated costs of travel and the opportunity cost of lost livelihood for both the patient and the accompanying family member. All of these costs add up to create a substantial financial impact. Private healthcare service providers in urban India are focused on the most profitable tertiary care segment. Thus, the large demand in the primary and secondary care segments is not addressed by the market (refer to Figure 2.1), especially the one that is generated in semi-urban or rural India. This creates the need for social enterprises like Vaatsalya Hospitals, which address markets that are financially unattractive for commercial enterprises. In the context of Indian healthcare services, private hospitals have naturally gravitated towards delivering tertiary care in high density urban locations in order to maximize their profitability. Therefore, Vaatsalya was set up to deliver primary and secondary care in semi-urban and rural locations. Vaatsalya's model, even while charging fees to the patient, reduced the TCH for them. Yet Vaatsalya, from the very outset, wanted to be a financially viable organization. This is the paradox embedded in the concept of financially viable social enterprises – they choose to operate in a space abandoned by commercial enterprises because of apprehensions about profitability, yet they strive to address the social needs of such markets profitably.

KEY DRIVERS OF VAATSALYA'S BUSINESS MODEL

There were several drivers that enabled Vaatsalya to establish a sustainable business model. One can group those under three broad heads – attracting medical practitioners, efforts at reducing cost and establishing a trust-based relationship with patients and the local community.

Since the poor have a limited capacity to pay, it was important for Vaatsalya to deliver its services at a low price. In the absence of any subsidy, the only way it could do so was to reduce costs. Perhaps the ingenuity of Vaatsalya lay in the fact that it took a broader view of cost and tried to reduce TCH services through three important means.

The first cost dimension that it dealt with was the cost that people from semi-urban and rural locations incurred in travelling to urban hospitals that were located far away. Vaatsalya minimized this cost by situating its hospitals in semi-urban locations. An alternative business model could have been to start low-cost hospitals in urban centres – while it could have minimized the cost of treatment, it would not have lowered the total cost of healthcare for the rural poor. In order to operationalize their model, Vaatsalya dealt with various trade-offs, the most important of which was the availability of qualified medical practitioners.

Vaatsalya realized that attracting and retaining doctors would be a critical enabler of its business model. Therefore, it looked for doctors who originally belonged to such locations where their hospitals were being set up and offered them a better career and compensation compared to what they were having in urban hospitals. Theories of motivation suggest that while a higher compensation can attract employees, they are hygiene factors. Employees get used to it very soon and they are not effective retention tools in the long run. Vaatsalya, therefore, complemented higher compensation by providing a greater decision-making authority to the doctors as well as by creating opportunity for treating a larger number of patients. For young doctors, getting the opportunity to treat a large number of patients was an important advantage for building their careers. Moreover, given the dearth of qualified medical professionals in these communities, Vaatsalya doctors earned a lot of respect for their contribution. Such intangibles catered to the social and esteem needs of these doctors.

It is necessary that employees in social enterprises remain committed to the social objective of the enterprise and Vaatsalya achieved this by constant interaction that the senior management team had with the doctors, by insisting on ethical practices, such as no-referrals, as well as by motivating the doctors to develop deep relationships with the patients that went beyond commercial transactions. Vaatsalya, therefore, made constant efforts to provide careers to its doctors that were intellectually stimulating, professionally attractive and socially meaningful, which went a long way in sustaining its business model. It is important to note that many of these practices were expensive to implement. However, Vaatsalya incurred these organizational expenses because they were deemed critical for its business model that would finally reduce the total cost of healthcare for its patients.

The second dimension was cost control through reduction of operational expenses, such as renting property instead of purchasing real estate, not having air-conditioning unless it was an absolute necessity and not having ambulances or a cafeteria. Even when Vaatsalya reduced non-essential expenses, it remained sensitive to the unique needs of its customers. This is evident from its decision to provide a common kitchen and cooking facilities to relatives of patients, who were usually more comfortable in cooking their own food than buying it from a cafeteria. However, the most important dimension of Vaatsalya's cost reduction was the variety versus scale trade-off that it made. The operational cost of services can be lowered by standardizing them which can only be achieved by minimizing the variety of services offered (Kellogg and Nie 1995). Thus, Vaatsalya chose a limited set of specialties that addressed about 70 per cent of all illness and sought to standardize such operations to the maximum extent possible. Mass delivery of a limited set of standardized services was at the core of Vaatsalya's operational strategy, though it had its own set of challenges. For example, as Vaatsalya grew, there might have been internal and external pressures to become a full-service hospital. If Vaatsalya moved in that direction, it would have serious consequences for their business model in terms of disproportionate amount of cost escalation. This was possibly happening in some of the older hospitals (Hubli) or those located in larger towns (Mysore) that had a larger number of specialties, as can be seen in Table 2.3.

Since Vaatsalya did not offer all services, it was necessary for it to leverage complementary assets. This is one of the important determinants of the location of Vaatsalya Hospitals, so that it could access the diagnostic facilities and blood bank of medical colleges that were located nearby. The case also talks about various other options that Vaatsalya explored, such as inviting an entrepreneur to invest in diagnostic facilities within the premises of a Vaatsalya hospital under a profit-sharing arrangement. Thus, at every stage, Vaatsalya needed to balance the marginal social and commercial benefit that it would get from the additional service with the costs that it would incur. For example, while Vaatsalya had earlier decided not to invest in pharmacies, it later reversed its decision, so that it had better control over the quality of medicines that were critical to its patients' welfare and presumably also to shore up its revenues. However, incorporating a pharmacy within its portfolio added to some of the overheads and operational complexity of Vaatsalya. The context in which Vaatsalya chose to operate was characterized by institutional voids (Mair and Marty 2009), that is, unavailability of complementary resources and institutions, leading to high transaction costs and market failures. Therefore, social enterprises like Vaatsalya needed to be creative in leveraging resources that could partially compensate for such voids, while at the same time make efforts in developing some of the critical institutions.

The third important dimension of Vaatsalya's model was establishing a trust-based relationship with its patients and local community. It provided greater motivation and job significance to its doctors. Vaatsalya also realized that its no-referrals policy, instituted as part of ethical practices, resulted in the reduction of overall cost of providing services even though it made it difficult for Vaatsalya to attract some of the medical practitioners to its fold, who were unwilling to give up such a source of income. However, at the heart of this philosophy was the realization that a doctor–patient relationship is characterized by information asymmetry and trust is an important mitigation mechanism to resolve the apprehension that patients have because of such asymmetry. This is also the reason that despite their lack of qualification and dubious practices, quacks have a stronghold over patients in semi-urban and rural India. Many such unqualified local practitioners also act as opinion makers for the local community. Therefore, Vaatsalya decided that in order to earn the trust of its patients, it needed to work with the local practitioners, rather than treat them as competitors. It realized that given the harrowing experience that many patients have with urban private hospitals, they would be apprehensive about the intentions of a private hospital like Vaatsalya. It would, therefore, not be too difficult for the local practitioner to increase such apprehensions if Vaatsalya antagonized them. Therefore, Vaatsalya meticulously planned its launch campaign where it had multiple interactions with opinion makers and the local medical practitioners to assure them how Vaatsalya was keen to work with them rather than compete with them. Once it was able to attract patients to its hospitals, its differentiated service, process transparencies and carefully developed culture of care for patients combined to deliver a high quality experience to its customers, as was evident from the various customer surveys that Vaatsalya conducted from time to time.

CHALLENGES OF SCALING

Vaatsalya had two options for scaling. It could continue to do what it had been doing and replicate its model in other geographical locations, within and outside the state of Karnataka. The second was to do things differently, such as offering additional specialties in existing hospitals, moving deeper into smaller towns and villages and addressing the healthcare needs of even poorer patients. These two options might not be mutually exclusive because there might be economies of scale and scope that could be sought simultaneously.

Possibly, the easier of the two scaling options would be to replicate Vaatsalya's existing model in other parts of the state and then move to different states of India. Vaatsalya had developed a reasonable degree of confidence in its processes and with the opening of every additional hospital, it was likely to experience the benefits of learning from its best practices as well as from past mistakes. Replication would also provide Vaatsalya with additional scale economies in functions such as purchase. However, there were certain aspects of its existing business model that were difficult to replicate rapidly, which was what set it apart from rapidly scaling commercial enterprises, such as fast food chains. The success of Vaatsalya's model was critically premised on identifying, attracting and retaining like-minded medical practitioners who were constantly kept in touch with the social objective of the organization through careful selection, interaction with senior management and collaborative decision-making. Such organizations are governed more by culture and values than by processes or output control mechanisms (Ouchi 1980). Cultural reinforcement and value-based governance required a human touch, which was difficult to scale or replicate rapidly. This is the reason why many social enterprises find it difficult to create meaningful impact beyond a limited size while others, having scaled, regret the loss or dilution of social objectives.

Each of the scaling options that required Vaatsalya to change its existing business model had seemingly insurmountable challenges of financial viability. Paradoxically, each of these options seemed compelling when evaluated through the lens of Vaatsalya's social objective. If a large proportion of the rural and semi-urban population suffered from kidney-related diseases and required dialysis, it was important for Vaatsalya to offer such services. However, even at cost price, such services were way beyond the paying capacity of a majority of its patients. Likewise, if Vaatsalya wanted to be truly inclusive, it needed to extend its services deeper into smaller towns and villages as well as address the healthcare needs of the bottom 30 per cent of the economic strata. Given the current state of technology and costs, it was impossible to address these dimensions and maintain financial viability of Vaatsalya's operations. One possible way of extending Vaatsalya's reach to smaller towns and cities was the hub-and-spoke model that it experimented with. However, it turned out to be unviable because it was difficult to attract and retain good quality medical practitioners to the spokes. Operating far away from the hubs, doctors felt alienated from Vaatsalya. Therefore, it seems imperative that Vaatsalya needed to work with partners and government institutions who could subsidize a significant portion of its costs if it intended to extend its services in the aforementioned dimensions. The concluding section of the case mentions the various efforts that Vaatsalya was making on those fronts. However, in the absence of other institutions, such as micro-insurance organizations or support from the government, it would be impossible for Vaatsalya to extend its services and still maintain financial self-sufficiency.

While Vaatsalya was able to establish a financially viable business model in a domain that was traditionally shunned by commercial enterprises, it seemed to have reached the limit beyond which there were not many ways of addressing needs through entrepreneurial and organizational innovations. Possibly, this is the point where one needs institutional and policy-related innovations or interventions if one is to serve the needs of those at the bottom of the economic strata. However, there are certain other inclusive healthcare models that are able to go further down the economic pyramid. We discuss them in the next section.

OTHER INCLUSIVE MODELS IN HEALTHCARE

We select two hospitals, Narayana Hrudayalaya Heart Hospital, located in Bengaluru, and Aravind Eye Hospital, located in Madurai in the south Indian state of Tamil Nadu. Both these hospitals cater to the needs of poor patients by following a model of cross-subsidization.[14]

Narayana Hrudayalaya (NH) provided high quality cardiac care to the masses by reducing cost, improving operational efficiencies, leveraging technology, such as telemedicine, to extend its reach, and by partnering with the government to augment its resources. It subsidized the treatment of poor patients from surplus generated by treating full-fee paying patients. Its innovations included creating intermediate-level medical specialists who could handle emergency and non-intervention cardiology to overcome the supply shortage of qualified cardiologists. In 2015, NH treated 1.97 million patients through its multispecialty hospitals, performed 51,456 cardiac procedures and 14,036 cardiac surgeries (Balachandran 2016). Aravind Eye Hospital (AEH) was able to deliver high quality eye care to millions of Indians every year by standardizing cataract eye surgery and by ensuring that surgeons, the resource in short supply, only focused on the non-routine task of surgery while all other routine tasks, such as preparing the patient for the surgery, were done by para-medic staff. This led to a dramatic improvement in productivity, which, in turn, reduced its costs. It achieved a virtuous cycle of scale and efficiency that enabled it to examine 2 million patients a year and conduct 250,000 eye surgeries. Nearly 66 per cent of patients visiting AEH were offered treatment free of cost or at a nominal fee.

---

[14]   Information about the operating models of NH and AEH can be obtained from secondary sources, such as 'Narayana Hrudayalaya Heart Hospital: Cardiac Care for the Poor', HBS Case 9-505-078 (2006); 'Healthcare for All: Narayana Hrudayalaya Bangalore', UNDP Case on Growing Inclusive Markets, 2007, or the company website. For AEH, information may be obtained from 'The Aravind Eye Hospital, Madurai, India: In Service of Sight', HBS Case 9-593-098 (2009) and 'Aurolab: Bringing First World Technology to Third-World Blind', HBS Case 9-507-061.

Comparing Vaatsalya with NH and AEH, both of which were having a large scale impact by making high quality healthcare affordable for and accessible to the poor, one can identify three dimensions of inclusiveness in Indian healthcare, namely affordability, availability and accessibility. While NH started with the objective of increasing affordability, AEH focused on the dimension of availability at the outset. However, soon both of them had to deal with the other dimensions because it was only by tackling all three dimensions simultaneously that they could achieve scale and the desired impact. How each of the models addressed these dimensions is depicted in Figure 2.2.

Vaatsalya was predominantly focused on the dimension of accessibility and was innovative in solving challenges associated with accessibility. However, many of the challenges that it started to grapple with subsequently arose from the other dimensions of affordability and availability. Unfortunately, Vaatsalya was not well suited to adopt the model of cross-subsidization followed by NH and AEH, primarily because it was unlikely to have many economically

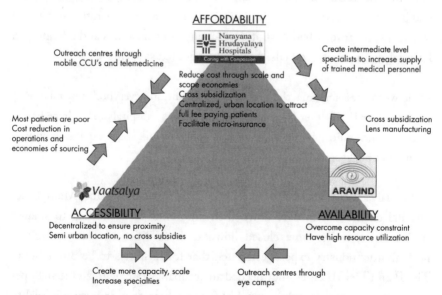

Figure 2.2 The Three Dimensions That Inclusive Healthcare Models Need to Address

Source: Representative diagram created by the author.

well-off patients who could be charged high enough fees that could subsidize poor patients. This was a direct consequence of its location, a choice it had to live with if it wanted to stick to its operating model of decentralized network of low-cost hospitals. One can speculate what would happen if a hospital like NH opened an outreach centre close to a Vaatsalya hospital. Should it result in two socially oriented hospitals directly competing with one another until the better one survived, as is typical of competitive markets, or should Vaatsalya proactively seek ways of collaborating with socially oriented healthcare service providers, such as AEH and NH, to extend its own reach and portfolio of services?

VAATSALYA HEALTHCARE – A JOURNEY OF DIFFICULTY

Vaatsalya had encouraging growth until about 2012, when it operated 17 hospitals across two Indian states and seemed well on course to establish 50 hospitals in other smaller cities across India. However, many of its hospitals failed to turn profitable and Vaatsalya started to face competition from larger and better resourced hospitals in the same cities where it operated or planned to operate. By 2019, it had to shut down many of its hospitals and operated six hospitals with about 400 beds. Ashwin was quoted as saying,

> Between 2008 and 2012, the hype was significant, and everybody was talking about Tier II and Tier III cities (as places to open hospitals). That hype has come down quite a bit. In Karnataka, people now talk about expansion only in select pockets such as Hubli and Shimoga.

Vaatsalya was not alone in curtailing their expansion plans. Many other hospital chains had to pare down their ambitions of expanding to smaller Indian cities, while some closed down their facilities because of lack of profitability. Industry experts estimated that for hospitals to be profitable in Tier II and Tier III cities, they needed an occupancy rate of greater than 85 per cent and an average length of stay (ALOS) of three days. However, in reality, the occupancy rate was around 70 per cent and ALOS was more than four days. This was because of low purchasing power of people as well as many people in such towns being covered by government schemes. Therefore, while Vaatsalya's decentralized model promised to provide healthcare in proximity to a large underserved population, thereby reducing their total cost of healthcare, their experience so far showed that it was difficult to make such a model financially sustainable or to scale.

CHAPTER LEARNING

There is a large demand for primary and secondary healthcare in Tier II and Tier III Indian cities and in rural India. Low-cost hospitals set up to address this need promise to be a viable business model.

Low-cost hospitals need to relentlessly focus on cost reduction through a host of measures, such as focusing on a limited set of specializations, not having non-core operations and investment in low-cost infrastructure.

Attracting and retaining good quality medical practitioners will be the biggest challenge in hospitals that are not located in Tier I cities or in a metropolis. Doctors who have roots in small towns or villages can be a viable source for recruitment. Providing them market-indexed salaries and giving them more autonomy and responsibilities can be good strategies for retention.

Low-cost hospitals will need to work with local medical practitioners to augment their capacity as well as to earn the trust of the local community. They may have to invest in developing capabilities of such local practitioners since some of them may not be professionally qualified. However, alignment of values with local practitioners may remain a challenge.

Low-cost hospitals need to have a lot of partnerships to overcome their inherent limitations of having to serve a population that has a limited paying capacity. This can include the government, other large well-resourced hospitals in urban locations or charitable foundations.

Inclusive models of healthcare need to address all three dimensions of the problem of inclusivity, namely affordability, availability and accessibility simultaneously. A model that is able to address all of these will be the one that can create sustainable impact.

3

GYAN SHALA[1]

Providing Inclusive Education

There are 1.5 million schools in India catering to 250 million students. Eighty-five per cent of these schools are located in rural India and 75 per cent of them are run by the government. However, the share of students going to private schools has been steadily increasing and the 25 per cent of schools that are run privately cater to little less than 50 per cent of students (Majumdar 2018; Nambissan 2012). While in developed countries, private schools typically cater to students from rich households, Indian private schools cater to students coming from a wide economic background, such as children of migrant labourers to those of company CEOs and rich businessmen. Low-cost private schools are a set of schools that cater to children from low-income households. They are often run by individuals from their homes, charging fees that are lower than those of government schools and sometimes even lower than the minimum daily wage, as earned by the parents of these children. It is unofficially estimated that about 92 million children are enrolled in about half a million low-cost private schools in India.

The need for such low-cost private schools that can educate children from poor households is likely to grow in India, given (a) the large-scale migration that continues to happen from villages to cities; (b) failure of the government to expand its schools in urban areas to keep up with the pace of urbanization; and (c) poor public perception of the quality in government schools. Migrant labourers typically settle in slums in the cities, places that are characterized by poor infrastructure, high population density and lack of basic amenities. Eijipura in Bengaluru, purportedly the largest slum in the city dubbed as

---

[1]   In Hindi, *gyan shala* means the school for knowledge or wisdom.

the Silicon Valley of India, is an example. It has 10,000 school-age children living within an area of 7.5 square kilometres. If one has to follow government regulations regarding minimum space that is required to set up a school, only two schools can be established in this area, which can cater to a maximum 2,000 children. Therefore, the need for the 8,000 remaining children can only be fulfilled by low-cost private schools.

In this chapter, we talk about one such private school, Gyan Shala, that was set up to educate out-of-school children from poor households, primarily in urban slums, with the aim of helping children in such low-cost schools match the educational outcome of schools for the elite. According to the Census of 2011, one in four children of school-going age in India had dropped out of school and there were about 72 million migrants from rural to urban India who worked as daily wage labourers. When children migrated with their parents, their chances of going to school declined dramatically. The Gyan Shala model of education has benefitted more than 200,000 children from poor families in the states of Gujarat, Bihar, Uttar Pradesh (UP) and West Bengal, and its practices have been adopted by about 10,000 government schools. Table 3.1 provides the number of students enrolled in Gyan Shala classes during 2018–19.

EARLY DAYS OF GYAN SHALA'S FOUNDER

Dr Pankaj Jain founded Gyan Shala as a not-for-profit in 1999 in the city of Ahmedabad in Gujarat. Pankaj believed that a significant failing of the Indian education system is its inability to create a scalable model of delivering good quality education at a modest cost. In the absence of such a model, India runs the risk of not educating millions of economically deprived children that would result not only in a lost opportunity for economic growth but also in social unrest. According to him, education that was targeted at out-of-school children from poor economic backgrounds should primarily focus on learning outcomes and not worry too much about school uniforms, food or certification, which were all peripheral to the core learning process.

Pankaj grew up in the Indian state of UP and having studied engineering from the Indian Institute of Technology (IIT) Roorkie, he went to work for the Indian Space Research Organization (ISRO). Subsequently, he enrolled for a PhD at the Indian Institute of Management (IIM) in Ahmedabad,

Table 3.1 Children Enrolled in Gyan Shala Schools during 2018–19

Grade / Standard	Ahmedabad	Surat	Lucknow	Farukhabad	Patna	Total
Grade 1	2,456	781	980	1,648	3,191	9,056
Grade 2	1,401	545	681	1,141	2448	6,216
Grade 3	1,107	354	399	886	1587	4,333
Grade 4	811			242	328	1,381
Grade 5	725			126		851
Grade 6	389					389
Grade 7	300					300
Grade 8	333					333
Grade 9	197					197
Grade 10	235					235
Total	7,954	1,680	2,060	4,043	7,554	2,3291

Source: Gyan Shala Annual Report 2018–19.

Note: These 23,291 students were taught in 939 classes.

where he started focusing on the development sector. Upon completing his PhD, even though he had an offer from Tata Consultancy Services (TCS), he joined the advisory team of Dr Verghese Kurian, the founder of India's largest and most successful cooperative, AMUL. Pankaj worked in Dr Kurian's office, preparing briefs for him to influence government policy that would facilitate the growth of cooperatives like AMUL. Dr Kurian acted as an inspiration for Pankaj and after two-and-a-half years, Pankaj joined the Institute of Rural Management in Anand (IRMA)[2] as a faculty member where he trained students on various aspects of rural management. He left IRMA in 1994 and went abroad where he taught and researched at various universities, such as the Massachusetts Institute of Technology (MIT), University of Leeds and the Institute of Development Studies (IDS), Sussex.

---

[2] IRMA was founded by Dr Kurian in 1979 to train professional managers who would catalyse rural development.

He also consulted for Grameen Bank and BRAC University in Bangladesh and for the state government of Andhra Pradesh, evaluating the education sector and suggesting improvements. As he started thinking of creating an organization that would provide quality education to children from poor households, Pankaj felt that he needed to have some background in education and learning theories. Therefore, he completed a course equivalent to Masters in Education (M.Ed) from the United Kingdom.

THE WORKING MODEL

Enriched with such a wide variety of experience and education, Pankaj returned to India and laid the foundation for Gyan Shala. He first focused on out-of-school children from Grade 1 to Grade 3 and wanted to create a model that would work within the existing resource constraints and deliver good quality education at low cost. In order to reduce the cost of physical assets, he chose a highly decentralized model that did not have any permanent school building or classes. Instead, classes were held in rooms of about 200–300 square feet that were rented in a home in the slum for a modest fee.[3] The room was available to Gyan Shala only for the time it held the class and was used by the family that lived in the house for the rest of the day. Gyan Shala ensured that the temporary classrooms had adequate lighting and ventilation. They were provided with colourful furniture and necessary electrical fixtures, making them attractive to the children and often more conducive to learning than most of the homes from where the children came.

While infrastructural costs are significant for running a school, the highest cost item is the salaries paid to the teachers. Moreover, schools located in urban slums and villages find it extremely difficult to attract and retain qualified teachers. Pankaj realized that a low-cost model of education could not depend on the availability of teachers with such qualifications. He, therefore, re-engineered the role of a traditional teacher, who he observed performing

---

[3] Rental was about USD 22 per month, according to Vachani and Smith (2008), INR 3,000 per month; see http://www.ashoka.org/en-in/fellow/pankaj-jain.

three distinct tasks: (a) preparing a curriculum and creating a sequence and schedule of teaching; (b) interacting with the students in class and facilitating simple learning exercises; and (c) answering difficult questions and solving complex problems. He realized that each of these activities required different levels of competencies, not all of which needed a highly qualified teacher and, therefore, some of it could be performed as well by less qualified teachers.

To make best use of the time of a qualified teacher, Pankaj set up a team of education professionals to design a curriculum and a schedule for daily classroom activities. However, he decided that the actual task of teaching in a class would be done by women recruited from the community who had tenth or twelfth grade school education and who would be paid USD 18 to USD 36 a month, depending on whether they taught one or two classes per day. This was very low when compared to schoolteachers in government or elite private schools who had higher qualifications and earned about USD 200–350 per month.

The design team made the community teachers ready for their classes by providing them with standardized lesson plans and recurrent training for implementing them. The daily lesson plans comprised methods and exercises, such as worksheets and small group activities for students that were deemed necessary for communicating a lesson. The students were taught four subjects, namely the local language, English, mathematics and environmental science to meet the state curriculum norms for these grades. Classes were held for three-and-a-half hours daily and the design team provided instruction to the teachers to implement the curriculum in chunks of 15 to 20 minutes each, to match the attention span of young children. For example, in Grade 3, the first 20 minutes were dedicated to signing a song, checking the date and neighbourhood news, reading a story or describing a picture. The next 30 minutes were allocated to language lessons comprising 15 minutes of teaching and 15 minutes of individual assignments on worksheets. A similar 30-minute pattern was repeated for mathematics. This was followed by a 50-minute group activity module where children worked in groups and rotated between activities. The last 20 minutes were dedicated to play and fun and homework instructions. Pankaj believed that this mode made the most effective and efficient use of class time, which is the most critical resource available in a school. While the design team ensured that Gyan Shala's curricula were in compliance with the official curriculum of the Ministry of Education, they sometimes adapted it by mixing it with exercises from higher grades to help students progress faster.

The pedagogy at Gyan Shala was highly interactive in nature, where the teacher acted as an enabler rather than an instructor. Children were induced to learn on their own through various group activities. Therefore, teachers spent less than 15 per cent of the time addressing the class and 85 per cent of the time was devoted to group activities. Children learnt individually and in groups on worksheets, closely supervised by the teacher who provided them personalized feedback. This was to operationalize Gyan Shala's design philosophy that made maximal use of the child's inherent capacity to learn well even with limited teacher support.

The design team was made responsible for overall programme implementation, including recruitment and training of the community teachers. Pankaj believed that the team needed to integrate of the design and management functions in order to ensure accountability and maintenance of desired quality. When it started, the design team members were paid USD 130 per month. The team worked for nine months putting together the programme and preparing materials before the first class was launched.

SETTING UP GYAN SHALA SCHOOLS

Gyan Shala's field staff visited various communities and conducted surveys to assess their suitability for establishing a class. When a community was identified, the staff explained their proposal to the community leaders and got their support. This was important for generating interest among the parents as well as for identifying teachers from the community. The staff enquired about young people living in the neighbourhood who were unemployed and were willing to work for them. They were selected based on their communication and interpersonal skills and general comfort level with subjects that were taught at Gyan Shala. Most of the teachers were women and Gyan Shala ensured their safety and well-being by investing time and effort in building a relationship between the community and their teachers.

The teachers were given two weeks of initial training that was designed to convey the high standards and professionalism that Gyan Shala strived for. During the training, the teachers were told about the students' learning schedules, how classrooms were to be organized and the nature and sequence of tasks to be followed in different subjects. They were trained so that they could explain the tasks to the students and act as facilitators of learning by providing guidance and support. Implicitly, they were exposed to theories of how children learn. The training the teachers received was often their first experience of a high quality programme. All aspects of the training, including the physical infrastructure, were maintained to communicate a positive ambience and a general sense of well-being. Apart from this introductory training, alternate Saturdays were dedicated to training in curriculum updates and teaching skills and two week-long workshops were conducted every year that reinforced Gyan Shala's values. All of these contributed to significant training expenses for Gyan Shala. Figure 3.1 gives a comparison of costs between Gyan Shala and a typical private school.

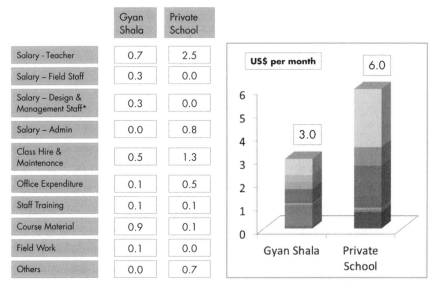

*Compensation of design team is amortized over 300 classrooms

Figure 3.1 Cost Comparison between Gyan Shala and Representative Private Schools

Source: Emerging Markets, Emerging Models, Monitor Group, 2009 / Author analysis.

SCALING UP

As Gyan Shala scaled up, it felt the need for an additional layer, the teacher-supervisor, who acted as an interface between the community teachers and the design team. These supervisors were experienced teachers with graduate degrees who supported the community teachers, assessed quality and ensured accountability. Each supervisor was responsible for about seven classes that they visited one day a week, reviewed teachers' and students' work, demonstrated effective class practices, answered complex questions that students might have had and helped the teachers deal with students who were falling behind in learning. The supervisors maintained contact with communities and families to ensure that children attended schools regularly as well as took care of administrative work, such as paying rent for the classrooms. They also provided feedback to the design team about which part of the programme was working well in class and which part was leading to challenges for the teachers or the students. The design team members also visited the classes sometimes to get direct feedback, which along with the feedback received from the supervisors enabled them to constantly develop and adapt the learning material to the context. After a few years, Gyan Shala created one more layer, that of senior supervisors, who assisted the design team and took care of school-level issues that supervisors could not handle on their own. Another important function of senior supervisors was to insulate actors at the level of classroom, that is, teachers and supervisors, from typical administrative and logistical chores, which are integral to any school programme, so they remained focused on curriculum tasks. These multiple levels provided a career growth path for junior members of the staff.

Gyan Shala operated with Grades 1 to 3 during the first five years of its operation. One teacher managed the students between the rotations to ensure that they did not get distracted or left the classes. Unlike government-run schools characterized by rampant absenteeism of teachers, classes in Gyan Shala were rarely cancelled. Teachers lost wages for unauthorized absence. An extra teacher was employed for every 10 classes, so any absent or on-leave teachers could be immediately replaced without disruption in the functioning of classes. Gyan Shala invested a lot to provide teachers and students with quality teaching and learning material, such as individual textbooks and worksheets.

Since Gyan Shala classes were held within communities, they were at walking distance from students' homes. Without such proximity, many of the children, particularly girls, would not have been able to attend the classes because of their parents' inability to bring them to school or being unable to afford any transportation. Since classes were three-and-a-half hours long, the children could help their parents after school hours. To encourage girls to attend classes, Gyan Shala appointed only women teachers. To ensure that parents had a financial stake in their children's education, Gyan Shala charged a nominal monthly fee of INR 100 per child in middle school. Education in primary school was free as per government regulation. All of these resulted in about 65– 80 per cent student attendance in Gyan Shala schools.

After five years of its operation, Gyan Shala decided to extend its model to middle school, that is, Grades 4 to 8. Pankaj had envisaged that input in the primary school should be enough to get out-of-school children admitted to mainstream education and eventually become a well-educated member of modern society. However, experience from the field was mixed and several of the Gyan Shala children who did well in the primary standards were found to be dropping out after they joined middle school. Learning theories indicated that children started to develop conceptual foundations only after they reached the ages of nine or ten, typically in middle school. Therefore, Pankaj hypothesized that to make a sustained impact, it was necessary for Gyan Shala to extend their mode of education to middle school. Subsequently, it took Gyan Shala several years to arrive at a curriculum for the middle school. Middle schools required Gyan Shala to change its mode of operation.

While in the elementary school, one teacher taught all subjects, in middle school, teachers were specialized by subjects and rotated between classes of the same grade, enabling a teacher to specialize narrowly in teaching one subject in one grade. This is because when concepts are being built, children require greater support from teachers, who, in turn, will need to have a greater capability to teach across multiple subjects in a grade, as in lower grade classes. Making a teacher specialize in the teaching of only one subject in one grade enabled a teacher with modest skills to still meet the higher curriculum skill requirement of middle school teaching. This also required that there was a cluster of classes nearby, so that the same teacher could walk across to teach in the same grades, thus fulfilling a typical quota of teaching four sessions daily to earn her monthly salary. To ensure that classes were not cancelled, for each group of four specialized teachers, there was one non-specialized extra teacher who could take over the classes in case someone fell ill. Therefore, she was trained to be up to date on all four subjects and taught one class every two weeks to maintain her teaching skills. The minimum qualification that was needed for middle school teachers was graduation. Fortunately, there were many college-going or graduate women available in the urban slums where Gyan Shala operated, who could be enrolled as teachers. Since the middle school programme was operationally more expensive, Gyan Shala remained conservative in scaling it. They also found it difficult to raise funds for it because there were donors for primary education and those that wanted to fund high schools that resulted in students getting a school certificate. But not many appreciated the importance of middle school.

IMPACT

Gyan Shala started with a fund of USD 17,000 from the Ratan Tata Trust. It started classes in nine slums of Ahmedabad in June 2000, with a team of 5 designers and 11 teachers. In 2001, Gujarat was hit by a massive earthquake that killed close to 20,000 people and destroyed infrastructure estimated to be worth USD 7 billion. With funding from VIDE, a USA-based non-profit organization, Gyan Shala established 45 classes in rural areas that were devastated by the earthquake. In 2004, Gyan Shala received funding from ICICI Bank, one of India's largest private banks. One of its expectations was that the recipient worked with the government to replicate its programme. Therefore, Gyan Shala started to work with the state government, who in 2004, in recognition of its innovative model, provided Gyan Shala with a grant of USD 40,000. This was a unique milestone because in India it is very rare for the government to provide funds to non-government schools.

Educating a child in Gyan Shala costs INR 3,800 in elementary school and about INR 7,000 in middle school, inclusive of class rent, learning material and stationery. Compared to that, the cost of educating a child in a government school could vary between INR 20,000 to INR 35,000 per year, excluding building, stationery expenses and the transport cost incurred by the students. Students in Gyan Shala attended 18 hours of classes per week, which was lower than those attending government schools. Despite lower classroom contact hours and its frugal structure, Gyan Shala students outperformed its government-school counterparts in all subjects – on average, Grade 3 students from Gyan Shala scored 63 in language versus 31 by those from government schools, and 87 in mathematics versus 40 by students from government schools. This was corroborated multiple times by reputed international research and funding organizations such as the Abdul Latif Jameel Poverty Action Lab (J-PAL) of MIT, Centre for British Teachers (CfBT) of UK and ASSET Educational Initiatives (EI) of India. It was, therefore, no surprise that Gyan Shala's model was adopted by government schools of other Indian states. The performance of children taught in Gyan Shala also matched those in elite private schools, where children receive considerable family support for education, and whose cost could be ten times or more.

Pankaj recognized that only the government or market mechanism have the capacity to reach millions of children who need quality education in India but cannot go to elite private schools. Introducing its model practices in government schools was always a strategic goal of Gyan Shala. It got an opportunity to work in 38 municipal schools in Ahmedabad, over 2008–11, to introduce its curriculum model and practices, which showed an improvement in test scores of more than half sigma in a randomized controlled trial (RCT)-based impact assessment exercise. In 2013–14, Gyan Shala was approved to introduce its model curriculum practices in 7,300 government schools in Grades 1 and 2 in the state of Bihar. However, the programme had to be discontinued due to the inability of the system to deliver the curriculum material, which was at the core of Gyan Shala's approach, to schools and children on time.

Gyan Shala used its lessons from these two initiatives to seek an approval to introduce its model curriculum practices in 1,000 government schools in UP. These experiences made Pankaj realize the typical implementation challenges of working with the government. While support from top bureaucratic levels is essential for overcoming the structural constraints, frequent changes at the top made progress slow and difficult. Recognizing the complexity of the challenge to impact the government system on a sustainable basis, the Godrej Foundation offered to support the introduction of the Gyan Shala model in low-cost private schools by offering the initial phase subsidy.

CHALLENGES

Tables 3.2 and 3.3 provide some financial figures and list of donors for Gyan Shala during the period of 2016–19.

Gyan Shala's greatest challenge during the initial years was to convince potential donors about the viability of its model that intended to deliver quality education while employing teachers with a modest qualification, since donors had heard from their education experts that teacher excellence was the main source of learning effectiveness. The traditional system of primary education gave a much more prominent role to the teacher who taught in class and it was not easy for the donors to accept Gyan Shala's unconventional model. The skepticism gradually disappeared as Gyan Shala was able to show the success of its model.

Gyan Shala's education was mostly free, as the nominal charge levied for middle school did not cover even 10 per cent of its modest cost. Raising funds to sustain the programme year after year remained a critical challenge, as most donors typically operated in a two-to-three-year grant cycle. The programme size, therefore, varied significantly over years, for example, from 45,000 children in 2015–16 to 25,000 in 2019–20, depending on success in funds mobilization.

Most low-cost schools cannot meet the formal regulatory requirements and often exist at the mercy of lower-level educational bureaucrats who have the power to de-recognize them. Pankaj refused to operate Gyan Shala through this widely practised approach. Instead, he used the rare provisions

Table 3.2 Key Financial Figures for Gyan Shala 2016–19 (in INR Million)

	2016–17	2017–18	2018–19
Earnings	124	113	97
Expenditure	124	107	96
Surplus	0.2	6.8	1.36
Total Assets	56	48	51

Source: Gyan Shala Annual Report 2018–19.

Note: Figures are rounded off to the nearest million.

Table 3.3 Donors and Funders 2016–19 (in INR Million)

	2016–17	2017–18	2018–19
Nalanda Foundation	10	22	27
SBI Foundation	–	13	18
E & H Foundation	9	11	12
GRUH Finance	3	4	–
Shroff Foundation	–	7	7
Bajaj Auto	–	7	3
Tata Trust	7	8	–
Macarthur Foundation	81	10	11
Delhi Project IC	6	5	–
P. K. Trust	2	2	–
Navin Fluorine	1	1	1
Parents	6	7	7
UBS Optimus Foundation	–	–	25
EAC-Doha	70	–	–
MSDF	22	–	–
Insaan, USA	3	3	2
Deshpande Foundation	–	–	2
Godrej Foundation GYF	–	–	1

Source: Gyan Shala Annual Report 2018–19.

Note: Figures are rounded off to the nearest million.

of existing laws to ensure that Gyan Shala's students got admission in other recognized schools and are at par with other children. This, however, created stiff opposition from local bureaucrats of the education department who complained about Gyan Shala defying the 'existing order'. Senior officers and courts had come to the rescue of Gyan Shala many times, but dealing with regulatory bureaucracy of the government remained a major challenge.

For example, a news item on 10 August 2019 in an Indian daily, the *Indian Express*, read 'Gyan Shala to discontinue high school classes on government orders'. Gujarat's education minister, B. Chudasama, was quoted saying,

Regularization of primary classes will not be allowed in Gyan Shala. They are depriving children of formal schooling. In most cases, government schools are right beside these illegal classes run by the NGO. As a result, the enrollment in our schools go down.

The education department ordered that all 350 students from Gyan Shala centres in Grades 9 and 10 be admitted to the nearest schools. About primary classes, Pankaj commented that they were working with the education department in order to regularize the centres.

It was not so long ago when the government of Gujarat had approached Pankaj to replicate his methods in government-run schools and he had run a two-year pilot in training teachers and teaching more than 8,000 students. With a change in political majority, the project was suspended. In 2013, Pankaj filed a petition in the Gujarat High Court against the state education department for denying general register (GR) numbers to 2,200 students who were taught at Gyan Shala centres. GR was essential for these children to get admission in government or private schools. The high court ordered to provide the GR numbers, which was duly implemented. However, in 2014, a five-member education reform committee recommended strict action against Gyan Shala for running illegal and non-approved classes that restricted children from getting enrolled in municipal schools. 'In city and rural areas, several organizations under the pretext of social work adopt illegal ways to stop children from getting admission in Class I and municipal government schools. Strict action should be taken against such organizations,' they recommended.

Thus, apart from the challenges of raising funds and scaling its model, Gyan Shala and Pankaj seemed to have a real problem at hand in dealing with unhappy government officials in its home state of Gujarat, which was threatening to close down or derecognize its centres.

DISCUSSION: INNOVATIONS IN GYAN SHALA'S MODEL

Like most inclusive business models, Gyan Shala was targeting a service at poor customers. Therefore, it was necessary for them to offer their service at the lowest possible price point, something that would be affordable for parents of children with low household income. It adopted several measures to reduce cost, such as renting rooms for a few hours in the neighbourhood rather than hiring or owning a school building. Apart from reducing costs and increasing availability, this ensured that children, most of whom were young, did not have to travel far to reach schools. This is very important in the context of providing education to the poor because children usually need to be accompanied by an adult to reach and return from schools, the opportunity cost of which would be high if schools are distant. Travelling over longer distances can also have security risks, especially for children and young girls, and is one of the key reasons cited for high dropout rates.[4] Moreover, such hired rooms in the neighbourhood were unlikely to have much maintenance costs, which reduced the overall cost of operation for Gyan Shala.

However, the most important innovation that Gyan Shala did was enabling adults with limited education to become teachers in the schools. In India, one needs to have at least a bachelor's degree and preferably an additional bachelor's in education to qualify for being a teacher in a government recognized school. This naturally restricts the supply of qualified teachers as well as increases their price. Teachers, all young women in Gyan Shala's case, had only completed high school education. How did Gyan Shala ensure that they would be suitable to teach the children without a formal qualification that was deemed necessary elsewhere? This was possible because Gyan Shala deployed the concept of para-skilling, an important lever of cost reduction that is witnessed in many inclusive business models.

Gyan Shala analysed that the most expensive and, therefore, constraining resource for them were the teachers. To reduce the cost of education, one has to reduce the salaries that were paid to them without reducing the quality. In a conventional system, a teacher is responsible for both the design and delivery of the academic content. Gyan Shala reasoned that in their context, while the design of academic content still needed expertise in education, the delivery of the content could be standardized and, therefore, be taught by someone who was not an expert. It was more a skill that could be learnt through training

---

[4]   Karamchandani A., M. Kubzansky and P. Frandano (2009), 'Emerging Markets Emerging Models', Monitor Group Report.

rather than needing any professional qualification. Just as Henry Ford created the blueprint of mass-manufacturing of automobiles by employing semi-skilled people in car manufacturing and standardizing the design that was created by experts, Gyan Shala created a model of delivering education at a large scale. In both these cases, the task was conceptually divided into two components, the routine and the non-routine. Experts were deployed to do the knowledge-intensive non-routine aspect of the task, the design, while low-cost resources, young women with high school education, were trained to deliver the skill-intensive routine aspect of the task. They were para-teachers, who not only needed to be trained for the job but also had to operate in a highly rule-bound environment to ensure that they were actually delivering the service as was designed by the team of experts.

An activity that is delivered by deploying para-skilled employees has high economies of scale. The expert designers will command a high salary, which is largely a fixed cost. Therefore, the greater the scale of operations, the more the ability of the model to spread this cost and reduce its incidence on per unit service that is delivered. It is, therefore, conceivable that as Gyan Shala increases its scale of operations, their unit cost of operations will reduce, and they will be able to become financially viable without charging higher fees. One of the disadvantages of this model is the monotonous nature of the routine aspect of the job. Since the para-employees were operating in a highly formalized environment, they had limited scope of creativity, which could lead to burnout and loss of motivation after a period of time. To address this, organizations like Gyan Shala have to make constant efforts to motivate its para-employees by multiple means, such as providing them training for upgrading their skills, addressing their personal concerns, creating a fun-filled environment where they could socialize with their colleagues, recognizing them for their efforts and, above all, reminding them about the noble purpose that they were serving – providing education to children who would have most probably remained illiterate and on the streets had it not been for their service. It is for this reason that Gyan Shala conducted biannual workshops that reinforced the values of the organization.

Aravind Eye Hospitals, which we referred to briefly in the last chapter, also deployed a para-skilled model to improve the productivity of cataract surgeons and reduce the overall cost of operations. Dr Govindappa Venkataswamy, the founder, would surprise people who wanted to know about his model by referring to the fast food chain of McDonald's and explaining how he wanted to replicate their process efficiency. Aravind created a process where the bottleneck resource, the cataract surgeon, was only utilized for the non-routine task, the surgery, while all the routine tasks, such as making the patient ready for surgery, testing and applying medicines to the eye, were conducted by para-medics. Patients were kept ready by the paramedics one after another almost like in an assembly line, so that the surgeon could move seamlessly from one patient to another, conducting a series of cataract removal operations. This process improved the productivity of cataract surgeons dramatically, allowing Aravind Eye Hospitals to scale up, reduce costs and cater to the huge demand without having to increase the number of surgeons proportionately.

Deploying young women from the neighbourhood as teachers had other advantages for Gyan Shala. Since they came from similar socio-economic backgrounds, it was likely that these teachers would be lot more empathetic to the students, and the young children would feel more comfortable in their familiar company. Being from the same community would also make the teachers more accountable to the parents of the children and research has shown that when parents and the community demand accountability from the teachers, the teachers spend greater effort in improving the learning experience of the students (Smith and Benavot 2019). All of these would have contributed to the better academic performance that students of Gyan Shala have shown when compared to students of other schools that had much greater resources.

Despite innovations in Gyan Shala's model, it is important to keep in perspective that Gyan Shala was preparing the children by providing them basic literacy, so that they could eventually join mainstream schools. Since Gyan Shala's was a very unconventional model, it is unlikely that it would be recognized by the formal system as school education. Therefore, for the children to have a formal educational qualification, they needed to join schools that were established by the different Boards of Education. In that sense, Gyan Shala was not a substitute for school education but a means for children from economically challenged backgrounds to gain enough knowledge so that they could join the formal education system eventually. The parents who were sending their children to Gyan Shala were making a trade-off and, given the myriad challenges that they faced, Gyan Shala provided them the best option for starting their children's education. This is an example of trade-offs that the poor are willing to make because of resource constraints. Innovative business models like that of Gyan Shala identify such opportunities and create products and services to address their needs, although partially, because they realize that addressing the needs fully would make the business model unviable. To a certain extent, this started to happen when Gyan Shala began to replicate their model in middle school. Because of various reasons explained in the case, the operating costs went up, which made Gyan Shala conservative with respect to its expansion plans.

BAREFOOT COLLEGE – AN ANTITHESIS OF FORMAL EDUCATION[5]

We next turn our attention to another innovative model of education, or rather the lack of formal education – the Barefoot College. Barefoot College was founded in 1972 by a group of like-minded professionals under the leadership of Bunker Roy, in the city of Tilonia in the state of Rajasthan. The 'barefoot' approach to development adopted by Roy is based on the belief that anyone can become a skilled professional, such as an architect or a solar engineer, without a formal education. Barefoot College, therefore, recruits their students, primarily poor women from rural India, and teaches them skills, such as installing, building and repairing solar lamps and water pumps. The students typically receive six months' training on technology, such as solar panels and storage batteries, before they return to their villages and start earning their livelihood by maintaining and repairing solar-based systems. Scholars have described this approach as demystifying high technology to the rural poor to show that with the right training even the uneducated and semi-literate can operate and manage seemingly complex systems, such as solar panels and water pumps.

---

[5] Information about Barefoot College has been collected from secondary sources, such as www.barefootcollege.org and YouTube videos such as https://www.youtube.com/watch?v=6qqqVwM6bMM.

Barefoot College also runs night schools for training students who work to support their families during the day. It uses Rajasthan's traditional art of puppetry to spread awareness about health, education and human rights among the rural poor.

Underlying the various activities of Barefoot College is the Gandhian concept of a self-reliant village. Roy's intention is to empower the rural poor, so that they can serve all their basic needs of education, health, drinking water and employment. The traditional approach in meeting the needs of the rural poor has been to invest a lot of resources by institutions and funding organizations to formally train urban educated professionals who can provide these services. By contrast, Barefoot College avoids urban educated qualified professionals for rural development. They identify para-professionals from the villages and utilize their wisdom, traditional knowledge and practical down-to-earth skills for identifying, analysing and solving developmental challenges of the villages.

Over the years, Barefoot College has trained barefoot doctors, teachers, engineers, architects, IT professionals, metal workers and communicators. Barefoot solar engineers, most of them illiterate women, have electrified thousands of houses in eight Indian states, while barefoot water engineers were the first to install hand pumps in Ladakh at an altitude of 14,000 feet, a feat that was considered technologically infeasible by urban experts. In 2012, Barefoot College partnered with UNESCO to train women from villages in rural Africa and, subsequently, from Fiji with skills to install solar electricity in their villages. Over the years, generations of trainees have returned to their communities in India and other developing countries with the knowledge and skill earned at Barefoot College that enabled them to construct rainwater harvesting tanks from local materials or to solar-electrify their villages at a fraction of the cost that is incurred by international aid agencies and their experts.

The positive impact created by Barefoot College makes one ask the question: when it comes to enabling the poor, which one is more important, providing them education as Gyan Shala is attempting to do or providing them with skills as Barefoot College is doing? One can argue that Gyan Shala and Barefoot College are not suitable for comparisons. Gyan Shala is providing primary education to children mostly in Grades 1 to 3, while Barefoot College is involved in providing training to adults. Notwithstanding such specific differences in the two models, the larger question that I am raising here is the relative importance of education and skills training for young adults who come from poor economic backgrounds. Should parents of children belonging to poor households invest in education or should they invest in skills training without worrying so much about their child's education? A formal education does not guarantee livelihood or jobs and requires constant investment from the parents over a long period of time. On the other hand, providing skills training, such as in plumbing, masonry or installation of solar lights, can create livelihood opportunities in the short run and thus provide financial stability. It is a difficult trade-off for a poor family who can choose only one of the two options and the odds are stacked heavily in favour of skills training. What then is the value of education for children from poor households, if at all?

Education gives one a choice and, therefore, the freedom to determine what he or she wants to be in her life. While skills provide pay-offs immediately, they also lock the skilled person in a specific trajectory. Poor people who receive training to be beauticians or plumbers are likely to remain so throughout their lives irrespective of whether they like their vocation or not. Given their lack of education, they will have limited choice in changing their occupation unless they are able to make substantial investments and are in a financial position to take risks. However, people who are educated are likely to have, in the first place, a better understanding of their own suitability for a particular occupation. If the education that they received provided them with a larger perspective about the world and a deeper understanding about themselves, they are likely to make a better choice about their occupation. More importantly, they are going to exercise greater freedom while making this choice – it is likely to be their own choice rather than being thrust upon them by someone else or through compulsion. Finally, their educational qualifications will provide them with more options in their career as they progress in their life and profession and they will have a better assessment about the risks and returns of the choices that they would make. Thus, in the final assessment, education caters to what we call as 'life needs' of an individual, whereas skills cater to 'livelihood needs'. While both are important for an individual, if one needs to make a choice between the two, it is a trade-off between benefits in the short and the long run.

COMPARING INCLUSIVE MODELS OF EDUCATION WITH HEALTHCARE

In the last chapter, we looked at the three models of inclusive healthcare and found them to be financially sustainable. Thus, healthcare represents an ideal case for inclusive business models where we find that despite their challenges, it was possible for the organizations to meet their dual objective of serving the needs of the poor and financial sustainability. In case of Aravind Eye Care and Narayana Hrudayalaya, they were even able to achieve the third desirable objective of being able to deliver their services on a large scale and thus create a greater impact than most other social enterprises. However, when we look at the education sector, most of the organizations that address the needs of the poor run in a charitable mode. Even though Gyan Shala charges a nominal fee, its primary source of funding is grants from charitable institutions. Therefore, it raises the question: why is it more difficult to achieve financial sustainability with inclusive models of education when compared to healthcare? Is there something fundamentally different about these two sectors that makes achieving financial sustainability significantly difficult in one? I would argue so.

It is easier to make a model financially sustainable if the person receiving the product or service is willing to pay the right price for it. The reason why it is relatively less difficult to achieve this in healthcare is because the benefits provided by a hospital or a doctor are measurable and can be felt in the short term by the patient. Patients are acutely aware of the loss of productivity or livelihood opportunities when they fall ill and, therefore, there is an inherent pull from them to get cured at the earliest. The benefit of recovery is tangible and the sooner they are able to seek treatment, the faster they would be able to go back to their work or taking care of their families, all of which have high opportunity costs. Therefore, patients will make difficult trade-offs, such as borrowing money at high interest rates to get treatment with the expectation that their sacrifice and suffering would be only for a short while, which will ensure better days sooner than later. This is also the reason why a model such as that of Barefoot College, which provides skills training to the poor, will have financial sustainability. The poor will be willing to pay for such training if they have the confidence that such training will provide them with increased livelihood opportunities in the medium term.

However, when it comes to education, the benefits can only be realized in the long run. Committing to educate a child is a long-drawn-out affair over at least 15 years when parents are needed to make economic sacrifices, unlike getting a treatment for an ailment where the economic sacrifice is expected to be for a limited period. Even in the long run, the benefits of education do not have a direct correlation with livelihood opportunities because in countries like India where there is severe competition for jobs, there are enough examples of educated youth not finding suitable employment. Even if education is offered free of cost, there are significant opportunity costs for the students, especially as they grow up. Grown-up children could start earning income or they could take care of the family when their parents are out for work, explaining the high dropout rates among children who come from poor households. Therefore, the need to educate children will have to come more as an internal drive from parents who realize the intangible benefits of education and are willing to make sacrifices over a long period of time for benefits that are uncertain and accrue only years later. Researchers have found that poor parents view their children's education more as a lottery or a game of chance and are, therefore, willing to take bets only with their most intelligent child, who is most likely to be male, since parents do not expect much from the girl child in the long run assuming them to get married (Banerjee and Duflo 2011).

The second reason why financial sustainability is difficult to achieve for inclusive models of education is the inability to offer cross-subsidy. As we saw in the case of Vaatsalya Hospitals, their inability to implement cross-subsidization was a key reason for their struggle to achieve financial sustainability, something that was achieved by the centralized models of Aravind Eye and Narayana Hrudayalaya. In a hospital, one can offer treatment to the patient who is poor along with a patient who is rich because treatment is an individualistic act where there is limited interdependency among the patients. How a doctor treats a poor patient has little or no bearing on and can be different from how the doctor treats the next patient who may not be poor. Therefore, the rich patients should not have any concern about the quality of treatment that they receive because the same doctor also treats poor patients. So long as the hospital in question is offering treatment at a reasonable price and cross-subsidy is not increasing the fees beyond the affordability of the rich patients, they will not have any concern. Given that hospitals have significant fixed costs, a greater number of patients reduces their unit costs of service and very often hospitals that can operate at a high scale are able to offer their services at an equal or even lower price to its customers when compared to hospitals that are commercially oriented, even if they cross-subsidize the poor patients.

However, it is completely different when it comes to education. Education is offered as a collective, in classes that have multiple students. While the marginal cost of adding, for example, 5 poor students to a class of 30 students who come from economically well-off backgrounds might be close to zero, having students from poor families would start impacting the way the teacher teaches in class. This is because the learning ability of the students is not only dependent on their intelligence, which one can assume to be independent of economic conditions, but also the physical and socio-economic conditions of the students. And learning does not stop inside the class when the teacher is teaching. Therefore, even if students from different economic backgrounds learn equally in class, those who come from privileged backgrounds go back to homes where they can eat nutritious food, sleep comfortably and focus on studying and preparing for classes the following day. However, all of these conditions are questionable for children coming from less privileged households, where the physical infrastructure might be poor, they might not be getting nutritious food and the overall environment at home that is likely to be much smaller and shared with more number of people might not enable them to concentrate on their studies. Many of them might also be expected to take care of household matters or help their parents earn livelihoods. Therefore, when the children get back to classes the next day, they might not be as prepared as the children from privileged backgrounds, neither would they be as mentally and physically alert. If this continues to repeat over a period of time, it is definitely going to show up adversely in their learning ability and academic performance in class. The teacher would, therefore, find it difficult to deal with the different needs of both these groups in the class and the best solution at that point of time would be to conduct classes separately for them, which will increase the overall cost of education. Thus, even if cross-subsidy is possible within schools, when compared to hospitals, it would be far more difficult to arrive at a working model that is financially sustainable.

CHAPTER LEARNING

A significant number of children from poor households drop out of school because of various reasons related to their socio-economic conditions. A school that provides education at a low cost can act as a bridge to enable them to get back to formal schooling.

The most significant cost component for schools is usually teacher salaries. Reducing teacher salaries without compromising learning quality can be an effective way to provide affordable education that is necessary for out-of-school children from poor households.

Separating curriculum and class design from in-class delivery can reduce the overall cost of education. While the design is still needed to be done by high-cost resources, the delivery can be done through low-cost ones, that is, teachers who can be paid lower salaries because of lower qualification and greater supply.

To ensure good quality, the delivery of such education needs to be highly standardized and the in-class teachers need to be trained to follow instructions meticulously.

Such low-cost schools need to invest significantly in design and study material to ensure good quality, even while they reduce other expenses, such as those on infrastructure. Locating schools within communities of poor households makes it easier for children from those households to attend classes.

Private providers of low-cost education need to manage their relationship with the government tactfully. Ideally, they should get into partnerships with the government, so that their model can be replicated at scale leveraging government resources. However, dealing with government systems can be challenging.

Creating a financially sustainable education model for children from poor households can be challenging because of the poor paying capacity of the parents as well as such parents often considering the benefits from education to be uncertain.

4

RANG DE

Creating a Platform for Social Investing

Microfinance, or specifically microcredit, comprises lending small quantities of money to the poor to address their entrepreneurial or personal financing needs. In developing countries like India, the poor do not usually have access to formal sources of credit, which prevents them from undertaking any entrepreneurial activity that has the potential of increasing or diversifying their income. Microfinance can be considered as the poster child of inclusive business models, thanks to the pioneering effort of Muhammad Yunus, who, in 1983, established Grameen Bank in Bangladesh that showed the world that it was possible to build a profitable bank whose sole purpose was to provide micro-loans to the poor.[1]

THE GRAMEEN BANK MODEL

Yunus, a professor of economics at the Chittagong University in Bangladesh, realized that small loans could have a significant positive impact on the lives of the poor during his visit to the nearby village of Jobra. There, he met poor women who were involved in making bamboo furniture. However, since they did not have access to formal credit, they needed to take loans from moneylenders to buy bamboo, the raw material. The moneylenders charged them such

---

[1]   Yunus or Grameen Bank, however, was not the first to start microlending. Organizations such as the Self-Employed Women's Association (SEWA) Bank in India and Accion in Latin America preceded Grameen Bank in microlending.

exorbitant rates of interest that the women could hardly make any profits and continued to remain poor. Yunus lent USD 27 to 42 such women, which resulted in them earning profits from their businesses for the first time. This led Yunus to investigate the systemic problems that resulted in the poor's inability to get formal credit and what could be done to overcome those problems.

There are several problems that prevent a poor person from getting credit from formal financial institutions, such as a bank. The poor usually do not have assets that they can pledge to the banks as collateral, nor do they have any credit history for the lender to rely on. Therefore, they are viewed as high-risk borrowers. Moreover, the loans that they need are typically of small denominations, which implies that the income that the bank can earn from the interest on such loans was meagre, compared to the transaction costs that the lender would incur in evaluating the borrower or for processing the loan. This compels the poor to borrow from informal sources, such as friends and family members, and, very often, from moneylenders. The moneylender charges very high interest rates, partly to cover his transaction costs and partly by being opportunistic and taking advantage of the desperate situation of the borrower. Many moneylenders develop long-term relationships with the borrowers and their community through interlinked transactions, which also enable them to make a better judgement about the borrower's capacity to pay. Most of them also do not hesitate to use strong-arm tactics to recover their loan amounts in case the loan becomes delinquent.

Yunus realized that in the absence of credit history or collaterals, the best person to evaluate the riskiness of a potential borrower was his neighbour or his community. Thus, he created a model of microlending where he would lend to an individual, but the person needed to be part of a group, of usually five members, all of whom needed loans. While the group did not give any formal guarantee for the loan, the group had to make sure that the money was repaid. This implied that the group members helped each other to repay the loan because they would not get any more loans unless all the payment commitments were met. It also meant that the group will not agree to have someone as their member if they felt that the person was a high-risk borrower and was unlikely to meet his financial commitments.

Based on this principle, Yunus set up Grameen Bank in Bangladesh in 1983 through a special act of parliament. Of the total equity of the bank, borrowers, mostly poor women, own 94 per cent and the balance 6 per cent is owned by the Government of Bangladesh, making Grameen a bank by the poor, for the poor. The Grameen model of microfinancing was an astounding success, showing the world that it was possible to create a financially sustainable business model while providing loans to the poor. As of 2018, Grameen Bank had distributed USD 21 billion in loans, out of which USD 19 billion have been repaid. Its loan recovery rate of more than 96 per cent is higher than most commercial banks in the world. In 2018, it provided services to more than 80,000 villages in Bangladesh through its 2,568 branches and had an employee strength of more than 20,000. Grameen Bank has also been profitable and it has not needed to depend on grants or financial aids for more than 25 years now. While it was initially asked by the Government of Bangladesh to use its profits for strengthening its balance sheet, from 2008, Grameen has been giving out 30 per cent annual dividends to its 6.2 million shareholders.

In the original Grameen model of microfinancing, a Grameen field worker initiated five-member groups for taking collateral-free loans, which were provided to the members in a staggered manner to create group liability. Eight such groups formed a centre, which conducted weekly meetings together. Loans were approved in these meetings and the Grameen field worker who attended the meetings provided the necessary service. The meetings enabled the field worker to develop familiarity with the borrowers and the group dynamics. Loans were provided directly to the individuals and loans needed to be repaid in 50 instalments. On a reducing balance basis, Grameen's interest rate on its loan was about 20 per cent, which was higher compared to traditional banks. Rules regarding loan size, repayment schedule, commission, membership fees and interest rates were all standardized by Grameen. Around 30 such centres were aggregated to create a Grameen 'branch', which was encouraged to be profitable. Over the years, the model underwent some changes and from 2002, Grameen introduced a model that had more flexibility. Grameen staff members were given discretion in designing loan products that were more responsive to member needs. Thus, the duration of the loan and the size of weekly repayments could be varied to match expected cash flows of the borrowers. If the borrower had genuine difficulty in paying back a loan, the repayments could be rescheduled. Grameen also introduced new products, such as loan insurance for borrowers and pension funds.

Yunus structured Grameen Bank in such a manner that it was not just a microfinancing institute but also a vehicle for social transformation. Thus, Grameen encouraged its borrowers to make regular savings, which not only lowered their cost of funds but also inculcated financial discipline. Every group and centre were required to exhibit a form of democracy and they elected their chairpersons and secretaries. Grameen members were also encouraged to vote in national elections without being influenced by the bank about which party to vote for. Grameen prioritized lending to women because it believed that it brought greater benefit to the family than lending to men. Yunus, when questioned about this policy which some regard as unnecessarily biased against men, is often heard saying that women have greater long-term vision and they make excellent managers of scarce resources. Grameen borrowers are encouraged to regularly recite and inculcate Sixteen Decisions, a set of practices for transforming their lives, which include sending children to school, keeping families small, not accepting and giving dowries at weddings, keeping family members and the environment clean and taking joint actions to help the community. It must be noted that there are a few critics of Grameen's Sixteen Decisions, which they view as indoctrination.

MICROFINANCE IN INDIA

The Grameen model of solidarity lending, where small groups borrow collectively and encourage each other to pay, has been adopted by different countries worldwide, including India. Initially, most of the microfinance institutions followed the Grameen model with a developmental focus. However, there was one big difference. Indian regulations did not allow microfinance institutions (MFI) to take deposits from their members. As a result, they had to borrow funds from banks, resulting in an additional interest burden. During the early days, the microfinance domain attracted not-for-profit (NFP) organizations who mostly acted as financial intermediaries linking self-help groups (SHGs) to banks. Often, the NFPs encouraged the SHG members to save and start inter-lending among members. Once the SHGs developed a certain corpus, the NFP linked them to a bank and facilitated their borrowing from the bank, leveraging their corpus. The NFPs provided the SHG members with training in finance, self-governance and group decision-making. While they borrowed from the bank at about 8 per cent, they lend internally at about 24 per cent and whatever profits they made were shared among group members. One of the reasons why this model, known as self-help-group bank linkage programme, became quite popular in India is because of the large network of bank branches in rural India that became accessible to the traditionally underserved community, thanks to the efforts of the NFPs. However, the loan amount that this model enabled the SHGs to borrow was modest, creating constraints for their growth.

Soon, the success of Grameen Bank and variations of the microfinancing model in India started to attract for-profit entities to this domain. Indian regulations[2] required them to have certain capital adequacy norms and a minimum entry capital of INR 20 million. While they still could not take member savings, they could attract equity funding from venture capitalists and borrow from commercial banks on the strength of their own balance sheets. Thus, by design they were commercially oriented and were keen to achieve scale as means to provide high returns or attractive exit multiples to their investors. In their quest to grow rapidly, they did not have either the time or the intention to evaluate the needs of the borrowers. Neither were they careful in evaluating whether the borrowers were utilizing their loans for creating income-generating activities or whether these loans were being used to fund their consumption. Eventually, it created an unsustainable situation where the number of borrowers in a state like Andhra Pradesh was more than nine times the estimated number of poor households, implying that the same borrower had borrowed from multiple MFIs. The borrower was borrowing from one MFI to pay off the loan from another MFI and such was the pressure of scaling on the MFIs that they did not hesitate to provide loans to such borrowers, fully realizing that they were over-leveraged and were in a financially unsustainable situation. Some such borrowers started committing suicides when they eventually ran out of lenders. It was a news item about one such unfortunate incident that made the founders of Rang De, our anchor case for this chapter, to take their plunge into social entrepreneurship in the domain of microfinance.

---

[2]   Reserve Bank of India Act, 1934, and Indian Companies Act, 1956.

RANG DE: INTRODUCTION

N. K. Ramakrishna and his wife Smita Ramkrishna founded Rang De in 2008 as an Internet-based peer-to-peer (P2P) microlending platform. Through its information technology-based platform, Rang De enables individuals to lend to the economically underprivileged and marginalized communities across India. By 2019, Rang De had channelized INR 800 million lent by 15,000 social investors, at affordable rates, to 65,000 individuals, to fund their livelihood activities or their children's education.

When Ram and Smita established Rang De, they aspired to create a sustainable initiative that offered affordable loans to low-income households, who hitherto found it difficult to do take loans because of prevailing high interest rates. Smita and Ram realized that a P2P lending model mediated through the Internet had the potential to bring down interest rates substantially. They founded Rang De as an NFP organization that had the ability to connect the lender with the borrower directly, eliminating intermediation. Lenders could be individuals or corporations and Rang De would work with field partners in order to reach the needy.

Eleven years since it started, Smita and Ram have established a sustainable business model. However, they have also realized that the need for microfinance was enormous and they have just begun to scratch the surface. Noted Ram,

> We would like to be able to reach out to people across all states in India and go deeper into the territories where we have started to work. We would also like to provide a wide range of social investing options to the investors and make social investing a norm.

THE GENESIS

Ram grew up in the city of Lucknow and went on to study mechanical engineering in a private college in Vijayawada, a city in the state of Andhra Pradesh. Even during his formative years, Ram felt deeply about social problems in India and looked up to Mother Teresa and Rippan Kapur[3] as his role models. While in his second year in college, Ram got a chance to organize an event to raise funds for the Missionaries of Charity. Even though Ram had no prior experience of that and Vijayawada was a relatively small town with no big corporations, Ram and his college mates were able to conduct the event successfully by raising funds and other resources from diverse sources such as IT training institutes, a car dealer, a local baker and faculty members of the college. Ram was thus able to see first-hand proof of what his idol Rippan used to believe – 'people who could make a difference existed everywhere. They needed to be asked with grace, boldness and conviction.' Moreover, that event was able to unite the students and faculty of the college for possibly the first time, who were otherwise split along lines of political affiliations and caste.

Inspired by the work of Swami Agnivesh,[4] Ram begun volunteering for an NGO, SKCV Children's Trust, that was working to rehabilitate street children. After getting his engineering degree, he started working in Bengaluru and continued to volunteer for different organizations that worked with underprivileged children and those with special needs. It was in one such programme that he met Smita, who was working for the Foundation for Action, Motivation and Empowerment (FAME) India, a school for special children. Smita, who had a master's degree in social work, had a strong inclination to work for the development sector. She had chosen to work for NFPs despite parental expectation of joining the administrative services. Through her experience, she realized that there was a general mistrust of NFPs, who were perceived to be lacking accountability and transparency, which acted as a major deterrent for developing a culture of philanthropy in India.

---

[3]   Rippan Kapur was the founder of a not-for-profit, CRY (Child Rights and You), which worked for providing justice to children.

[4]   Swami Agnivesh was a revered person and a social activist in India. He was the winner of the Right Livelihood Award in 2004. He was known across the globe in general and India in particular for his campaigns against bonded labor. See http://www.swamiagnivesh.com/about-swamiji.php?PHPSESSID=490e3d0dcd5baadca6b3abc8a67b47cd.

It was not before long that Ram and Smita realized their common passion and intentions. They got married in 2004 and went to the UK where Ram worked for a software company and Smita volunteered for Oxfam and then went on to work for the Oxfordshire County Council. Unlike in India, they found the NFPs in UK much better organized and professionally managed. They had a lot of time there to reflect on their next career move and how they could do something meaningful that would have a positive impact on the lives of the economically underprivileged. They considered various options, such as adopting a backward village in India and solving their problems, prevention of child labour and creating door-step rural employment.

In 2006, Yunus won the Nobel Peace Prize for his work on microcredit. This was an eye-opener for Smita and Ram because until then, they were not aware that financial inclusion was a big problem in developing nations like Bangladesh and India. While doing their research on microcredit, they came across news items that borrowers of an MFI that charged 50 per cent interest rates had committed suicide. They also learnt that the repayment rate in the industry was close to 99 per cent. Noted Smita,

> We were unable to figure out how all of these added up, how one could talk about eradication of poverty by lending money at more than 50 per cent interest rates.

Soon they came across two international organizations, Zopa and Kiva, that introduced P2P lending, connecting retail and institutional investors to consumers who needed loans. Kiva's model of leveraging technology and working with field partners to connect the lenders with low-income entrepreneurs appealed to them and they realized that they could lower the cost of microcredit if they followed a similar model of raising money from civil society. They chose to name their organization Rang De, which they thought would have a pan-India appeal, was meaningful[5] and had a call for action.

---

[5] Rang De figurately implies filling lives with colour or spreading the colours of joy. It is derived from a longer expression, *rang de basanti chola*, which implied giving a part of oneself for the sake of one's country and had a connection with India's freedom struggle.

THE FOUNDING OF RANG DE

The cost of running a microcredit organization had two primary components – the cost of capital and the cost of operations. Organizations that charged high interest rates justified it by citing the high cost of operations because lending was a high-touch business. However, technology could play an important part in reducing the cost of operations, reasoned Ram and Smita. Benchmarking themselves with Grameen Bank, they planned to keep their operating cost at 5 per cent and did not plan to provide any returns to the social investor. With a high-level plan in place, they started looking for financing. After being turned down by several organizations, they put together a seed capital of GBP 6,000 from their own savings. Their immediate need was to identify a technology partner who could build their platform and after talking to several organizations they got introduced to a group of software developers who had just quit Infosys to start their own consulting business. They went on to become Rang De's technology partners. Niyati Technologies, a boutique creative agency, joined the team to help Rang De with branding and creative collaterals.

In August 2007, Ram and Smita decided 26 January 2008 as a target date to launch Rang De. However, they were still grappling with a lot of uncertainties. There was no commitment for funding from anyone, they were unsure whether Rang De should be launched as a trust and, more fundamentally, they were not even clear whether Indian regulations allowed P2P lending. In October 2007, they chanced upon the opportunity to attend India's annual Microfinance Conference, where they took up a stall so that they could meet people in the domain and identify a few field partners. They got an overwhelming response at the conference and they both had to forgo even their lunches to explain their model to the stream of visitors that included several big names from the industry. They had offers from three private equity players but decided against going with them.

Ram and Smita identified a few potential field partners from the conference and they spent the next few months visiting NFPs in the states of Maharashtra and Karnataka to know the potential partners better. Three such partners were shortlisted, and they were provided training at IIM Bangalore's Centre for Entrepreneurship. The technology platform was ready in three months but two of the partners backed out and Rang De was left with only one field partner. Given multitudes of such uncertainty, Ram and Smita continued to have doubts about the feasibility of their enterprise. They had already spent their GBP 6,000 and were only a few months away from going live. The uncertainty was finally resolved when they got a chance to meet Nachiket Mor of ICICI Bank on 26 December 2007, a month before the launch. Nachiket was setting up ICICI Foundation (ICICIF) that would work for inclusive growth and rural development. He was impressed with Ram and Smita's ideas and committed to not only fund them but also help them make the model work. In return, he wanted Ram to work for ICICIF as head of technology. Ram was, however, also allowed to work part-time for Rang De

Ram took up the offer and they relocated to Chennai in February 2008 and Rang De was launched as a trust with Smita as a partner. ICICIF gave them INR 5 million, of which they paid INR 1 million for legal advice and the rest was used for developmental costs. In April 2009, Ram joined Rang De on a full-time basis and submitted another proposal for funding to ICICIF, which they perceived would make them break even as an organization by 2012. Meanwhile, Rang De had also started hiring and building their organization.

THE MODEL

The model that Rang De put in place involved working with small NGOs and NGO MFIs as field partners who did not have the resources to raise enough capital for their operations. After a while, Rang De stopped working with NGO MFIs because they found most of the MFIs to be focused only on providing credit, which did not align with Rang De's core value of looking at credit as an enabler of impact and not as an end in itself.

Rang De raised funds from social investors and channelled it as credit to the field partners. The field partner identified the borrowers and uploaded their loan application on Rang De's online portal. Rang De approved the profiles and published the stories of the borrowers on their website, so that social investors could identify with their needs and choose the borrowers they would like to provide credit to. Rang De decided on an interest rate of 8.5 per cent. Smita explained,

> We realized that 5 per cent was a reasonable margin for the field partner, provided they were able to scale up. That left us with the cost of borrowing and our own expenses. Initially, we thought that if people are lending for a cause, we need not give them any returns. But later, we decided to provide a 2 per cent flat rate, which was roughly equal to rates from a savings account. Finally, we added 1 per cent as our cost of operations and 0.5 per cent as contingency to arrive at 8.5 per cent.

On the field, borrowers paid between 6 and 10 per cent flat as interest on various loan products. The field partners were not allowed to charge any additional loan processing or documentation fees. The investor could lend in multiples of INR 100. Once the profile of the borrower was uploaded, Rang De waited for 20 days to raise the full loan amount. The loan amount was then transferred to the field partner who disbursed it to the borrower within the twenty-fifth day. The repayment started after a month and the field partner could collect it on a weekly or monthly basis, or even based on the business cycle of the borrower. The field partner transferred the repayments on a periodic basis to Rang De, which was uploaded on the website and the social investor's account got credited accordingly. Social investors could choose to reinvest the repaid amount in other borrowers or could withdraw the funds. Despite the second option, cases of redemptions were low, varying between 15 per cent in 2009–10 to about 5 per cent in 2012–13, indicating that a majority of the social investors were motivated by the desire to help others rather than earning financial returns on their investments. It also testified the trust that they developed in Rang De based on their experience of engagement.

As Rang De evolved, it started to provide different kinds of loans, such as those intended for business, education and micro-ventures. While loans for business ventures were charged an interest rate of 8.5 per cent, those for micro-ventures were charged 10 per cent. The scale of micro-ventures was typically higher, which needed a greater size of loans. Therefore, the interest charged was higher than that of smaller businesses. Rang De also provided educational loans at 5 per cent interest rates. Where the social investor did not seek any returns, the field partner was provided 4 per cent and Rang De kept 1 per cent for itself. The interest rates of educational loans were kept lower because, unlike business, these loans were not connected to any income generating activities. Even within education, the cost of servicing a primary or secondary educational loan was higher than that of higher education and, therefore, the share of the partner was kept higher. Table 4.1 provides the different rates of interest that Rang De typically charged for different kinds of loans.

Table 4.1 Interest Rates Charged by Rang De

Loan Product	Margin for Field Partner (%)	Margin for Rang De (%)	Return for Social Investor (%)	Contingency (%)	Interest Rate – Flat (%)	Interest Rate – APR (%)*
Livelihood/ Income generating activity	5.5	2.0	2.0	0.5	10.0	18.0
Higher Education	2.0	2.0	–	0.5	4.5	8.4
Primary Education	4.0	2.0	–	0.5	6.5	11.8
Micro-venture	2.0	2.0	2.0	1.0	7.0	12.6
Working Capital for Artisans	–	2.0	2.0	1.0	5.0	9.0
Special Loans**	5.0	2.0	2.0	1.0	10.0	18.0

Source: Provided by Rang De.

Note: * APR interest rates are calculated on a monthly repayment schedule.

** Includes loan for sanitation to construct toilets and field staff loans.

MANAGING FIELD PARTNERS

Since field partners were a critical part of Rang De's operations, it took great care in selecting and developing them. Their due diligence comprised understanding the field partner and its strengths and assessing whether the field partner would be able to work with Rang De's model of operation and meet their expectations.

At the outset, Rang De screened a potential partner based on their application. Rang De was clear that the partner needed to have other sources of sustenance, so that Rang De was not the only source of funding for them. This was followed by field visits to understand the kind of communities they worked with as well as their levels of skills, such as those with information technology that was necessary for Rang De to manage their interactions. Finally, all of these were consolidated, and the senior leadership and Rang De's advisors took a call whether to induct the partner. Noted Smita,

> In the early days, we would get very emotional with the partnerships. We felt that if the head of the organization was passionate about the cause, there was not so much need for due diligence. Things will fall in place. But later, we realized the value of processes. Rapport with the community was not enough; we needed to follow the process. Field visits are, therefore, very important where we get a first-hand feel of their team, their values and how much they know about the community.

While Rang De started its operations with only one field partner, it was not long before a large number of NGOs started applying to become their partners. As a result of the rigorous process that Rang De applied in selecting its field partners, the conversion rate, that is, field partners chosen from a pool of applicants, was typically under 10 per cent. Rang De also set up a partner selection committee to bring in more objectivity into the process. In 2017, Rang De worked with 25 partners across 15 states. Other considerations, such as the need for development in a geography, also went into selecting the partners. For example, Rang De realized that there were significantly more credit-providing institutions in south Indian states compared to those in northern or eastern India and, therefore, chose to work with more partners in relatively underserved areas. Many of Rang De's partners started to work in other geographies with these loans. These were places that they were unable to serve earlier because of the higher interest rates they used to charge. Rang De's lower interest rates enabled them to serve those communities.

Rang De evaluated its partners on a quarterly basis and took decisions on whether to scale up activities with the partner. Further, loans were not provided to the partners if there was a default. Rang De investigated the reasons behind such defaults and if they found that there were genuine reasons, such as illness, death or a natural calamity, the loss was shared by Rang De, the field partner and the social investor.

Rang De realized that credit by itself was not enough to help borrowers emerge out of poverty. It was necessary for the borrowers to get complementary support in the form of technical knowledge, such as how to improve farm or dairy productivity, and managerial knowhow, such as how to scale or diversify a business. Therefore, Rang De started to evaluate its partners based on the complementary services that they provided to the borrowers, so that the borrowers could utilize the loans effectively to bring about positive impact in their lives. Said Smita,

> We started to carefully handpick organizations who had a focus on entrepreneurship and community development, building capacity such as through mentorship or providing market access. These organizations consider credit as an enabler of impact. We spend time to understand how credit provided by Rang De impacts people in their livelihoods. We also work with partners to understand and arrive at the impact narrative for each of them.

Rang De interacted with its partners regularly, enquiring about the challenges that they faced and suggesting possible solutions. A point of contact from Rang De's leadership team, who was responsible for continuity in the communication, was allocated to every partner. Rang De shared their monthly performance report with the partners and kept them updated about delays in processes, if any. This was complemented by quarterly impact newsletters that Rang De sent to its partners informing them about new projects and partnerships.

Rang De provided field partners with regular trainings on how to monitor and evaluate borrowers, maintain proper financial accounts as well as run a professional organization. Rang De organized an Annual Field Partner Meet, which was an important occasion for knowledge-sharing and building relationships. Rang De used this platform to educate field partners about new initiatives and interventions relevant for the partners. Other stakeholders, such as social investors and volunteers, also participated in these meets.

In 2014, Rang De introduced an incentive scheme for their partners based on their quarterly performance. Rang De increased its interest rates from 8.5 per cent to 10 per cent and increased the partner's share from 8 per cent to 8.5 per cent, making the additional 0.5 per cent dependent on their performance. The performance rating, shared transparently with all the partners, was dependent on parameters such as on-time submission of profiles, disbursal of loans and repayments. Rang De noticed an improvement in partner performance after the incentive scheme was launched. Partners also provided Rang De with positive feedback, explaining that transparent ratings enabled them to identify problem areas and take steps to resolve them.

All of the above contributed to lower dropout rates among the partners. Apart from performance-related issues, Rang De's partners dropped out if there was a mismatch of vision and mission between them and Rang De or if the project objective was met and the desired impact was created.

VOLUNTEERS

Over the years, Rang De started to develop a large community of volunteers. Most of these volunteers were social investors who got inspired by Rang De's work and wanted to get involved beyond their financial contribution. Rang De enabled them to form chapters across various cities and let them decide what they would like to do to promote Rang De's causes. The members would work as extended team members of Rang De. Their activities involved creating awareness about Rang De as well as reaching out to social investors and borrowers in their areas. They made online and offline campaigns, organized fundraisers, made corporate presentations, represented Rang De at different events and some of them made field visits to understand the impact of Rang De's loans. These field visits were often life changing for them.

TECHNOLOGY

Right since its inception, information technology played a key part in Rang De's operations. Their online platform enabled their social investors to choose specific beneficiaries who they would like to give their loans to, make the investment, track repayments and re-invest or withdraw their loans. Likewise, field partners used the platform to upload the loan applications, receive approvals and track the loan amount that they received from Rang De, along with the disbursal to the borrowers and repayments. It substantially reduced paperwork and automated calculations of instalments to be made by the borrowers on a monthly or weekly basis. Based on data collected from the portal and performing continuous analysis, Rang De was able to maintain an organization-level dashboard that provided a snapshot of field partner performance, repayments, fund transfers and loans raised as well as created reports that were required periodically. The online portal reduced the time for submission, selection and approval of borrower profiles from 20 days to 7 days and ensured that the time needed for processing of loans from approval to disbursal was between 35 and 40 days.

While Rang De had initially outsourced the technology function, they subsequently integrated it within their organization. By 2020, technology function comprised the largest team in Rang De.

EVOLUTION AND DIVERSIFICATION

By 2010, Rang De allocated loans to more than 2,000 rural entrepreneurs across 10 states in India, channelizing funds from about 1,000 social investors. The entrepreneurs came from a wide variety of initiatives, such as clean energy, water and sanitation. They worked with 20 field partners and disbursed about INR 12 million. The key challenge for scaling up was to earn the trust of the investor. Noted Ram,

We are overcoming this challenge by focusing on some of our non-negotiables, which are transparency and communication. We go out of our way to communicate to our social investors. Be it good news or bad news, keeping the communication channel open is very important.

Rang De scaled up its operations during the next five years and by 2015, it had raised and disbursed INR 400 million through 25 partners across 16 states that helped 38,000 low-income households. Driven by the objective of reaching out to communities that never had access to credit from financial institutions, Rang De diversified into sectors such as handloom weaving, handicrafts and waste segregation and provided loans to people with disabilities. In the process, they started to customize their interventions to suit the specific needs of individuals and communities. For example, Rang De increased the moratorium period for some individuals involved in goat-rearing since their business did not give immediate returns. That customized loan product was offered to certain vulnerable communities in the Bundelkhand region of Madhya Pradesh and Uttar Pradesh where livelihood opportunities were severely affected by three consecutive years of drought. In another instance, Rang De increased the loan ticket size from INR 10,000 to INR 35,000 for farmers who reared cattle when discussions with them revealed that they had to borrow from other sources at much higher interest rates.

The Rang De team made a lot of effort in reaching out to people who were in real need of credit but did not have access to it. They chose field partners in areas that were underserved and those who had access to marginalized communities. An analysis in 2013 showed that about 88 per cent of Rang De's loans were disbursed in areas where the penetration of other microfinance organizations was between 1 and 2 per cent and another 10 per cent where penetration was between 2 and 5 per cent.[6]

Almost 50 per cent of Rang De's borrowers were first-timers. For example, Rang De, through their field partner Self Employment Voluntary Association (SEVA) in Manipur, provided a loan of INR 8,000 to Minarani Devi from Wangkhei Angom Leikai, a place in Imphal, who was involved in making knitted winter wear. Minarani, a widow with four children and the sole

---

[6] Rang De Social Accounts 2012–13.

breadwinner of her family, used the loan to buy raw material in bulk and avail discounts that enabled her to scale her business. Likewise, Rang De's loan of INR 40,000 to Krishna Ayyakanu through Hasiru Dala, a waste pickers' association, helped Krishna set up a dry waste collection centre in Bengaluru. Krishna had been a waste picker since he was eight years old, segregating and selling waste to support his family. Hasiru Dala provided him with waste management training and the necessary equipment, and Rang De's loan enabled him to make the necessary investments to start his business.

Talking of another dimension of their diversification, Smita explained,

> In the agricultural sectors of emerging economies like India, capital is the key. It dictates power and ownership and therefore providers of capital capture lion's share of surpluses created in agribusiness value chains. Now a new investment model which employs *participative capital* is challenging the status quo. Hence, we revised our strategy to partner with producer companies, cooperatives, self-help-groups and help them raise working capital to amplify their impact.

When Rang De offered loans to communities such as those of artisans, they could offer it at even a lower rate of 5 per cent because in such cases Rang De directly partnered with the borrowing entity and there was no need to charge the 2 per cent that was otherwise kept as margins for the field partner.

Over the years, Rang De realized that the rural poor not only lacked access to credit but also did not have basic financial literacy. The lack of financial literacy made these individuals, especially women, susceptible to fraud and exploitation by moneylenders who charged them exorbitant interest rates. Therefore, in 2016, they launched Swabhimaan, an initiative to provide financial literacy and requisite skills to women so that they could make well-informed financial decisions. As part of the programme, the women would be eligible for individual loans from Rang De only after they completed their financial literacy training and cleared an assessment. Rang De generated a credit score for these women and their loans could be customized to their specific needs in terms of ticket sizes and tenure. Thus, loans could range from INR 2,500 for household expenses with a repayment tenure of 1 month to INR 20,000 for livelihood with a repayment tenure of 12 months. The loans were disbursed directly to the borrower's bank account without the assistance of a partner organization. This had the additional advantage of making the borrower conversant with banking transactions and reducing her dependency on intermediaries. Rang De was delighted to note that some of these women decided not to take a loan despite being eligible for it, attesting the effectiveness of the financial literacy programme.

CORPORATE PARTNERSHIPS

Rang De forged different kinds of partnerships with corporations to raise funds. It started in January 2015, when one of them donated INR 2.5 million for the traditional weaving community through their CSR fund. Since corporations donated money to Rang De from their CSR funds, these were used as corpus or revolving funds to provide lower cost credits, such as for education and livelihood projects. They were also used to fund any deficits in fundraising. Donations from corporations and from high net worth individuals, typically foreigners, had a compound effect because once a borrower repaid the loan, it could be used for providing credit to other borrowers. Corporate partnerships were often the result of referrals from social investors to CSR departments of their own organizations. Once such a relationship was struck, it had the multiplier effect of inspiring other employees of the organization to become social investors. Rang De thus ran several campaigns in organizations, such as Rang De story sessions, payroll giving programmes and field visits with employees, that created awareness, converted many of the employees to investors and some of them even became active volunteers. Some organizations also matched the total amount that was invested by their employees.

Rang De's Mumbai chapter of volunteers were very active in reaching out to corporates, creating awareness and encouraging their employees to raise funds. In one such initiative, the volunteers reached out to Axis Bank and inspired 65 employees to run the Mumbai Marathon[7] as ambassadors of Rang

---

[7]   The Mumbai Marathon is the largest marathon event in India.

De. That event acted as a catalyst for engaging Axis Bank Foundation as well and showed Rang De the potential of such events to raise funds.

In 2013, Rang De received financial support from the National Bank for Agriculture and Rural Development's (NABARD) Microcredit Innovations Division to carry out an action research project in the states of Maharashtra, Bihar and Madhya Pradesh to understand borrower behaviour. The project also provided some revolving funds that could be used to provide credit to beneficiaries identified for the research. It was found that borrowers who were mentored as part of the project reported greater increase in savings as compared to non-mentored borrowers.

In 2014, Rang De received funding support from Tata Trusts that helped them scale up their organization and invest in their technology platform. Tables 4.2a, 4.2b and 4.3 give data about Rang De's social investors, investments, loans and borrowers over the years.

SOCIAL MEDIA CAMPAIGNS

Since its early days, Rang De tried to leverage social media to raise awareness and to get the attention of social investors. In 2011, they used the excitement around the Cricket World Cup to raise funds, where every time a successful action would happen at the game, people would pledge funds as social

Table 4.2a Social Investors and Borrowers
(Figures for a Particular Year, Not Cumulative)

	09–10	10–11	11–12	12–13	13–14	14–15
Number of social investors	925	1580	882	1,183	2,516	2,516
Social investment raised (INR millions)	11	25	32	65	85	64
Number of borrowers	2,103	4,517	5,155	7,952		

Source: Provided by Rang De.

Note: * APR interest rates are calculated on a monthly repayment schedule.
　　** Includes loan for sanitation to construct toilets and field staff loans.

Table 4.2b Social Investments and Loans

	On 31 March 2013	13–15	15–17
Number of active social investors	4,752	6,494	10,617
Number of loans	20,192	14,120	20,214
Number of women borrowers	95%	13,073	18,493
Number of occupations funded	257	308	412

Source: Provided by Rang De.

Table 4.3 Investments (in INR Million)

	31-03-2013	13–15	15–17
Outstanding portfolio	46	62	131
Individual social investments	104	32	94
Corporate grants	30	37	6
Other grants	0.8	3	44

Source: Provided by Rang De.

investments through Twitter. In two weeks, they were able to raise INR 1 million from 155 pledges on social media. Their campaign titled Rang De World Cup Fever received a lot of media attention and won several awards for its creativity.

In 2012, Rang De launched the Light Up India campaign during Diwali, where people were invited to purchase a sky lantern for INR 100 and that amount was invested by Rang De on their behalf. Rang De was able to attract 267 new social investors through this campaign. In 2015, Rang De used a similar campaign around Diwali to engage employees of specific organizations that resulted in INR 0.7 million investments from about 500 social investors.

Rang De's Influencer project enabled an individual to refer someone they knew and trusted to receive a formal loan. It was a project that was based on empathy and was a powerful invitation for citizens to influence change in the life of someone they knew. In 2019, they launched the #Myeverydayhero campaign where they invited social media influencers to join the Rang De team and share a selfie with someone who was their 'everyday hero', a person that they admired, respected and trusted, and would be happy to support. They reached out to about 300 social media influencers on Twitter and Instagram, out of which about 60 people opted to participate in the campaign. On the day of the campaign, traffic to their platform increased by 67 per cent though only three of the social media influencers actually participated.

BECOMING A NON-BANKING FINANCIAL COMPANY (NBFC)

The demonitization[8] of the Indian economy in November 2016 brought forth the need for digital financial inclusion. The promise of digitally serving the unbanked segments of the economy led to an influx of fintech companies to the sector, which, in turn, made the Reserve Bank of India (RBI) create regulations for P2P lending in October 2017. The new regulations required Rang De to become a private limited company from being a public charitable trust and it had to apply for an NBFC P2P licence from the RBI. It could no longer raise grants but had to fund the new entity through equity investments. Ram and Smita were worried whether private investors would expect them to change their operating model that could dilute their social mission. Recollects Smita,

> On the cusp of turning 10, when RBI's regulations for peer to peer lending hit the headlines, Ram and I were not sure if we were ready for this new adventure. Were we left with any energy to redo this all over again? We did what was required of us – the painful task of communicating to our 14,000+

---

[8] On 8 November 2016, the Government of India announced the demonetization of all INR 500 and INR 1,000 bank notes and issuance of new INR 500 and INR 2,000 banknotes in exchange. This action intended to curtail the shadow economy and reduce the use of illicit and counterfeit cash to fund illegal activities. The announcement was followed by prolonged shortage of cash, which compelled citizens to adopt digital modes for financial transaction.

community of social investors that the future was uncertain. We also knew that we had to start winding down the operations of RangDe.org if we were not able to comply with the regulation. While people were congratulating us for completing 10 years, we were wondering if there would be a Rang De 2.0 in the making.

Fortunately for Rang De, 23 of their social investors volunteered to become equity investors and by January 2018, Rang De was able to raise INR 20 million that was needed to file for the licence. The social investors were well aligned with the terms and conditions that Rang De suggested for maintaining the social mission of the organization. Commented Ram,

> We have shied away from taking commercial equity, as we are not promising high returns and want to continue with the philosophy of social return. We did not want to become a shareholder maximizing entity at the cost of our social mission and, therefore, looked at several inclusive business models to decide what should be our new operating model. With encouragement from our mentors and after some iterations, we seemed to have got the model that we want.

To arrive at their new model, the Rang De team talked to both their social investors and field partners. The social investors unequivocally communicated to them that the two aspects that they valued most and did not want to compromise were Rang De's ability to serve people at the last mile and deliver credit to them at a low price. And they were willing to pay a small membership fee for the service that Rang De provided them so long as these two objectives were fulfilled. In the absence of Rang De's platform, their field partners used to spend a lot of time and effort arranging for credit. Thus, they were also willing to pay Rang De a fixed membership fee because they no longer incurred many of the transaction costs. The field partners were also able to convince their donors about the utility of paying fees to Rang De to get on to their platform and avail their services. Rang De was thus able to create these new revenue streams that would enable them to remain financially sustainable. And since none of these costs was passed on to the borrowers, it enabled Rang De to remain focused on their mission. Wherever possible, Rang De waived the fees for the social investor, such as in case of interest-free loans. Moreover, Rang De was also ready to help their field partners raise funds in case they found it difficult to pay the fees.

It was mandatory for Rang De to have a strong technology platform in order to qualify for an NBFC P2P. All transactions had to be digital and funds had to flow directly from the account of social investors to the account of borrowers through an escrow account. Rang De was also required to collect know your customer (KYC) documents from all their social investors. Since not all communities met these requirements, Rang De had to work closely with them to meet the necessary requirements. Some of Rang De's social investors were not comfortable sharing their details as mandated by KYC documents and hence had to discontinue.

From 2018 to 2019, Rang De took a gap year where they modified their platform to suit the new guidelines as well as to bring in new investments. It went live once again in September 2019 and was able to raise INR 9 million by December 2019. Looking back at their journey so far, Smita commented,

Our journey has been extraordinary because we have this committed community of social investors who are now family. It is their power, belief, passion and perseverance that translates into Rang De's strength. They were the strong pillars that helped Rang De raise a fund of INR 20 million in a record 20 days. We draw all our strength and inspiration from them. And it is to them that we owe Rang De 2.0. The Rang De team has been through two years of trials and tribulations, rethinking, reinventing, questioning and celebrating change. Only time will tell whether we will be able to get closer to our dream of an inclusive India. For now, we are just content that we have put in everything that we have and there is no stone unturned.

DISCUSSION

What was the key problem that Rang De wanted to address? Smita and Ram, possibly because they were outsiders to the microfinance domain, started with a very basic question: why were the interest rates of lending to the poor so high? Even in case of Grameen Bank, which has been a role model for microlending, the interest rates of lending to the poor was higher than that was charged by commercial banks. This implies that a poor person was paying a 'poverty penalty' for getting a loan, being charged higher interest rates than the economically well-off person. When Grameen Bank charged high interest rates to its poor borrowers and declared a profit at the end of the year, it did not raise many questions because the bank was owned by the borrowers and the profits went back to the borrowers as dividends. However, Indian MFIs had two sets of problems. First, their interest rates were higher than Grameen Bank's because they could not take member savings and had to borrow from commercial banks. Second, they were owned by individuals, the private equity investors who were presumably very well-off. Therefore, when an Indian MFI charged a high rate of interest to poor borrowers and declared profitability at the end of the year that resulted in increase in net worth for its rich owners, it looked blatantly exploitative.

We have already discussed why the microlending model structurally has a higher cost of operations, the key ones being the higher riskiness of providing collateral-free loans and greater transaction costs incurred because of the small size of loans and the repeated transactions needed to service them. But how much premium should an organization charge to cover the costs of additional risks and higher transaction costs? The high recovery rates in case of Grameen Bank and most other MFIs indicate that probably the risks were overstated and the poor turned out to be far more dependable borrowers than they were expected to be, despite the fact that the loans were provided collateral-free. Thus, Grameen Bank's interest rate, which was about 20 per cent, provided Ram and Smita some idea about what a suitable interest rate could be to cover the cost of operations. However, in the Indian context, they had the additional cost component of borrowing from a bank. Therefore, they intended to innovate on two fronts. Being from the information technology industry, Ram was aware of its power to automate operations and reduce costs. They felt that if information technology could be leveraged such that the processes of evaluation, disbursement and tracking could be automated, operational costs would reduce substantially. Second, they wanted to introduce the model of P2P lending where loans would be raised from well-meaning individuals rather than banks, who would be willing to lend small sums of money without charging any interest. This would combine their intention of doing good even while not having any major financial impact because they would be getting back their principal amount. And for Rang De, it would significantly reduce the borrowing cost, which could be translated into lower interest rates for their borrowers. While this model was followed by organizations such as Kiva internationally, Rang De was the first to introduce it to India. Thus, by reducing operational costs by leveraging information technology and borrowing costs by adopting a P2P lending model, Rang De was able to reduce the overall interest rates of micro-credit to levels that were unheard of in the industry. This enabled them to reach people who were underserved even by existing MFIs.

What were the key elements of their model that needed to work to make it successful? What did Rang De do to make those elements work well? Apart from information technology, the critical elements in their model were the implementation partners and the social investors. Rang De had to attract social investors in large numbers to raise enough money as well as ensure that its field partners were able to disburse the loans and make recoveries on time. The challenge with attracting social investors was that the concept of providing small loans by individuals was completely new in the Indian context. Individuals are accustomed to being approached by NGOs for donation and in a country like India, where the needs are many, individuals encounter requests for donation quite often. However, Rang De was approaching them for loans and not for donations. This by itself was a new proposition, which individuals may take some time to realize or get familiar with. Thus, Rang De had to spend a lot of time and effort in creating awareness about this new mode of P2P lending. Unlike most donation seeking organizations, they did not have employees on the field who could visit potential creditors or even interact with them over phone. Therefore, Rang De had to depend a lot on social media campaigns to create awareness. They complemented this by holding events in organizations, so that they could motivate its employees to become investors. Moreover, they developed a large network of volunteers comprising typically young boys and girls who wanted to do more for Rang De's cause than investing. The volunteers helped Rang De conduct both online and offline campaigns to increase awareness and attract social investors. It is difficult to say whether all of these were enough for Rang De to meet their aspirations because a significant part of their loan portfolio comprised money raised from corporations as grants and donations.

The third important element in Rang De's models were their field partners. Rang De was connected to the borrower through the field partners and was critically dependent on their efficacy in choosing borrowers, disbursing loans and collecting repayments. Therefore, they evolved an elaborate process of partner selection, judging their knowledge about local conditions, the processes that they followed and whether they will be able to work with Rang De in terms of their skills to deal with information technology and their alignment with Rang De's values. Rang De realized that it was necessary to make a first-hand evaluation of the partners through direct interaction and hence they made field visits to understand any potential partner. They also realized that passion alone was not enough to ensure the suitability of the field partner and developed a thorough process of due diligence, including the appointment of an independent advisory board who could analyse the data that Rang De collected about potential partners and provide a dispassionate view. Rang De also realized that they needed to work closely with the partners, providing them training and improving their skills and professionalism. Finally, they developed a transparent evaluation system for the partners that was used to provide them with incentives for better performance. As noted by some of the partners, this evaluation system acted as a good feedback mechanism, informing them about the areas that they needed to improve. While Rang De had some turnovers among its partners, they could develop fairly long-term relationships with most of them. Moreover, they received proposals from a large number of organizations who wanted to become their partners, both of which indicate that Rang De was fairly successful in managing partner relationships.

How did Rang De evolve? Rang De's evolution can be traced along two dimensions, namely diversification and customization of loans and their realization that loans alone were not enough to help people overcome poverty. Rang De intended to keep its cost of operations low. This necessitated standardization of operations as much as possible because a variety in operations increases costs. However, over a period of time, Rang De realized that the credit needs of different communities were different as was their ability to pay back, especially in terms of frequency and timing. Therefore, as Rang De started to work with different communities, they started to customize their loan product to suit the cash flow and business needs of the borrowers. This has been the experience of most organizations that try to address the needs of the poor – one size does not fit all and to be most effective, one needs to customize the products and services to suit specific needs. Rang De was also sensitive to the fact that some of their borrowers would not be able to pay back on time because of events beyond their control, such as droughts, and in such cases, they gave pay-back holidays to their borrowers. Rang De also improvised and worked with producer communities and cooperatives directly, which enabled them to reduce interest rates further, since they did away with the intermediate layer of the field partner.

The experience of working with their field partners and borrowers made Rang De realize that while credit was necessary for the poor to build and sustain their micro-enterprises, it was not sufficient. This was because entrepreneurship was inherently risky and many of the borrowers did not possess financial skills or business acumen that was necessary to run a business. And unless the borrowers were able to build successful businesses utilizing the loan amount, it was impossible for them to improve their financial condition. Rang De, therefore, started focusing on providing such skills over and above credit to their borrowers. This was done primarily through field partners where Rang De started to select and evaluate field partners not only for their ability to connect the last mile for loan products but also for the additional services that they were able to provide to the borrowers that would increase their chances of success with their business. Rang De by themselves also started the Swabhiman programme that provided financial literacy to women borrowers, with the intention that it would result in better utilization of the loan amount. Rang De's evolution along these dimensions was similar to Grameen Bank's, which also customizes its loan product and looks at credit more as means to social transformation rather than an end in itself. However, Rang De's interventions in terms of providing financial literacy and business acumen were narrower in scope than the social transformation agenda of Grameen Bank. Thus, one can speculate which of the two would be more effective for building an inclusive business model and which of the two would be able to create greater social impact.

CHALLENGE OF CONVERTING A VISITOR
TO A LENDER

Rang De has been using its information technology platform extensively for reaching out to potential lenders. But its challenge has been that less than 10 per cent of the visitors to its site become lenders. While their conversion rate of 7–8 per cent average is way higher than other sites, it is still not enough for them to generate adequate funds to meet demand. This challenge will increase even more given that now they have become an NBFC and, therefore, cannot receive grants from CSR funds of organizations. How can Rang De convert more of their visitors to lenders? One of the possibilities is to understand what kind of visitors are becoming lenders. Through their platform, they can ask a question to all their lenders about what made them finally decide to lend. It is possible that visitors who are eventually becoming lenders were not casual visitors but were referred by a friend or family member who was herself a lender. This implies that lenders were mostly getting to know about Rang De from someone whom they trusted and was visiting the website to seek additional information, such as to understand the mechanics of lending. Or it was possible that lenders were typically from organizations where Rang De carried on a campaign that engaged the employees. Both of these implied that Rang De's platform was not enough to make someone decide to lend. It was acting as an implementing tool when people have already made up their mind about lending. If this is the case, Rang De should increase its engagement with organizations and follow up with their employees immediately, so that they make up their mind in favour of Rang De. They should reinforce their reference programme if word of mouth is found to be the key factor in converting visitors to lenders.

Information technology-mediated platforms increase reach at little or no marginal costs, but they are not good for carrying rich information (Evans and Wurster, 1997). Richness is defined by the amount of complex information that can be carried, the degree to which the information can be customized and extent of interactivity that is possible. Therefore, Rang De should ask itself the question: what does it take for someone to commit to lending money at very low interest rates? It is an intensely personal as well as emotional decision.

For some, it might need some kind of convincing, a little bit of pressure to decide in favour of lending and finally a smile of gratitude when the decision is made. All of these is possible through personal touch, through someone who is interacting with the lender, customizing the messages while trying to understand the levers that will make the person commit. This is what is done in a traditional model when an organization seeks donations for a noble cause. They interact with the potential donor over the phone and follow it up with a personal visit. When a person from the organization is sitting in front of the potential donor or lender and asking for money for a noble cause, it gives very little excuse to the lender to delay the decision. This personal touch is lacking in Rang De's model. It saves them an enormous amount of cost and also enables them to reach out to an unlimited number of people. But they should ask themselves if there is some way of combining their reach with some personal touch that can increase the richness of the interaction and thus improve the conversion rate. By itself alone, an impersonal platform might not be enough to convert a visitor to a lender.

CHAPTER LEARNING

It is of utmost importance for the poor to get access to low-cost sources of credit. However, existing financial systems, such as retail banks, find it difficult to provide collateral-free micro-loans to the poor at low interest rates, despite empirical evidence that such loans rarely become non-performing assets.

Even successful models of microlending, such as that of Grameen Bank, charge relatively high interest rates when compared to those charged by commercial banks. The poor, therefore, end up paying a poverty penalty.

Interest rates charged to the poor on micro-loans can be reduced significantly by reducing the borrowing costs of the lending institution. This can be achieved by borrowing from social investors who are lending for a social cause, rather than to have a steady income or a financial gain.

Interest rates can also be reduced by leveraging technology that reduces the transaction costs of lending.

Microlending organizations who are primarily dependent on technology-mediated P2P lending platforms must seek multiple means to attract a large number of social investors and commit them to investing. This can include high-decibel social media campaigns and recruitment of volunteers who can act as evangelists and ambassadors for the platform.

Partnerships with grassroots organizations who work closely with underserved communities can be an effective way of overcoming last-mile problems of reach with minimum expenses. Such partners, however, need to be selected carefully to ensure that they are well aligned with the social mission of the organization.

5

LABOURNET

Empowering Informal Sector Labourers

Close to 90 per cent of India's working population belongs to the unorganized sector, people who are typically poor, consumption deprived and socially vulnerable.[1] During the last two decades, even while the number of people below the official poverty line has reduced, the number of people consuming less than INR 30 per day has increased within the informal sector. A majority of people working in the informal sector are rural migrants who come to the city in search of livelihood because of dwindling opportunities in the villages. India's sprawling cities are able to absorb many of them because of the booming construction sector as well as an increasing tendency among Indian corporations to outsource their non-core activities. However, in the cities, the migrant labourers face hostile conditions and the wages they receive are grossly inadequate to make ends meet. Thus, if India wants to solve its poverty and inequality problem, it needs to squarely address the needs of informal sector workers. LabourNet, a for-profit social enterprise, is trying to address these needs. M. Gayathri, the Managing Director of LabourNet, noted,

> Even though cities attract them in large numbers, cities do not assimilate the poor migrant labourer. Arriving from the villages, they do not have any place to stay, do not get the kind of food that they were used to. Without

---

[1] This was estimated by the Report of the Committee on Unorganised Sector Statistics, National Statistical Commission, February 2012. Other estimates such as Das (2019) indicate that the informal sector comprises 79–85 per cent of India's nearly 500 million work force.

an identity, they are unable to prove their BPL[2] status. Thus, they may be living in the cities for fifteen years, yet they do not belong to the cities, being always at the receiving end of its hostilities and exploitation. One needs to think about catering to some of their fundamental needs that would enable them to survive the harsh realities of cities. This is what LabourNet intends to do.

ORIGIN AND EARLY DAYS

The roots of LabourNet lay in MAYA (Movement for Alternatives and Youth Awareness), a Bengaluru-based NGO founded in 1989 with the intention of dealing with the problem of child labour. MAYA wanted to send children working in the streets back to school and its founders along with volunteers spent the next several years spreading awareness among children, youth and communities about the evils of child labour and enrolled working and street children into non-formal education schools. During this period, MAYA was also instrumental in creating several movements and initiatives, such as the Campaign against Child Labor and Prajayatna, a programme aimed to monitor and improve the quality of education in elementary government schools. It was not very long before the founders of MAYA realized that the root cause of child labour was poverty and the poor needed to be provided access to better livelihood opportunities if they were expected to send their children to school. MAYA enrolled older children in vocational training institutes and once again confronted the issue of livelihood when it wanted these trained children to be gainfully employed. Subsequently, MAYA set up enterprises in the domains of carpentry, automobile repair and screen printing, which were owned and managed by youth trained through MAYA. Although, many of these micro-enterprises, such as automobile repairing, could sustain themselves on their own, others like toy manufacturing needed continuous investments for skill upgradation, design improvements and marketing. In early 2000, MAYA Organic Support Services (MOSS) was set up as a Section

---

[2] Below poverty line (BPL) citizens received some benefits from government-managed welfare programmes, such as subsidized food and healthcare.

25[3] company for providing marketing and business support to worker-owned enterprises. MAYA Organic India Private Limited (MOIPL) was set up as a private company that could secure investments and act as an aggregator marketing company for MOSS.

It was, however, difficult to address the livelihood needs of urban informal workers through micro-enterprises. Their challenges were unique, given that most of them were migrant labourers. Reduced opportunities and increased pressure on agricultural land in rural India drove millions of villagers to the cities in search of employment. A significant proportion of them got employed as daily labourers in the construction industry, thanks to the real estate boom in urban India.[4] Such daily labourers moved from one place to another, were seldom recognized by the government as a community of workers and were not provided with either any security or benefits by their employers apart from their daily wages. As they typically originated from the economically impoverished areas of rural India, they did not possess any assets and invariably ended up as slum dwellers in cities. Their forced mobility prevented their children from going to school. From its experience, MAYA learnt that for the same level of income, the children of a domestic help, who was permanently based in the city, were more likely to go to a school than the children of a migrant labourer. As a consequence, the second generation of migrant labourers had much lower chances of improving their economic conditions through education. Moreover, the temporary and informal nature of their work prevented them from being regulated by labour laws. A builder outsourced work to a big contractor who, in turn, outsourced work to smaller contractors and agents who were responsible

---

[3]   In India, non-profit/public charitable organizations can be registered as trusts, societies or a private limited non-profit company under Section 25 of the Indian Companies Act, 1956. Such companies are usually not allowed to sell any products or services, unlike a company that is registered as a private limited company. This is same as Section 8 of the Indian Companies Act, 2013.

[4]   According to the National Commission of Enterprises in the Unorganised Sector (NCEUS) report in 2005, 424 million Indians were employed as informal labour, out of which about 25 million were engaged as construction workers.

for recruiting daily labourers from villages. This series of outsourcing diluted and nearly eliminated any responsibility that the employer (that is, the builder) needed to take for the welfare of its employees. Thus, while the construction industry provided significant employment at an aggregate level, the individual labourer was highly disaggregated, resulting in large-scale exploitation.

LabourNet was conceptualized as an organization that would create and enhance income opportunities for workers in the unorganized sector. Beginning as a project under MAYA, it was registered as a for-profit business in 2008. Although, there was a significant demand for labour provided by workers from the unorganized sector, the labourers had limited means of knowing the points of demand for their services. Therefore, it was estimated that they spent close to 35–40 per cent of their workday being economically inactive, waiting or searching for employment opportunities.[5] Their unfamiliarity with the market compelled them to depend on several layers of intermediaries, who often were exploitative and cornered a fair share of their income.

LabourNet started off by creating a database of workers with the objective of linking them to potential customers. Their market research indicated that urban customers often found it difficult to hire reliable workers for household work. LabourNet, therefore, decided to create an information technology-based search engine that could enable the urban customers to locate reliable workers with minimum effort. LabourNet employees travelled to slums and collected information about potential workers to decide the kind of jobs they could be deployed in. Once this information was captured in its database, LabourNet made it available to potential customers and charged them a fee. While in its early days LabourNet charged the customers an access fee of INR 200, it was later changed to a transaction-based fee.

PROVIDING IDENTITY AND OTHER SERVICES

LabourNet's efforts at registering workers, their skills and linking them with potential employers was aided by the boom in cellular phones that was

---

[5] Report on Employment in Informal Sector 2013–14, Ministry of Labour and Employment, Labour Bureau, 2015.

witnessed in India from 2006. Since India had one of the lowest usage charges, it was possible even for a poor worker from the informal sector to purchase and use cellular phones. This made it easy for LabourNet to communicate with them, register their information and link them to the markets. Realizing that migrant labourers were excluded from any kind of formal financial services, LabourNet decided to provide the registered workers with a bank account and accident insurance.

However, for delivering any of these services, a proof of identity, such as a ration card or a driver's licence, was necessary. This turned out to be a problem because most of the workers either did not possess such proofs of identity or had left them behind in their villages, often at distant places, before they migrated to cities.

Moreover, it was difficult to convince insurance companies to provide individual insurance to construction labourers since they were considered as a 'high risk' category. After two-and-a-half years of negotiation, LabourNet convinced Oriental Insurance Company[6] to provide group insurance to the construction workers. LabourNet took up the responsibility of administering and monitoring the product since the cost of dealing with individuals was very high for the insurance company. It even partly financed the premium.

LabourNet registered the first 800 workers free of cost. Thereafter, to instil the importance of registration and its renewal in the workers, LabourNet shifted to a fee-based model. Workers were charged an annual fee of INR 75 for registration and another INR 75 for accident insurance. Since every insured worker received a card bearing his name, address and photograph, it served as a proof of identity for them. In the beginning, registration was slow, about a hundred a month, and it required a lot of convincing by LabourNet to get the workers registered and insured. LabourNet also realized that very often, it was the labour contractors rather than the workers who were getting registered.

Simultaneously, LabourNet continued its efforts with the banks, convincing them to provide bank accounts to the labourers. This turned out to be much more difficult than procuring accident insurance. LabourNet approached

---

[6] Fully owned by the Government of India, Oriental Insurance Company is one of the leading non-life insurance providers in India.

several banks as well as the Reserve Bank of India (RBI), so that they could loosen their norms of customer identification and other criteria for opening a bank account. Although, there was provision for opening a no-frills account within RBI guidelines, most of the banks did not show much interest in opening accounts for workers in the unorganized sector who, they perceived, would add a huge transaction burden to the bank's operation without contributing to its asset base. Finally, LabourNet was able to convince Punjab National Bank by offering to take care of the processing and documentation needs that were essential for opening a Mithra (a no-frills account that had no requirement of maintaining a minimum balance) account. LabourNet provided the bank with all the necessary details of the registered workers and acted as their introducer. The bank provided the workers with an ATM card along with a bank account to minimize in-branch dealings with the workers.

Subsequent to this, LabourNet saw a steep rise in registration, from the erstwhile hundred-a-month to about thousand a month. LabourNet modified its registration policy and started to provide each worker with accident insurance and a bank account for a fee of INR 105. With an increase in the number of registrations, LabourNet decided to start four Worker Facilitation Centres (WFCs) in Bengaluru, realizing that the workers expected to see a proper office if they were to pay for the services delivered by LabourNet. These WFCs provided account-opening and accident insurance services to start with and later offered additional services such as training.

Table 5.1 provides the number of workers that LaborNet registered during the period of 2004–11. While LabourNet started to register workers in thousands from the informal sector annually, re-registering them became a challenge. Workers either forgot to renew their policies or believed that what they had paid was a one-time fee for their entire lives. Some of them, having established their own networks, did not perceive much value in renewing their registration. Thus, the onus of reminding and convincing the workers to renew their registration was on LabouNet. LabourNet issued reminders through text messages sent to their mobile phones. This was effective only if the worker could read text messages and had not changed his mobile number, which was a common phenomenon.

LabourNet negotiated with several health insurance companies for a policy that would cover both out-patient and hospitalization expenditure

Table 5.1 Number of Labourers and Customers Registered by LabourNet

Year	Labourers Registered	Customers Registered
2005–06	518	100
2006–07	1,237	436
2007–08	2,662	1,386
2008–09	5,452	1,455
2009–10	8,881	507
2010–11	2,676	161

Source: Provided by LabourNet.

for registered employees. Most of the products available in the market were expensive and not geared towards addressing the needs of the poor. In a particular year, 2,000 workers bought health insurance and INR 700,000 was paid as premium. However, utilization was only for INR 95,000. As a result, it became difficult to convince the workers to buy health insurance the next year. Workers believed that they were in the prime of their health and failed to see the utility of paying premiums that might be as high as INR 700 per annum. LabourNet continued negotiating and working for better health insurance products and believed that they might become viable if linked to loans.

By providing bank accounts to the registered workers, LabourNet became a key enabler of financial inclusion for workers from the unorganized sector. However, LabourNet discovered that in some cases, there were middlemen who were charging the labourers fees to withdraw money from their ATM accounts since the labourers themselves were apprehensive about operating the ATM kiosk. Moreover, not all workers could provide the necessary documents that were needed for opening the bank accounts, howsoever minimal the requirements were. This made LabourNet modify its registration policy – while the identity card and accident insurance were mandatory for all registered workers, bank accounts and health insurance were made optional to ensure that even those who could not provide necessary papers derived some benefits from LabourNet.

BUSINESS MODEL AND MARKET DEVELOPMENT

By 2008, LabourNet had nearly exhausted the initial funding that it had received from Ford Foundation. Therefore, it had to approach new donors with a fresh business plan. Having created a database of workers, the task was to generate adequate demand for their skills and meet such demand in a timely and cost-efficient manner. LabourNet gathered the requirement from the customers through its Internet-based portal. Its software matched such demand with the available skills in the database. The workers were informed about job openings through multilingual messages sent to their mobile phones. The target customers were young professionals for household activities and small enterprises for housekeeping and other semi-skilled labour.

LabourNet proposed to offer clients enhanced safety compared to conventional ways of hiring labour, primarily because LabourNet workers had proper identification. A key value proposition was to ensure customer satisfaction. Therefore, there were provisions for the customers to provide feedback to LabourNet on the quality of work and the labourer. Thus, if a client was not satisfied with the work done, they could report the same to LabourNet through its call centre. Feedback had an impact on the worker's ratings. If completely dissatisfied, the client could ask for a replacement. LabourNet sent an executive to assess the situation. If it was the worker's fault, the client often got a replacement worker. To ensure better quality of service, LabourNet provided soft-skills training to the registered workers, teaching them the norms of professionalism. However, the fact that LabourNet could have very little control over fulfillment without incurring high monitoring costs posed a big challenge for ensuring good quality service.

In its early days, LabourNet had mandated that all payments made by the customer to the workers be routed through the company. Workers were also told that their membership might be cancelled if they bypassed the system and received payment from the customers directly. In practice, this system became difficult to implement because LabourNet did not have cost-effective means for monitoring and verification on the field. There were instances when the customer refused to pay a worker because of alleged poor quality of work. At some construction sites, the workers were made to sit idle because the supplier did not deliver construction material on time. Yet the contractor refused to pay

LabourNet workers because the work was not completed. In all such instances, the workers expected LabourNet to compensate them for the foregone wages and LabourNet was in no position to understand what actually went wrong and who should bear the responsibility for the lost wages. Technology-mediated means of payment through smart cards or Internet-based payment gateways seemed unfeasible in this particular sector because of its informal nature.

In order to generate adequate demand for its registered workers, LabourNet devised various marketing strategies. LabourNet was one of the earliest organizations to advertise on auto-rickshaws, an inexpensive and effective means of disseminating information. It visited information technology companies, which employed a large number of young professionals who, LabourNet reasoned, would have much demand for household services. However, it turned out that young professionals had a high demand for domestic help and early childcare providers but did not have much need for plumbers or electricians since most of them did not own or run households. LabourNet's next port of call was maintenance managers of apartment complexes who needed plumbers, electricians and repairmen. However, the demand there was much lower than expected. Moreover, many of these apartment complexes charged them high fees for setting up a registration desk, something that LabourNet could ill-afford at that point in time.

Despite their efforts, LaborNet could not register an adequate number of customers. Table 5.1 gives the number of customers that LaborNet registered during 2004–11. The number of registered customers were far less than was needed to provide employment to the number of workers that they had on board. Overall, LabourNet realized that while there was some demand for domestic help and childcare workers in the household sector, it needed to target other segments for its construction-related workers.[7]

This led LabourNet to explore large commercial enterprises, especially organizations involved in large-scale construction, for generating demand. Large enterprises looked attractive as a segment because demand was concentrated and the revenue per customer was higher. LabourNet was able

---

[7] Construction-related workers include electricians, plumbers, carpenters, masons, painters, welders, tile layers and fabricators.

to deploy 30 of its construction workers at a large project in Yelahanka, close to Bengaluru. The total revenue earned was INR 300,000, more than 90 per cent of which was paid to the workers. Although LabourNet faced some difficulties in collecting the money from the customer, it was the company's first breakthrough with a large customer. Many of the construction companies expressed eagerness to hire workers from LabourNet because they appreciated LabourNet's welfare motive and wanted to run their business in a socially responsible manner. However, during commercial negotiations, they were unwilling to pay any premium for LabourNet services and agreed to pay only market rates to the construction workers. They were not inclined to release the workers for training or provide LabourNet the opportunity to conduct training on-site, defeating LabourNet's intention of skill upgradation of its workers. This attitude of the large construction companies made the workers wary of undergoing training that LabourNet was imparting – either the workers were not getting any value for their training or they had to forgo income opportunities.

In 2009, LabourNet developed a partnership with Biome Environmental, a Bengaluru-based organization involved in sustainable building designing and rainwater harvesting. Biome trained LabourNet's registered workers in rainwater harvesting and employed them in projects. However, there were complaints about the quality of work. Moreover, many of the trained workers, after having received their money from the project, severed their relationship with LabourNet. After a while, LabourNet called off the partnership.

TRAINING AND SKILLS DEVELOPMENT

One of the first projects that LabourNet undertook soon after its inception was to provide market-relevant training to about 800 construction workers. Upgradation of skills through training was deemed important for increasing the income of informal sector labourers. It would also act as a differentiator for workers who were registered by LabourNet. J. P. Solomon,[8] founder and core team member of MAYA, noted,

[8] Public address, 24 June 2010, at Summer School on Computing for Socio-Economic Development organized by Microsoft Research, India.

The construction industry has hardly seen any innovation in the last 150 years in the style of working and in the tools being used. It is labour-intensive, there are very little work standards and training is on the job. The employers think that the employees are there only for a short while. Therefore, they do not want to invest in training.

LabourNet's training project, however, did not meet with much success, first, because the company was not clear about the kind of training that needed to be imparted and, second, because in the absence of any well-defined work standards, workers trained by LabourNet failed to command any additional price from the market for their skills. However, LabourNet continued to explore options for imparting training to workers in the unorganized sector because that was the only means by which such workers would be able to enhance their competencies and improve their potential for earning a higher income.

LabourNet found out that the Directorate General of Employment and Training (DGE&T), a government body, certified workers from the unorganized sector if they had attained the ministry's standards of competence. For example, if a construction worker, such as a carpenter, underwent 300 hours of specific training, he was certified as 'Assistant Carpenter'. With the intention of getting its workers trained and certified, LabourNet tied up with several industrial training institutes. These were government-managed institutions under the Ministry of Labour constituted to provide training in the technical field. Batches of workers thus trained were invited to LabourNet's facilitation centres, where they were examined and certified by the DGE&T-approved certification agency. To its surprise, LabourNet realized that the certification agency was not interested in examining worker skills. Instead, it was keen on doling out as many certificates as possible because DGE&T paid the agency based on the quantum of certificates it issued.

The workers, however, were satisfied with such a process. The certificates were an important identification document that could also help them to secure jobs, especially in the Middle East. However, in reality it did not differentiate them from the other workers in the industry. Moreover, the training imparted by the full-time training institutes was not geared towards addressing market realities. The focus was on giving designations such as Assistant or

Associate Carpenter, which had little utility unless the person was taking up a government job. Further, the more sophisticated skills that were required of a modern painter or plumber to deal with latest materials and gadgetry were missing from the curriculum.

The situation presented a moral dilemma for LabourNet. Two of LabourNet's objectives were to improve the skills of workers and provide them with identification. Easy certifications provided a form of identity and indicated, through governmental sanction, that skills have improved. Thus, LabourNet could 'prove' to its stakeholders that it had achieved its social objectives. Indeed, LabourNet was a pioneer in terms of large-scale worker certification and during the period of 2008–09, a majority of construction workers certified in Bengaluru were LabourNet-registered. Yet LabourNet knew that it had neither intrinsically improved worker skills nor met the needs of the market. By the end of 2009, LabourNet decided that there would be no more DGE&T or any other certifications until a proper training modality had been worked out.

Thereafter, LabourNet experimented with various methodologies for imparting training to the workers. Leveraging some kind of technology was important for rapid scaling. A study conducted by Microsoft India Research Centre on the behalf of LabourNet found that training through video film was effective, especially when it involved communicating work methods through stories and examples. This led LabourNet to invest in making video films for training in various activities, such as painting and tiling. However, producing a good quality film was expensive and any compromise on quality reduced the effectiveness of the training module. Moreover, results were mixed when such training was tried out in the field. LabourNet realized that further research needed to be done, especially with inexpensive technology, such as mobile phones, to make it viable.

ALLIANCE WITH THE GOVERNMENT

In 2009, LabourNet started exploring options of expanding its operations to other cities in India. It reasoned that the experience of working in other cities will provide valuable learning that would enable them to develop their business model further. During this time, the state government of Haryana approached LabourNet for registration and training of construction workers. The Haryana government had collected a 1 per cent tax from every construction project in the state to be used for worker welfare. However, the government was struggling with the identification of legitimate recipients just as they were yet to figure out what might be some of the schemes that they needed to introduce for worker welfare. As a result, the money that was collected was largely lying unutilized with them. The Haryana government was impressed with LabourNet's approach of registering workers and providing them with training and insurance, and it wanted LabourNet to replicate the same in Haryana, utilizing the money that the government had collected.

The Haryana government's offer was attractive because it provided LabourNet with an option of geographical extension without significant financial risk. However, there were apprehensions about working with the government and running a business model that was largely dependent on grants. LabourNet finally decided to accept the offer of partnership, primarily because Haryana as a state had a large number of migrant workers employed in the unorganized sector and LabourNet believed that it could make a difference to their lives through this partnership. It was decided that the Haryana government would bear two-thirds of the cost of the project, while LabourNet would fund the balance using a grant from one of its funders, CHF International.

Registrations in Haryana rose rapidly, with almost 9,000 workers registered in a short period. This was partly because while LabourNet in Bengaluru had to approach dispersed individual workers and convince them, the alliance with the Haryana government enabled them to go to any given builder's site and register all the workers. However, it was not long before LabourNet and the Haryana government started to have philosophical differences, and when LabourNet found it difficult to run the operations the way they thought was most beneficial for the labourers, it called off the partnership. Gayathri summarized by saying,

> They wanted us to be their agents rather than their partners. If we want to work with the government, we will have to be their vendor. The government is the largest spender; they are sitting on these funds that can be deployed

for worker welfare. Therefore, it is imperative that we work with them for maximum impact. It is probably too much to expect that we can change their way of working. Even though our alliance did not work out, we were able to introduce notions of accountability into the system.

CHALLENGES AHEAD

Notwithstanding such setbacks, LabourNet continued to work assiduously to improve the living conditions of migrant labourers by providing them with identity, training for skills development, financial inclusion and by linking them to markets. Within the first five years of its operation, LabourNet mainstreamed 43,000 informal workers by registering them and issuing identity cards, provided accident insurance to 32,000, opened 14,000 bank accounts, imparted training to 5,300 and were able to link more than 8,000 of the registered workers with jobs. It planned to extend its reach to several other Indian cities in the next few years.

However, growth remained a critical challenge for LabourNet. Given that there were close to half a million migrant labourers in and around the city of Bengaluru itself, LabourNet's ambition was to talk in terms of 'millions of registrations' across India, rather than the thousands that it had achieved over the years. Rapid scaling would also enable LabourNet to become financially sustainable, a goal that had constantly eluded them.

One of the unique features about LabourNet had been the common philosophy that bound the senior leadership, even though individuals such as Solomon moved on to other development organizations. For example, after considerable discussion among senior management, LabourNet decided that it would not sell the database of the workers to mobile telephone companies even though that would have provided LabourNet with a steady source of income. The leaders were not comfortable with breach of privacy that might occur. Looking back, Gayathri felt that such collective decision-making resulted in LabourNet making significant social impact. She said,

We have been able to bring the issues to the fore and our advocacy functions have far overtaken our reach in terms of registration. The Andhra Pradesh and Karnataka state governments are talking to us to replicate our WFCs. They recognize that these centres are a necessary intermediary if they want to deliver services to the informal sector. We have also been working with the RBI and the UID[9] team to lay down a blueprint for financial inclusivity. Thus, if MAYA was a pioneer in its campaign against child labour, LabourNet has been pioneering several issues pertaining to the livelihood of migrant workers.

Brian English, Managing Director of CHF India, one of LabourNet's funders, agreed,

We would like to continue to support LabourNet because they squarely meet our objectives of increasing income, improving living conditions and giving a voice to the urban poor. Unlike some of their other funders, we do not expect any returns from our investment. With our money, they can take risks and experiment. Over a period of time, we expect such experimentations to reduce. But till that time, we have to be patient.

Jayakumar, former CEO of LabourNet, expressed views that were even stronger.

Social enterprises can never attain complete financial sustainability. They go where market forces do not prevail. Therefore, they develop markets, while incurring losses. Once they become profitable, commercial enterprises will take over and the social enterprise will move on to address other market failures. They need to sustain themselves through grants and work with the government for funds. LabourNet is supporting an uncompetitive segment of producers in a competitive market. How can such a developmental activity be done in a financially sustainable manner?

However, it would not be very long before LabourNet and its senior management would have to worry about creating a sustainable source of

---

[9]   UID stands for Unique Identification, an initiative by the Indian government to provide unique identification numbers to all Indian citizens.

income stream if they were to realize their dreams of creating large-scale impact. Some of their existing funds were nearing the end of their terms and any effort to raise fresh investments would require plans for generating demand for LabourNet-registered labourers as well as exploring revenue streams for the organization. Many of its strategic questions, such as an addressable market and investment on training, remained unanswered. LabourNet also needed to evolve a model for working with government agencies, if at all, because it could ill-afford a repetition of its Haryana experience. There is no doubt that all these issues would keep the senior management engaged and worried for some time, even as they continued to deliver essential services to migrant labourers.

DISCUSSION: TRADE-OFFS BETWEEN ACHIEVING SOCIAL IMPACT AND FINANCIAL SUSTAINABILITY

LabourNet's case brings forth the dilemma that many social enterprises face between maximizing social impact and earning enough commercial returns to be financially self-reliant. Because LabourNet was conceptualized as a for-profit organization, it was keen to identify revenue streams that would reduce its dependency on grants. However, most of its efforts that created positive impact on the lives of the informal sector worker could not be monetized because LabourNet's target segment – the informal sector labourer – was poor and could not afford to pay fees for the services that LabourNet rendered. Moreover, LabourNet did not deem it ethical to leverage some of the monetization opportunities that came its way, which would have possibly made them financially self-reliant. Realizing the various trade-offs that LabourNet had to confront can make one understand the complexities of creating business models that address the needs of the poor as well as are financially self-reliant. It is possible that there are certain sectors where it is almost impossible to achieve both. In the following sections, we will analyse LabourNet's model of value creation and discuss whether it is possible for it to become financially self-sufficient without diluting its key objective.

LABOURNET'S MODEL OF VALUE CREATION AND IMPACT

LabourNet's value creation activities can be divided into two parts: (a) providing services related to identity creation, financial inclusion and skills training to informal sector labourers and (b) acting as a multisided platform (MSP)[10] that connected informal sector labourers to potential employers.

LabourNet realized that one of the serious challenges faced by the informal sector workers, especially those who migrated from villages, was the lack of any document that proved their identity. In the absence of an identity card, the informal sector workers were excluded from government welfare programmes, neither could they have bank accounts or any kind of insurance, many of which were causes behind their inability to get better livelihood options or have protection against exploitation. Thus, LabourNet could do significant value addition to their lives and make them better prepared for earning their livelihood if they could bring such labourers into the mainstream. Data from the case indicates that LabourNet had succeeded considerably in their effort in this direction, which also resulted in their being invited by the Haryana government for registering construction sector workers as well as by the governments of Andhra Pradesh and Karnataka. LabourNet had also ventured into providing training to the registered workers for upgrading their skills. LabourNet deemed such training to be essential for the workers, so that they were able to command a better price for their efforts and thus increase their income. However, LabourNet had met with limited success in this regard because, given the demand–supply situation in the labour market, employers were unwilling to pay a price premium for labourers who were trained by LabourNet. Neither were they willing to provide the labourers with time away from work that was necessary for the labourers to get trained.

The second dimension of LabourNet's activity was creating a platform that connected the informal sector labourers with potential employers in an efficient manner. The labourers LabourNet dealt with were mostly migrants

---

[10] An MSP is defined as an organization that creates value primarily by enabling direct interactions between two or more distinct types of affiliated customers. LabourNet can be considered as a two-sided platform, a special case of MSP. For a detailed discussion, see Hagiu and Wright (2011).

from rural India. Significant numbers of such migrant labourers were involved in the real estate sector as construction workers, while many of them also catered to the household sector as helpers and drivers. While there was a large demand for the services that they rendered, such labourers did not possess any bargaining power because they were disaggregated, the jobs that they did were mostly unskilled or semi-skilled, they lacked information about potential markets as well as because of the presence of several intermediaries who were responsible for bringing them to the cities from villages and linking them to employees. Many such intermediaries provided them with safety nets, such as lending them money and providing them a place to stay, while at the same time such intermediaries were exploitative, who charged them high interest rates and often retained a significant portion of their wage as their service charge. As a consequence, the income of migrant labourers was meagre; they had to continuously struggle with the inhospitable and unfamiliar conditions of urban India and were often exploited by the intermediaries, their employers and even the local law enforcers.

LabourNet's objective was to act as a benevolent intermediary by connecting the migrant labourers with potential employers. The platform that they created matched labourers and their skills with demand for their services. From a modest beginning, LabourNet was able to register close to 30,000 labourers and about 4,000 customers that resulted in 8,000 labourers getting jobs. It is possible that the number of jobs procured by the registered workers was higher because many of them had used their own connections to get better jobs after they had made the initial connections with potential employees through LabourNet. Thus, LabourNet had been successful in realizing its objective of providing livelihood opportunities, though the number was possibly much lower than what they would have liked it to be, given that they had registered 30,000 labourers on their platform.

Through which of these activities was LabourNet creating a greater impact in the lives of the informal sector labourer? LabourNet was fundamentally a social enterprise that wanted to alleviate poverty that was endemic among informal sector workers. When LabourNet provided them with jobs by connecting them to potential employers, it resulted in a source of livelihood. That LabourNet did not retain any share of the money that the labourers earned implied that the workers were able to earn more because of LabourNet, even if they were able to procure similar jobs through other intermediaries. Therefore, there is no doubt that LabourNet created value by acting as an MSP for the informal sector labour market.

On the other hand, when LabourNet provided the labourers with identities, helped them to have bank accounts, get insured and developed their skills through training, it enabled the labourers to be self-reliant and be able to face the harsh realities of urban life. Once the labourers were 'mainstreamed' by LabourNet, it became easier for them to search for jobs on their own, have some kind of security through the insurance and not get exploited by the intermediaries. Development economists such as Amartya Sen (1999) have argued that while providing income can be an effective way of helping the poor, it is more important to develop their capabilities, so that the poor can have greater choice in their lives and be self-reliant. Thus, one can argue that the services that LabourNet was providing in the form of identity creation and enabling financial inclusion were quite unique and probably there were no other organizations that would do the same. Since there were several placement agencies that acted as MSPs and linked labourers to service markets, that dimension of LabourNet's value creation was not unique. Thus, LabourNet was doing quite well as a social enterprise in delivering a unique service to the informal sector workers that would enable them to access the markets. Did LabourNet need to do both, or could they have only stuck to the activity of providing the labourers with proof of identity, financial inclusion and training and not venture into creating a platform to provide them with jobs? It was possible, but it would have made their task of becoming financially self-reliant even more difficult. This is the topic of discussion in the next section.

BECOMING FINANCIALLY SELF-RELIANT

Let us analyse each of LabourNet's activities from the possibility of financial viability. In this context, it implies whether LabourNet can create a sustainable business model and not depend on grants and charities to achieve its objective.

If LabourNet wanted to achieve financial sustainability through providing services to the informal sector labourers, it could resort to a fee-based model. However, such fees cannot be very high, given the low paying capacity of their customers. Therefore, unless LabourNet generated very large numbers, it was unlikely that such fees would pay for the expenses incurred in running the operations. Moreover, given that the labourer was unlikely to come back to LabourNet for repeated registrations, an annual fee-based model did not seem to be a practical option. LabourNet will have the opportunity to charge the customers only once when they come for registration the first time. Thus, it seems unlikely that LabourNet could become financially self-reliant based on the registration fee alone. To augment its income, LabourNet could get into revenue-sharing arrangements with other organizations. However, even there the options do not seem to be many. The banks were unlikely to share any revenue with LabourNet because informal labourers would not be a profitable segment. Banks were also providing services to this segment mostly to discharge their corporate social responsibilities. The insurance companies might agree to share some revenues with LabourNet if it was able to provide them with a large number of customers. Thus, the practical option before LabourNet seems to depend on grants and donor funds. Over the years, LabourNet has developed competence in delivering these services and have been able to satisfy their donors even though it was yet to figure out a way of working with the government for a long term. In this mode, the demand for its services would be primarily generated from welfare schemes of the government and LabourNet could evangelize and make the labourers aware of such schemes, apart from partnering with the government in delivering those services. As argued in the earlier section, this line of activity would enable LabourNet to make a meaningful impact, but it would be very difficult for them to become a financially self-reliant organization.

If LabourNet wanted to build its MSP business, it was necessary that it created a lot more employment opportunities, which would draw the informal sector labourer to LabourNet. It could effectively become a job portal for the lowest end of the employment market, given that there are already several players in the middle and upper end. LabourNet would function as an aggregator, reduce search costs for the potential employers and reduce information asymmetry for the labourers. However, in this segment, it would have to deal with competition – mostly from local intermediaries – and it would need to charge economical prices. Local intermediaries could resort to flexible pricing because of their personal relationships with the labourers. The local intermediaries had a strong control over the labourers and even though they were exploitative, they ensured continuity and had credibility with the employers – something that LabourNet had found difficult to establish. In the absence of that, LabourNet was unlikely to get a price premium from the employers, which would pose serious challenges to its business viability. It is unfortunate that LabourNet was operating in a market where intermediaries made themselves viable by exploiting the labourers and, given the large supply of migrant labourers to the cities, it was nearly impossible for a social enterprise such as LabourNet to establish a viable business model without depriving the informal labourers of their share of wages. The employee database was one asset that LabourNet could monetize, such as by selling it to telemarketing companies. However, LabourNet's founders did not find that to be an ethical proposition.

Which of the two options – service provision or MSP – should LabourNet concentrate on? While operating as an MSP seemed to have the potential for LabourNet to attain financial self-reliance, LabourNet was delivering significantly more value by providing identity and financial inclusion. Moreover, as an organization that had its roots in MAYA, the founding team seemed to be much more welfare-oriented than commercial-minded. This implied that even though they wanted to be financially self-reliant, their core objective lay in touching the lives of the labourer in a more meaningful manner and creating a long-term impact in their lives, rather than providing them with only jobs through the LabourNet portal.

The case, therefore, raises the question of whether LabourNet needed to be financially self-reliant or whether they should abandon the objective of financial sustainability and continue to depend on donor money for their activities. The two comments towards the end of the case – one by Brian English and the other by Jayakumar – are insightful in this respect. Brian did not seem to be worried about the fact that LabourNet was not financially self-reliant. He and CHF were happy with the work that LabourNet was doing and they understood that it was not easy to monetize such work. According to him, donor money was for taking risks and doing experiments and they were ready to be patient until LabourNet was able to figure out a suitable business model. Likewise, Jayakumar commented that LabourNet was addressing a market failure – of providing financial inclusion and identity to the informal sector worker – and it was unrealistic to expect that LabourNet could attain financial self-reliance even while addressing it. Thus, one can argue that the goal of financial self-reliance need not worry LabourNet much for the time being because as an organization it was creating significant value for its target community. Identifying revenue streams that could enable it to meet some of its expenses might be desirable, but that should not distract them from continuing to do the good work that they have been doing so far.

EPILOGUE[11]

The detailed case study on which this chapter is based was written in 2012. Tracing the evolution of LaborNet through that case helped us to understand the trials and tribulations that organizations with inclusive business models go through. Some of them struggle to deal with the challenges as has been the case with Vaatsalya and RuralShores, while others like SELCO are able to successfully tide over them. Fortunately, LabourNet falls in the second category. In fiscal 2017–18, LabourNet reached a turnover exceeding INR 1 billion and a profit of INR 88 million. Table 5.2 gives LabourNet's financial performance during financial years 2016–18. By 2018, it had trained 700,000 laborers and developed 135 certification courses for 28 industries. Its training was delivered from 150 livelihood centres and from 912 work sites of organizations. It also conducted vocational training in 700 schools and, along with providing employment in organizations, LabourNet also helped develop entrepreneurs.

However, their journey was a difficult one. Gayathri was quoted as saying how in 2011, when LabourNet had a turnover of INR 40 million, she realized that their existing model of removing information asymmetry in the market for informal labour would not be enough for LabourNet to grow as an organization. Moreover, customers preferred labourers with experience rather than those who had certificates. Gayathri, therefore, decided to focus LabourNet on training that would bridge the gap between skills and market

---

[11] Based on input from secondary sources such as Chakraborty (2018), Bhargava (2019) and https://unreasonablegroup.com/companies/labournet/#video.

Table 5.2 LabourNet's Financial
Performance (in INR Million)

Year	Turnover	Profitability
2015–16	738	(–) 48.4
2016–17	828	6
2017–18	1,087	88

Source: From *Forbes India* article by Sayan
Chakraborty (2018).

needs. Apart from its own training centres, it started to provide technical and vocational training on work sites and in schools.

To fund its growth, Gayathri raised INR 350 million in equity from angel investors, such as Acumen Fund and Michael and Susan Dell Foundation. Till date, LabourNet has worked with around 100,000 workers at work sites and shop floors that have included construction sites, leather companies and rubber manufacturers. Typically, these workers who were originally earning between INR 9,000–10,000 per month managed to increase their wages by about 15 per cent because of the training they received.

LabourNet trained another 100,000 workers through its training centres in Karnataka, Tamil Nadu, Maharashtra, Himachal Pradesh and Haryana. These courses were for two to six months and included beauticians' work, welding, auto services (2–3 wheelers) and electrical services. While some of those trained have joined full-time employment, others have become micro-entrepreneurs.

LabourNet ran a four-year vocational training programme in schools. It began by helping students identify their areas of interest from Grade 9 onwards and guided them towards suitable training after Grade 12 if the students did not want to pursue academics. It worked with about 30,000 students in 700 schools in Punjab, Haryana, Himachal, Odisha, Assam and Chhattisgarh.

Around 2013, LabourNet started working with micro-entrepreneurs so that they could run their businesses better. LabourNet provided them training in areas such as accounting, human resource and inventory management. Over the next five years, it trained around 7,000 micro-entrepreneurs, some of whom managed to raise their incomes by 20–25 per cent.

By 2018, LabourNet developed a capacity for training 200,000 people and Gayathri hopes to expand that to 1 million by 2022, which would give LabourNet a revenue of INR 10 billion and a cumulative impact of creating livelihood for 10 million labourers. Commented Gayathri,

> We want to formalize the informal sector. The idea is not to give doles and benefits, but to empower people to make a better living.

Commented Naga Prakasam, partner at the Acumen Fund, which was one of LabourNet's investors,

> LabourNet has grown more than many skilling companies and non-profits. A private company in this space, taking equity investment and reaching INR 100 crore in revenue, is fantastic. The next thing that Gayathri needs to prove is that this scale is also possible without aid from government programmes like Skill India, and have people pay for it. For people to pay, the outcome needs to be clear. If they see the scope for earning more by taking up a course, they will pay. An NIIT or an Aptech[12] thrived because people were willing to pay as they got jobs.

CHAPTER LEARNING

Migrant labourers who move from villages to cities in search of jobs are caught in a vicious cycle of poverty because most of them are engaged in low-paying jobs that demand low skills. One way of improving their economic condition is to upgrade their skills so that they can command better wages.

Migrant labourers often do not have proof of identity that prevents them from accessing different services such as banking or insurance. They

---

[12] NIIT and Aptech were Indian organizations that provided information technology-related training to millions of graduates, which enabled them to find employment in India's information technology and software services industry. Training providers like them are often considered a key element of the ecosystem that enabled India to create an important position for itself in the global information technology industry.

also do not have information about employment opportunities. For all of these, they depend on intermediaries, who are often exploitative.

An organization that intends to improve the economic conditions of migrant labourers need to connect them to employment markets and help them to get access to financial and other services, apart from upgrading their skills.

Since upgradation of skills and connections to suitable employment opportunities can lead to enhanced income for the labourers, it is possible to create an inclusive business model around such services because the labourers are likely to pay for such services. However, other services such as providing them with identity cards or access to banking and financial services will be difficult to monetize and can create a problem for financial sustainability of the business model.

On the demand side, connecting to businesses such as real estate organizations or manufacturers might generate more employment than connecting them to individual households.

Organizations working in this domain need to be flexible in offering training from multiple types of locations, including premises of employers, since not all employers will be willing to spare the labourers from their work to upgrade their skills.

Governments have significant funds allocated for skills training of labourers, which can be accessed by organizations who intend to provide such services. However, dealing with funds provided by the government may lead to different challenges such as mismatch of intentions.

Inclusive organizations that intend to create positive impact on the lives of poor labourers need to make trade-offs at multiple levels. Some of the services that yield income for the labourers such as skills training and connection to employers can create a financially sustainable business model. While others such as providing them access to financial services, even if creating significant long-term positive impact on the lives of the labourers, will not be suitable for creating a financially sustainable business model. Therefore, organizations intending to create inclusive business models might need to make a difficult choice of not providing services that are non-monetizable, despite their positive impact.

6

SELCO

Inclusive Model for Energy Access

According to the Indian census in 2011, 81 million households in India suffered from energy poverty, of which 71 million were in rural India. Energy poverty is defined as households having less than adequate consumption of energy, using a polluting source of energy or spending excessive time in collecting fuel. While the Government of India took an aggressive target of connecting every Indian village to the grid and declared in April 2018 that, with the electrification of Leisang village in the state of Manipur, India has achieved 100 per cent rural electrification, connection to the grid did not imply that households in a village had access to electricity. A village was declared electrified if 10 per cent of the households could access electricity along with public institutions, such as health centres and schools. Hamlets and the residences of poor households were not considered in this calculation. Thus, even if a greater number of households might have obtained access to electricity post the 2011 census, a significant part of rural India and considerable part of urban India continue to have unreliable and intermittent access to electricity, if at all. Dr Harish Hande founded SELCO in 1995 to sell solar lights to the poor with a belief that access to solar energy would significantly improve the productivity of rural households. By 2010, SELCO had sold solar lights to more than 120,000 rural homes and 4,000 institutions, such as orphanages, clinics, seminaries and schools, in the state of Karnataka. Additionally, through its partnership with the Self-Employed Women's Association (SEWA),[1] it had provided energy-efficient cook-stoves and solar lamps to another 80,000 poor

---

[1] Its partnership with SELCO is explained in a later section on product diversification.

consumers in the state of Gujarat. In this chapter, we look at how SELCO evolved as an organization, the various challenges it faced along the way and the unconventional ways by which it overcame them.[2] We end the chapter by discussing what may be some of the lessons that social enterprises can learn from SELCO's journey.

THE EARLY DAYS

Harish got the idea of bringing solar lighting systems to rural India when he was doing his PhD on sustainable energy at the University of Massachusetts in the USA. During a field visit to the Dominican Republic, he was surprised to find poor villagers using solar lighting and reasoned that if it was possible there, he should be able to bring solar lights to the rural poor in India too. In early 1993, having made up his mind to focus on solar lights as a means for rural electrification for his PhD, Harish travelled to the remote sugarcane growing village of Galgamu near Anuradhapura in North Sri Lanka with his scholarship money, carrying with him a few solar panels and his solar-powered laptop. He wanted a first-hand experience of issues and realities of villages that had no access to electricity in order to figure out how he could solve some of their problems. He lived there for the next six months, understanding the connection between poverty and energy until his stay ended abruptly because the village was stormed by an armed rebel group who took away all his solar panels.

Subsequently, Harish went back to Massachusetts where he met Neville Williams, a former Green Peace activist, who founded Solar Electric Light Fund (SELF), a not-for-profit organization that intended to promote the use of solar energy in developing countries. In 1993, SELF received a grant of USD 40,000 from the US-based Rockefeller Foundation to install solar lights in 100 rural homes and Neville asked Harish to lead and implement the project in the Western Ghats region of India. Harish saw that as a great opportunity to validate his thesis. He was, however, apprehensive about being dependent on grants for his endeavour and was keen to establish a financially

---

[2] According to secondary sources, by 2018 SELCO served 675,000 houses and 12,000 institutions.

self-sustainable organization, so that there was continuity in operations. He believed that the poor would be willing to pay for technology if they found it useful. Moreover, Harish and SELF faced several regulatory hurdles in bringing the money in the form of a grant into India. Therefore in 1994, he founded SELCO Photovoltaic Electric Private Limited as a for-profit enterprise that would sell solar lights in rural India.

Solar lights were not new to rural India. Almost every year, in the month of March,[3] the Indian government used to install solar-powered streetlights to utilize funds devoted to non-conventional energy. However, in the absence of an organization to assume responsibility, very little effort was subsequently put in for proper maintenance of these lights. March was followed by the Indian summer when abundant sunshine often resulted in overcharging of the solar panels and drying up of distilled water in the batteries. By the time the monsoons set in July, many of the lights stopped functioning, thereby creating a perception among villagers that solar lights were fragile and unlikely to function for more than three to four months.

Harish realized that he would have to change this negative perception about solar technology and decided to take the responsibility of maintaining some of the solar streetlights in Dakshin Kannada[4] that were installed earlier. He intended to demonstrate that the technology could be made to work on a sustained basis. He also trained some of the local villagers, typically those involved in television or cycle repair, on how to maintain those lights. In the process, he started creating a pool of technicians who could take on the responsibility of maintaining and repairing solar lights as and when SELCO would install them in the future.

SELCO, however, had no access to funds, even for its working capital. Harish struggled to convince suppliers to provide him with solar lights on credit. It was around this time that Tata BP Solar[5] was setting up its rural

---

[3]   March is the last month of the financial year in India and there is heavy pressure on the government departments to exhaust their budgets, so that their budgets are not cut in the next financial year.

[4]   A rural district in southern Karnataka.

[5]   A joint venture between Tata Power Company and BP Solar, having a revenue of INR 11 billion in 2009, of which INR 9 billion is earned from exports.

infrastructure division with the aim of developing markets for its products targeted at rural Indian customers. Harish was able to impress them with his ideas and they decided to provide him with solar lights on credit, one or two systems at a time. Thomas Pullenkav, a young manager at Tata BP, who was responsible for developing their rural infrastructure business, recalled,

> I was less convinced than my organization about the viability of Harish's plans. However, I was impressed by his dedication and conviction and realized that giving him a system or two on credit was not much of a risk for a large company like Tata BP, even if all his plans failed. Moreover, I was convinced that Harish would pay back all his dues, even from his own pocket if he failed to recover any money from his customers.

Harish sold his first solar light to a wealthy betel nut farmer on the sly! Since the farmer had never heard about solar-powered lights, Harish was unable to convince him about its utility. However, Harish found the farmer's 72-year-old mother listening to him attentively and realized that he might be able to persuade her. Therefore, a few days later, Harish approached the elderly lady when the farmer was away and installed the solar lights in his fields. At night, when the farmer saw his fields light up, he was ecstatic. When Harish returned a week later, the farmer happily handed over his USD 300 as payment for the light.[6] During the next several months, Harish travelled across rural Karnataka, taking solar lights on credit from Tata BP and installing them in homes of farmers who could afford them. To save costs, he travelled by bus and sometimes even slept inside them overnight. Thomas, meanwhile, tried various means at his disposal at Tata BP to help Harish's cause, including convincing his other dealers to extend credit to Harish. In the process, he grew close to Harish, decided to leave Tata BP after about a year and joined SELCO, with the aim of creating an organization that could fulfill Harish's vision. M. Ramachandra Pai, one of the dealers at Tata BP, who had seen Harish's work from close quarters, also joined SELCO.

---

[6] Adapted from the article 'A Bright Idea That Helped India's Poor', written by Amy Kazmin in *Financial Times*, 25 February 2009.

Thus, SELCO started operating as an organization from 1996 even though it had no finance, could not afford any office space and could only employ the services of an accountant on a part-time basis. The next one year, SELCO faced a hand-to-mouth existence – Harish continued to live and operate from his aunt's place, while Thomas moved in with Pai to save costs on rent. Meanwhile, Harish convinced Neville that it would be better to invest money in SELCO, rather than depend on grants. Neville, therefore, registered SELCO in the US as a commercial entity in 1997, so that he could raise money from investors there. Apart from India, Neville set up various SELCO subsidiaries in other developing countries, such as Vietnam, China and Sri Lanka.

Towards the end of 1996, SELCO received a conditional loan[7] of INR 5 million from USAID through its partner Winrock International. That loan enabled SELCO to hire employees, invest in printing brochures and, most importantly, secure a greater number of solar lighting systems on credit. That increased SELCO's stature in the eyes of its suppliers. It was also the first time that Harish and Thomas received their salaries. Around the same time, the television repair market in India nosedived with the launch of several maintenance-free durable televisions and many of the technicians who had earlier worked for Harish on a part-time basis joined SELCO as employees. SELCO set up its first three rural service centres, which they deemed essential for creating a sustainable rural delivery model. Between 1999 and 2001, SELCO India received USD 750,000 from equity investors in the US and in 2003, a loan of USD 1 million from International Finance Corporation (IFC).[8] Table 6.1 through Table 6.4 show SELCO's assets and liabilities position and financial performance during 2004–09.

---

[7]   This loan was obtained after Thomas and Harish had sent a proposal to USAID/Winrock, who were evaluating projects on the commercialization of renewable energy for funding. The loan was provided specifically to set up three service centres.

[8]   IFC had created a Photovoltaic Market Transformation Initiative fund for India and Harish had applied for funds from them. This money was provided in three tranches, which SELCO was supposed to pay back

Table 6.1 SELCO's Profit and Loss Account (All Figures in INR Million)

	FY 04–05	FY 05–06	FY 06–07	FY 07–08	FY 08–09
Revenue	130	66	63	78	120
Material Cost	86	43	42	53	77
Sales Promotion#	8	4	4	5	8
General Admn Costs	32	29	36	28	32
Financing Costs	2	3	4	2	0.5
Profit/Loss	3.15	-12.3	-23.13	-8.39	1.36

Source: Provided by SELCO.

Note: # Includes market awareness creation programmes, demos, Interest subsidy costs, sales commission, and so on.

Table 6.2 SELCO's List of Shareholders as on 31 March 2009

Shareholders	No. of Equity Shares (Face Value INR 1)	Paid Up Share Capital in INR Million	Per Cent (%) of Shareholding
Solar Electric Light Company, USA	4,140,448	4.14	7
E+Co., USA	9,774,243	9.77	16
Lemelson Foundation, USA	14,000,000	14.00	23
Goodenergies Foundation, Switzerland	34,000,000	34.00	55
Harish Hande, Managing Director	253,859	0.25	0.41
K. M. Udupa, Director	20,000	0.02	0.03
Total	62,188,550	62.19	100

Source: Provided by SELCO.

Table 6.3 SELCO's Balance Sheet (in INR Million)

Parameters	FY 04–05	FY 05–06	FY 06–07	FY 07–08	FY 08–09
Fixed Assets	3.5	3.35	1.95	1.53	1.43
Current Assets & Investments	103.7	91.84	63.39	55.03	122.29
Current Liabilities	37.57	23.11	19.19	20.27	31.25
Secured & Unsecured Loans	30.8	45.88	45.86	44.62	18.22
Share Capital	45.94	45.94	45.94	4.59	62.19
Reserves (Net of Accumulated Losses)	-7.11	-19.74	-45.65	-12.92	12.06

Source: Provided by SELCO.

Table 6.4 SELCO's Secured Loans (External Commercial Borrowings) as on 31 March 2009 (Figures in USD)

Lender	Total Loan Amount	Loan Availed	Outstanding as on 31 March 2009
IFC	1,000,000	1,000,000	435,000
Lemelson Foundation	250,000	125,000	125,000

Source: Provided by SELCO.

FINANCING SOLAR LIGHTS

For a majority of SELCO's customers, solar lights were the most expensive equipment that they ever purchased. Even though they spent an equivalent amount of money in buying kerosene to meet their energy needs, making an upfront investment of an amount that was a few multiples of their monthly income was beyond their means. Explained Harish,

by 2009. The repayment date was extended after SELCO's financial restructuring in 2007.

One of the best financial lessons that I learnt was from a street vendor who told me that she could afford to pay INR 10 a day, but would find it difficult to pay INR 300 every month! That was when I realized that to sell solar lights the poor needed to be provided with financing such that payback patterns were synchronized with their income patterns.

However, SELCO realized that getting finance for the purchase of solar lights, even from the rural banks, was difficult. Rural banks provided loans for income-generating activities and it was difficult for them to conceptualize that home lights could be used for generating income.

After two-and-a-half years of untiring effort, Harish was finally able to convince Malaprabha Grameen Bank to sanction INR 1.5 million for financing 100 solar lights. SELCO showed the bank's internal notice, informing its branches about the decision to finance solar lights, to other rural banks. Since Malaprabha Grameen Bank was viewed as a progressive bank in rural Karnataka, some of the other rural banks did not hesitate to emulate it, convinced that Malaprabha Bank would have done its due diligence. The fact that the internal notice did not mention the bank's upper limit of INR 1.5 million or 100 systems helped SELCO's cause. However, it was still not easy to convince the loan officers at the bank branches to sanction the loans because the banks were treading into new territory and were unfamiliar with the technology of solar lighting. For the next several months, SELCO's staff organized field trips for bank officials to demonstrate to them the viability of solar lights and how they could make a difference to the livelihood of the rural poor. While some of the bank officials were sympathetic to the idea and were flexible enough to sanction loans to a variety of customers – from the paddy farmer to the *beedi* roller to the peanut farmer – others were apprehensive and reluctant. Therefore, SELCO even started tracking the transfer of sympathetic officials within the rural banking system and planned its own expansions accordingly.

SELCO, however, decided to stay away from financing the customers themselves, even though, as the business grew, there were such suggestions from their investors. Both Harish and Thomas strongly believed that there would be conflict of interests if they ventured into financing. SELCO's technicians developed close relations with their customers in the process of selling and maintaining their systems. They often shared their meals with their customers and sometimes even slept at night in their customers' homes because they would have missed getting on to the only bus that reached the remote village. Such emotional connections that were essential for understanding the exact needs of the customer were counter-productive when it came to collecting money. Therefore, it was decided that SELCO would work with rural banks, credit cooperatives and microfinance agencies to make necessary arrangement of credit for their customers but would not get into financing themselves. However, there were instances where SELCO stepped in to provide a bridging loan if it felt that a particular community or an individual was so poor that they could not even arrange the margin money.[9] Even in such cases, the collection of the amount that was due to SELCO was done through the agency that provided the rest of the finance to avoid any situation of conflicting interest.

CUSTOMIZING PRODUCTS

Although solar lights per se appear to be a standardized product, lighting solutions had to be carefully configured keeping in mind the needs of the customers and their capacity to pay the loan installments. Harish said,

> We could have gone in for some one-size-fits-all system, but we didn't. When it comes to the poor, everyone wants to standardize solutions to save cost, but not us. We have a significant amount of pre-sales activity, all of which is done by the technicians because they are in the best position to understand the context as well as the solution that can meet the requirement. We do not have any marketing budget. We put all our efforts into pre-sales and post-sales services, which is marketing for us. All our customer service agents don the mantle of marketers when they are dealing with the customers. We

---

[9] Apart from exceptional cases, the Reserve Bank of India did not allow banks to do 100 per cent financing and stipulated that the consumer would have to provide 10–25 per cent margin money as down payment for availing any loan.

encourage them to interact with the neighbours and the local community, so that they have a deep understanding of the problems that the people face.

SELCO serviced its customers from 25 service centers spread all across rural Karnataka. A typical sales cycle for SELCO started with an understanding of how much a customer could pay towards loan instalments every month. SELCO's technicians discussed with the customers the various costs incurred while providing light in their homes, in terms of both out-of-pocket expenses and foregone opportunities. For example, a family might be purchasing INR 50 worth of kerosene every month, which they would save if they purchased solar lights from SELCO. Therefore, a financing model that required them to pay less than INR 50 every month would be affordable. Once the instalment payments were made, they would be owning an asset, which could be used to secure further loans if necessary. Moreover, there would be non-quantifiable benefits in terms of better health, increased hours of study for the children as well as saving time that was otherwise spent in procuring kerosene or sourcing forest-wood. In another instance, solar lights might increase the business hours of a restaurant owner and the additional income earned would be enough for paying the instalments.

Sometimes, SELCO technicians came up with innovative solutions to address specific needs of a customer. For example, a family might think that they needed four lights for their house comprising a kitchen, bedroom, living room and cowshed. However, they could only afford to pay INR 150 per month as the loan instalment, which was just enough to procure a two-light system. When SELCO's technicians interacted with the family to understand their needs, they realized that all four rooms need not be lighted simultaneously. The wife, who looked after the cows and cooked food, needed lights either in the kitchen or in the cowshed at any one point in time. It was also unlikely that the family would need lights in the bedroom and in the living room at the same time. Therefore, SELCO technicians would complete the wiring in all the rooms, provided four points where the lights could be fitted, but supplied only a two-light system that met both the budget and the needs of the customer. They would ensure that the lights could be easily fixed and removed from each of the four points, so that the family could carry the two lights with them from one room to the other depending on where they needed them. Sometimes, the internal structure of the house would allow fixing a light at the intersection of two rooms, ensuring that two rooms were illuminated with one light. Thomas said,

> It is very important that our technicians have a genuine concern for the customer. Fortunately, we have managed to create a team of dedicated personnel over the years, many of whom have been with us right from the inception. These were people who were earning their living by repairing televisions and bicycles – who Harish had trained himself to be technicians for solar lights. Today, they run the service centres on their own. Even though our competitors offer them higher salaries, we have very little employee attrition, especially from our service centres. Once people understand our philosophy, they love working for SELCO, even though the task never gets easy, be it getting finance for the customers or enduring a long sales cycle.

SELCO charged INR 250 as an annual maintenance contract for a four-light system, which entitled a customer to two maintenance services and one emergency service on call.[10] SELCO's technicians checked every solar installation twice a year to ensure that they were in proper working condition. Since the livelihoods of many customers were critically dependent on the solar lights supplied by SELCO, the technicians tried to respond to every breakdown as fast as possible. This was a challenging task, given that most of the installations were in remote areas. SELCO was able to respond to 65 per cent of these calls within 24 hours and they constantly worked on measures to improve their response time.

SELCO was instrumental in creating several entrepreneurs in rural Karnataka. Besides home lights, SELCO manufactured solar lights that could be used by street vendors who usually sold their products in the evenings. Since street vendors did not need the lights for the entire day, SELCO identified entrepreneurs who would buy solar lights from them and rent them to the vendors daily. Although no bank would have been willing to cater to the needs

---

[10] Apart from annual maintenance charges, SELCO customers incurred INR 50–80 as operating cost per year to buy distilled water needed for topping up the batteries.

of the street vendors, the entrepreneur was able to provide both finance and service to them. Harish recounted,

This guy (the entrepreneur) in Hasan[11] started with 30 lamps and put the solar charging station on the roof of his house. He would charge the batteries daily and rent the lamps to the vendors at 5.30 p.m. Then between 9.30 p.m. and 10.00 p.m., he would collect the lamps back and a rent of INR 12 per lamp. The vendors would thus save INR 2–3 per day since they were earlier spending INR 15 on kerosene. Soon, he purchased another 30 and then another lot of 30. Now, he felt the need to purchase a tempo[12] to carry the batteries around and eventually employed two people to transport the batteries. Then one day he came back to us, saying that his technicians were getting exhausted lifting so many batteries daily – it would be of help if we could make the batteries lighter. We went back to the drawing board and designed lighter batteries – it's amazing how he made us realize a fundamental problem and led us to solve it.

SUPPLIER RELATIONSHIPS

As an organization, SELCO believed in developing long-term relationships with its suppliers. A solar light comprised four key components – the solar photovoltaic module (solar cell/panel), the battery, the charge controller and the lighting system (lamps and fans). The relative costs of these components for a four-light system are provided in Table 6.5. SELCO sourced 90–95 per cent of its panels from Tata BP, continuing their relationship that developed even before Harish founded SELCO as an organization. Although cheaper alternatives were available, SELCO preferred Tata BP primarily for two reasons. Their products were of very good quality and despite Tata BP's stringent internal processes, they were quite flexible with SELCO in terms of schedule and batch size of orders. Moreover, having a local source of supply

---

[11] A place in the northern part of Karnataka.

[12] A small commercial vehicle for carrying goods.

Table 6.5 Cost Breakdown of a 4-Light
System (Figures in INR)

Photovoltaic module	8,000
Battery	4,500
4 lights @ 800	3,200
Installation & wiring	1,300
Total	17,000

Source: Provided by SELCO.
Note: The sale price of the above system was INR 20,000.

helped SELCO reduce inventory levels by about 25 per cent, which was substantial given that they had to maintain inventories worth INR 15 million across their service centres. SELCO purchased panels from other suppliers only when Tata BP was unable to meet their demands. Similarly, batteries were purchased largely from Shakti Electronics, who worked closely with SELCO to customize batteries to suit the needs of SELCO lights.

SELCO sourced all its other electronic items from Anand Electronics located in Mangalore, Karnataka. It was a small-scale manufacturing unit run by two entrepreneurs who had been exclusive suppliers to SELCO since 1997. SELCO felt the need for Anand Electronics to improvise when it realized that the technology available with Tata BP was designed for European conditions. For rural India, SELCO needed electronic components that were rugged, even if that meant making trade-offs in technical sophistication. Anand Electronics was earlier involved in television repairing and was finding survival difficult in the late nineties with the advent of more reliable televisions at lower prices. SELCO convinced them to become its supplier. Being a small-scale unit, Anand Electronics did not have to pay excise duties and was able to keep its overhead costs low. Moreover, its long-term and exclusive relationship ensured that it could design and produce items to SELCO's exact specification, including experimenting with new product designs. SELCO kept track of the market prices of comparable products to ensure that it did not overpay for the relationship or flexibility that it enjoyed from its suppliers. SELCO had a high degree of transparency with all its suppliers and was ready to help them in case of constraints and challenges. Thomas said,

As an organization, we strongly believe that we should stick to our suppliers, especially those who have been with us during our difficult times.

And SELCO had seen difficult times not so long ago, almost to the point that most of its employees thought it to be the end of road for the organization.

THE DIFFICULT TIMES

SELCO broke even for the first time in March 2001, and during the next three years steadily increased its revenues. It made a profit of USD 88,380 by the end of the financial year in March 2005. Sustained good performance enthused SELCO to plan for expanding its operations into the neighbouring states of Andhra Pradesh and Maharashtra. SELCO also decided to appoint business associates in Karnataka, since many entrepreneurs had expressed interest to become its associates after witnessing SELCO's success during the past few years. SELCO planned to move its own employees to the new markets of Andhra Pradesh and Maharashtra and decided to address the needs of Karnataka through an associate network since it had already developed the market in rural Karnataka and established the rules of running a viable business. Around the same time, SELCO also took a decision to diversify its supplier base, so that it could get cheaper alternatives, especially for solar panels.

Unfortunately for SELCO, this was the time when Germany started providing high subsidies to solar power. This resulted in an increasing demand for solar panels of higher wattage in Germany and all major manufacturers started to cater to the German market, since there were higher margins in selling solar panels of higher wattage. Consequently, there was a shortage of solar panels in markets in the rest of the world, leading to a steep price rise of nearly 47 per cent. SELCO was caught completely unawares! It did not have enough material to service its customer demands. It no longer enjoyed the comfortable relationship that it once had with Tata BP given its decision to diversify to other low-cost suppliers. Its new suppliers did not have any obligation or relationship to provide SELCO with material when the German market looked far more lucrative. Even if they had, SELCO was not in a position to pass on the price increase to its customers. Thus, SELCO's new offices in Andhra Pradesh and Maharashtra were starved of supplies and the business associate model in Karnataka started to fumble. SELCO started making losses and in the next two years, ended up wiping almost the entire net worth of the company.

It was troubled times for SELCO in the US too! Apart from India, all its other subsidiaries had performed poorly and shareholders wanted to cash out. Harish's request for fresh funds was rebuffed and met with demands for retrenchment in India. Recalling those hard days, Thomas said,

> We were sitting in November (2006) with money that would last only till next March (2007). We had no option but to go into a mode of shutting down operations. I asked Harish which investor in their right frame of mind would lend money to a company like SELCO that has burnt the money received from the first set of investors? However, Harish was optimistic even in such trying circumstances. He promised us that if we could somehow make SELCO survive one more year, he would get fresh investments. I do not know why, but we all believed in what he promised – that is something only Harish can do! Our whole mindset changed. It was like rebuilding the organization. We focused on reducing costs and improving collections. We were able to stabilize operations and tide over the crisis, even before a fresh set of investments came.

Fortunately for Harish, IFC, which had provided a USD 1-million loan to SELCO, strongly supported SELCO India and enabled Harish to raise fresh funds from a new set of socially oriented investors, such as E+Co, Lemelson and Good Energies Foundation.[13] Meanwhile, prices of solar cells started to

---

[13]   IFC had funded a project with Gaia Kapital in Vietnam. Prior to the restructuring, Gaia was SELCO's major shareholder. Since Gaia was not fully aligned with SELCO's social mission and expected high rates of return, IFC helped Harish to buy out Gaia's majority share. Consequently, Gaia was reduced to a minority shareholder and they exited (Jayashankar 2012).

reduce, increasing availability. SELCO decided to postpone its expansion plans into neighbouring states and recalled its own employees to offices in Karnataka. It also realized that the associate network model, which was purely commercial in its intention, was unsuitable for an inclusive business such as selling solar lights to the poor. Most significantly, SELCO repaired its relationship with Tata BP and reverted to its earlier philosophy of having long-term relationships with one trusted supplier. The turnaround was complete when SELCO posted increased revenues and operating profits in March 2008. In retrospect, Harish felt that those difficult days helped SELCO not only to refine its business model but also to have a better set of investors whose philosophy was aligned to that of SELCO. He said,

Howsoever in need you might be, it is important to be careful about the kind of person you take money from. You should always have control of the company for the sake of the mission. Never take money from someone whose mission is not aligned with yours.

PRODUCT DIVERSIFICATION

In 2006, SELCO was approached by SEWA Bank to be its technology partner. Ela Bhatt founded SEWA in 1972 in Gujarat, with the objective of empowering poor women. In 2010, it was the largest single trade union in India with a membership of 900,000 women. SEWA Bank was established as its affiliate in 1974 to provide financial services to its members. Its services included taking deposits, providing credit and insurance as well as financial counselling. SEWA Bank initiated Project Urja[14] for its 300,000 members to have access to reliable and affordable sources of energy. It estimated that chronic shortages of cooking fuel, reliable lighting and electric power were the key reasons why the underprivileged were unable to break the vicious cycle of illiteracy, unemployment and poverty. SEWA chose SELCO to provide it

---

[14] *Urja* means energy in the classical Indian language of Sanskrit.

with technological solutions that addressed the energy needs of its members. Thomas noted,

> Project Urja was a dream come true for us. It immediately provided us with access to a largely diverse clientele away from our home base in Karnataka. Since it was SEWA, we did not have to worry about creating the infrastructure for providing finance to the customer. But most importantly, SEWA showed us the path to become an energy solutions company from a solar lighting company that SELCO was.

In the next two years, SELCO designed several solar products in consultation with SEWA. This included solar lanterns for the vegetable and fruit vendors who could use it for extending their working hours, head lamps for midwives and flower pickers, solar caps for labourers and masons and a smokeless stove for cooking. Most women in rural India did not have access to hospitals and used the services of midwives for their delivery within the privacy of their homes. In the absence of grid electricity, such deliveries were often done with the help of a mirror that reflected sunlight to the place of delivery inside the house. Such an improvised arrangement was not possible during night or on a cloudy day when the midwife had to use a kerosene lamp or a candle, which sometimes led to fire-related accidents during delivery. SELCO wanted to create a solar light that would be useful during such conditions and minimize chances of accidents. Harish recollected,

> We sat with midwives for two to three days to understand the delivery process. They taught us to cut the umbilical cord. People laughed at us, but we told them that we needed to know the process well to design the energy intervention. There were usually only two women at the time of delivery – one who is pregnant and the midwife. The midwife had a candle or a lantern, which she balanced with one hand during the delivery. We, therefore, decided to design a solar head lamp, so that both her hands were free and there was enough light in the room.

In the same locality, SELCO worked with flowers pickers, who collected flowers from midnight until 3 a.m. It was difficult for them to balance both the flower basket and a petromax lantern in one hand and pluck flowers with the other hand. It slowed down their efficiency. With solar head lamps, they were able to pluck double the quantity of flowers in the same time. SELCO appointed entrepreneurs who rented out the solar lamps to the midwives and flower pickers on a daily or an hourly basis, ensuring higher usage of the lamps and greater income generation. Harish said,

> Unless we work closely with them, we will not be able to identify their needs. Today, when we design a solution for a midwife, a vegetable vendor or a mason, we begin with the precept that the solution must pay for itself. It should be financed from the additional income that it generates. There is a big difference between creating a want to sell a product and identifying a need and designing a solution to fulfil it. We always want to focus on the need.

While SELCO started primarily as a company providing home lighting solutions, Harish estimated that in 2010, for more than 20 per cent of their customers, SELCO lights were a direct source of increased income generation through greater productivity. And their partnership with SEWA Bank provided them with a major fillip in that direction.

Women in both rural and urban India depended on the use of kerosene, liquefied petroleum gas (LPG) or firewood for cooking. LPG was expensive, and both kerosene and firewood were highly polluting and inefficient sources of energy. The smoke caused cough, skin diseases and irritation to eyes. Moreover, women typically spent an enormous amount of time sourcing kerosene or firewood, time that could be spent in income-generating activities. Therefore, with input from SEWA, SELCO designed a smokeless gas stove and named it Annapurna Stove. It was a brick and cement stove that used a minimum amount of firewood and retained the essential nutrients in food. Some of the women were also trained by SEWA and SELCO to construct these stoves so that they could earn a living by selling their services.

Such experience in working with the diverse energy needs of the poor inspired Harish to set up an innovation department and an incubation laboratory as an experimental arm of SELCO. The mandate for these departments was to explore and generate new ideas that could be developed into products and services to address the needs of the poor. Some of their new products included specially designed gloves for rag pickers and an energy-efficient pushcart for vegetable vendors. Although many of these products were not commercially viable at the outset, the innovation department acted as the locus for developing a culture of experimentation that Harish wanted to foster in SELCO. Its incubation centre had drawn considerable interest and attention from other organizations and institutions worldwide. Many socially oriented enterprises which could not afford to have research and development centres of their own approached SELCO to do product research on their behalf. There was also a beeline of students from various Indian and international technology and management institutions who wanted to do their internship with the centre.

SCALING THE BUSINESS

SELCO was on course towards achieving its key objective – of establishing a viable business focusing on the energy needs of the poor that was inclusive in every sense of the term. Harish said,

> We set up SELCO to bust three myths – poor people cannot afford technology, poor people cannot maintain technology and it is not possible to run a commercial venture that fulfils a social objective. SELCO's 15-year journey shows that if you can provide doorstep financing and doorstep servicing, you can create a sustainable business model that addresses the needs of the poor.

An impact assessment study by World Resources Institute in 2007[15] indicated that 86 per cent of SELCO's poor customers indicated significant savings in energy costs as their primary benefit of using SELCO products,

---

[15]   See N. M. Koppa and S. Willoughby (unpublished), 'Base of Pyramid Impact Assessment', World Resource Institute, 2007. This was obtained from SELCO's archives.

while the rest pointed to their children's education as the primary advantage. For their efforts, SELCO and Harish were awarded the Ashden Award (2005, 2007), Social Entrepreneur of the Year Award (2007), and the Financial Times Arcelor Mittal Boldness in Business Award (2009). Armed with investments worth USD 1.7 million[16] from three social investors, namely the Good Energies Foundation, Lemelson Foundation and E+Co, SELCO planned to light up 200,000 rural homes, covering a wider geographic area, in the next few years.

However, success raised expectations and Harish and the leadership at SELCO were asked very often about their plans of scaling their business. After deep introspection and taking into consideration their failed experiment with the associate network model, Harish and Thomas concluded that a small business model was ideally suitable for the kind of work that SELCO did. Harish said,

> It is better if we focus on developing other SELCOs suited to the context where they would operate, rather than trying to grow this SELCO.

And Thomas agreed with Harish,

> Ideally, we should create an organization that can become an investment partner for entrepreneurial entities – the SELCOs of the future. We can provide the seed capital and pass on to them our knowledge, things that we learnt the hard way. However, the new entities will have complete independence in the way they would develop their business, because their specific model needs to be suited to their context. We would like to do this in other parts of India first and thereafter, maybe, across the globe.

SELCO had been conservative even while scaling its business in Karnataka. Harish argued,

> One of the obvious ways to scale is to put aggressive targets on the sales team. Such targets would instinctively make them chase low-hanging fruits – they will go after customers who will buy faster and who will buy larger systems.

---

[16] This comprises a debt of USD 300,000 and equity worth USD 1.4 million.

But are these the customers whom we really want to sell to? SELCO exists to provide solar lights to the poor – the one who can probably afford a small system and that too on credit. If one mixes the social objective with the commercial objective, it is most likely that the commercial objective will dominate.

Thus, the SELCO sales team and regional managers were evaluated on the quality of customers to whom they were selling over and above quantitative targets. It was of great satisfaction to the senior management that over the years, their average invoice value had reduced, implying that they were selling smaller systems to the poorer sections of the society. Moreover, more than 90 per cent of their customers purchased their systems on credit.

For SELCO, any form of growth and scaling involved attracting and retaining talented individuals who were dedicated to their social objective. Being a social enterprise, SELCO was not in a position to pay the kind of compensation that engineering and management graduates from reputed Indian institutions commanded from other for-profit organizations. Thus, SELCO needed to figure out a way of leveraging high-quality talent even while its paying capacity was below the market. In 2010, SELCO seemed to be on the threshold of an inflection point. Pai, one of the founding members, moved on to become SELCO's exclusive dealer for manufacturing solar water heaters, targeted largely at the institutions and urban markets. And Thomas was planning to go on a sabbatical not quite sure about when he was going to come back. All these years, Thomas had managed operations of SELCO and built the organization that was necessary to realize Harish's vision. He wanted to ensure that when he went on his sabbatical, SELCO was able to run smoothly. Therefore, his successors were identified and Thomas gradually withdrew himself from most operational matters. Harish felt that Thomas's sabbatical was probably the ideal opportunity for him to step back from the management of the company and let the younger leaders take on their roles. Harish recounted,

All these years, Thomas and I have been perfect critics of one another. We could speak whatever came to our mind, because we knew that if it was a wild idea, the other will be forthright in telling so. With Thomas gone, there will be nobody to tell me that my ideas are wrong – therefore, this will prevent me from thinking freely. After 15 years at the helm of the company, it is time we step back. We have built this company to a size of about INR 150 million. There is enough opportunity in rural Karnataka itself to take SELCO to INR 400 million or INR 500 million. But we are not the ones to do it – we need fresh ideas, fresh legs to travel up and down the country in order to motivate people. This job needs a lot of that. I feel the difference now as I travel upcountry – while the older folks were far more comfortable in talking to me as peers, the younger ones treat me as their managing director. They are new; I am not very familiar with all of them as I used to be in the past.

Moreover, for creating greater impact, Harish felt the need to influence policy makers, who seemed to be giving a short shrift to small and medium decentralized energy solution providers like SELCO.[17] Given the recognition that SELCO received from national and international press, Harish felt he was in a good position to move into such a role of an evangelist if someone took charge of managing the organization.

DISCUSSION: KEY LEARNING FROM SELCO

SELCO's evolution has several lessons for social enterprises. We will talk about three in the following section, namely the importance of creating products and services for the poor that can improve income opportunities for them, the need for developing associated services, such as financial access, in order to sell such products to the poor, and the trade-offs involved in addressing the real needs of the poor.

---

[17]   In 2009, the Indian government launched the Jawaharlal Nehru National Solar Mission (JNNSM) to create an installed capacity of 20 Giga Watt by 2022 through grid-solar and off-grid solar applications using both solar thermal and photovoltaic technology. However, the detailed policy framework that emerged from JNNSM seemed to favour large centralized production, primarily because of small and medium enterprises' inability to influence policy makers.

Many of the so-called bottom-of-the-pyramid products look at the poor as consumers and consider 4 billion poor people in this world as a large market. In the process, some of these products and services get focused on creating 'wants' and 'desires' among the poor and then fulfilling them. However, SELCO's experience teaches us that a more sustainable approach is to understand the basic 'needs' of the poor and then address those needs by creating suitable products and services. This requires a deep understanding of the context in which the poor lead their lives and identifying the key enablers that would make them realize their potential and improve their income. Such missing enablers include access to healthcare, education, credit and sustainable sources of energy – the last one being the focus of SELCO. If the poor are provided with these essential enablers, they will become productive, have more income and will have the economic independence of choosing other products and services for consumption – be it a low-cost water purifier or a single-serve shampoo. However, if the focus remains on the product and the poor as a consumer, such products might not help to fundamentally improve their economic conditions.

The second learning is that for the poor to derive maximum benefit from a product or a service, it is often necessary to develop complementary services in a cost-effective manner. The socio-economic set-up of the poor is characterized by either an absence of institutions or presence of high-cost intermediaries. As a result, the transaction costs of reaching a product or a service to the poor is extremely high – either the intermediaries (for example, brokers, moneylenders and middlemen) capture most of the value or the developer of the product or service needs to incur high costs to overcome institutional voids, which makes the business model unviable. SELCO exemplifies how it is possible to build relationships with institutions and intermediaries such that it becomes easy for the poor to access its products and services. This also calls for a deep understanding of the context as well as dealing with some of the inherent trade-offs. For instance, given the presence of several microfinance institutions (MFIs) in Karnataka, it would have been easier for SELCO to tie up with them for financing the solar lights. However, Harish was not entirely sure whether the MFIs would be aligned with the social objective of SELCO and, therefore, chose the much harder path of raising credit from the regional rural banks.

The third learning is to develop an appreciation of the trade-offs involved in scaling up a business model that is premised on creating customized solutions for the poor based on a deep understanding of their context. SELCO's founders wanted to address the specific energy needs of the poor, which involved a considerable amount of customizing of their product and offering services around it. This, however, made it difficult to rapidly scale their business model, a necessity to address the energy needs of 80 million poor households in India. Scaling requires standardization, but standardization is often unable to address the unique needs, and the SELCO founders made a conscious choice of not offering a standardized solar product because they were convinced that in the long run, such products would not address the real need. In the following sections, we visit each of these issues in greater depth as we look at the factors that contributed to SELCO's success, the evolution of its business model and how SELCO can increase its impact without scaling its organization

WHY SELCO SUCCEEDED

Three factors can be cited as contributing to SELCO's success so far, namely Harish's focus on building a financially sustainable business model for delivering solar lights to the poor, ensuring that such solutions are affordable for the poor by facilitating availability of finance and complementing the product with suitable services and customization to ensure that it addressed the specific needs of the customer. The second and the third factors were a direct result of the deep understanding that Harish and SELCO developed about the socio-economic context of its potential customers.

The success of an entrepreneurial venture such as SELCO is often dependent on the vision, commitment and perseverance of its founders – in this case, Harish's. Right from its inception, Harish was keen on developing a financially viable business model for providing solar lighting to the poor. He was convinced that the poor would be willing to pay the right price if he were able to meet their needs. Therefore, instead of depending on grants, Harish created a business model that was based on loans and investments.

This forced him, and subsequently SELCO, to be organized and managed on sound business principles like any other commercial venture. There are several manifestations of such business principles throughout the case, such as SELCO's decision of not getting into financing its customers to avoid conflict of interest, having a few suppliers and developing long-term relationships with them to reduce transaction costs as well as encouraging experimentation and innovation to create an entrepreneurial culture within the organization. Since SELCO's success and survival depended on its ability to satisfy the needs of its customers (as opposed to convincing donors to provide them with grants), it enabled the company to remain constantly engaged with the real need of the customer – that of generating income and being more productive.

Right from the days of his PhD studies, Harish was keen to live and experience the environment that his customers encountered in order to understand their needs. This gave him the confidence that the poor could maintain technology and would be willing to pay for it, provided it addressed their real need. However, for the poor to be able to afford solar lights, they needed to be provided with credit. The poor did not have the money to make an outright purchase of solar lights. Neither did they have assets or the confidence of banks that could have provided them with loans at reasonable rates. As a result, they often end up paying a 'poverty penalty', that is, paying more than even the rich for many of the products that they buy. Harish understood that if he had to sell solar lights to the poor, he had to ensure that they obtained loans from banks such that the cash flow from their income matched the loan repayment pattern. This led SELCO to work perseveringly with rural banks and convince them that solar lights were a creditworthy purchase for the rural poor and they would be able to repay their loans through enhanced income or cost savings. Similarly, while working with street vendors, SELCO created micro-entrepreneurs who rented out solar lights whereby the enhanced income and/or reduced cost more than compensated for the rental.

SELCO also realized that most of its customers needed customized service in order to get maximum benefit out of solar lights. Because this technology is relatively new to the customers, they needed some amount of handholding, in the absence of which solar technology might remain unutilized. This was precisely the case of solar lights that were installed by the government in the same villages where Harish operated. The government's installation of solar lights was driven more as a policy rather than by any intention of creating a viable business model. As a result, government officials did not understand the need for handholding and services that were necessary for making the poor accept and utilize the new technology. Harish realized that SELCO's responsibility did not end with creating and selling a product. In order to meet the energy needs of the poor, they had to ensure that the product was correctly used by the customer. This made him develop a team of service and repair engineers from local television repairmen, who were later on inducted as permanent employees. They were trained to develop a deep understanding of the customer context, so that they were able to configure lighting solutions that matched the needs and purchasing capacity of the customer. An example would be when SELCO engineers met the lighting needs of four rooms by configuring a two-light system for one of the customers.

Harish and SELCO's example convey the important lesson that entrepreneurs and organizations who want to develop novel technological solutions for the poor have to spend a considerable amount of time and effort in understanding the specific context the poor encounter. More often than not, their needs are very diverse, calling for considerable amount of customization on multiple dimensions, including product configuration, maintenance and support as well as complementary services such as finance. Even when a product organization is not willing to get into a diverse set of complementary activities, it needs to act as a facilitator for the development of the entire value chain. If this is not done, the high-cost intermediaries and the institutional voids present in such markets will make the business model unviable, despite the technological merits of the product.

EVOLUTION OF SELCO'S MODEL FOR VALUE CREATION

How did SELCO's model evolve over the years? The case depicts a three-stage evolution of SELCO's business model – from providing solar lights to its customers to becoming a critical enabler for income generation to the poor and finally redefining itself as an energy solutions organization. Although it is debatable whether all social businesses need to evolve along similar lines, SELCO's evolution seems to be in the right direction because as the company deepened its understanding of customer needs, it was able to create a greater impact in their lives.

In its first stage of existence, SELCO's focus was on selling solar lights to customers who did not have access to grid electricity. Harish's sale to the betel nut farmer, as mentioned in the case, was driven more by the motive of proving that solar lights were viable than by any concern for poverty alleviation. At this stage, SELCO was still looking at poor people as its consumers and their lack of access to grid electricity as a potential market. Thus, many of the earlier customer examples have little or no reference to how the solar lights had any impact on income generation.

SELCO's evolution happened when it started to focus on solar lights as facilitators of income generation or enhanced income for the poor. SELCO moved beyond looking at the poor as its consumers and started to find ways by which solar lights could make the poor more productive. Part of this was driven by the fact that banks were unwilling to lend money to the poor for the purchase of solar lights if it did not lead to additional income. This made Harish and his team think deeply about the constraints to productivity of the poor, ways by which a solar lamp could enhance their income, the financial condition of the poor, their income patterns and how the credit terms could be structured so that it became relatively easy for the poor to repay the loan. The fruition of this approach is seen in the example where solar lamps were rented out to street vendors by an entrepreneur who bought several of these lamps from SELCO based on loans obtained from a rural bank. Not only did the solar lamps enhance the business potential of the street vendors, it was also instrumental in creating an entrepreneur who, over a period of time, was able to generate further employment, as is described in the case. It must be noted that SELCO continued to sell solar lights to consumers where such sale was not directly related to income enhancement. But increasingly, SELCO focused on customers where solar lights would enhance their income and a majority of such customers were from the lowest rungs of economic strata.

SELCO's second evolution started to happen during their technology partnership with SEWA Bank where they felt the need to create innovations that went beyond solar lights, such as a smokeless stove for cooking. SELCO started to redefine itself as an 'energy solutions' company, rather than a company that provided solar lights. This partnership also pushed SELCO to make many innovations even within its core domain of solar lights, so that it could cater to a wide variety of customers. Although SELCO's earlier focus was largely on rural Karnataka, innovations such as solar headlamps or solar caps had widespread use even in semi-rural or urban areas. The fact that in this partnership, SELCO did not have to worry about arranging for finance helped it to focus on technological innovation and experimentation. It was thus a very important milestone in SELCO's journey where partnerships, such as the one with SEWA Bank, held the promise of enabling SELCO to scale through a combination of product diversification and standardization.

INCREASING IMPACT AND SCALING BUSINESS

How can SELCO scale its business model and create greater impact? Although all stakeholders would like an organization like SELCO to scale so that it can create widespread impact, most social enterprises struggle to replicate their model at a large scale. Ironically, one of SELCO's causes for success, namely being able to customize solar lighting solutions addressing specific needs of the poor, can become its biggest hurdle to scaling its business. There is an inherent trade-off between customization and scale – it is usually possible to scale businesses where products and services are fairly standardized. As their comments in the concluding section of the case reflect, the founders of SELCO firmly believed that a standardized product was not suitable for addressing the real needs of the poor. Therefore, they were keen to continue with their business model of customized solar lighting solutions because they were apprehensive that if they pursued scaling as their business objective, the commercial objective of increasing sales would dominate the social objective of poverty alleviation.

Is it possible to create large-scale impact in ways other than scaling SELCO's organization? That was the path that SELCO's founders wanted to pursue. They decided upon two ways by which they could create greater impact – first, by nurturing entrepreneurs who were motivated to start businesses focused on providing energy solutions to the poor and, second, by acting as research partners for organizations who wanted to create products and services for the poor.

SELCO's founders felt that it was difficult to replicate their model in other geographies because the conditions are very different from one place to another in a vast country like India. However, entrepreneurs who were motivated to provide energy solutions in other geographies could gain significantly from the knowledge and insights that SELCO's founders had gained, thereby improving their chances of success at an early stage. SELCO also felt that having operated in rural India for more than a decade, it had developed insights about the needs of the poor and was in a good position to act as a testing site or as a centre for proof of concept for products and services that other organizations develop for the poor. SELCO, therefore, set up their innovation laboratory, which could be used by other organizations for developing, testing and refining their products intended for the poor.

It is interesting to note that SELCO's alliance with SEWA Bank led to the creation of products that were more standardized than what they had been selling in rural Karnataka. Therefore, the assumption that solar lights needed to be customized in order to meet the needs of the poor might not hold true for all the markets.

For example, in the case of urban poor, the needs for products like solar head lamps might be fairly similar, even from people employed in different occupations. And given the concentration of demand in these markets, it would be easier for SELCO to achieve the scale that was necessary to become financially viable. Such opportunities can provide SELCO to scale its business, even though they might face competitive pressures in such markets.

We end the discussion on SELCO by dwelling a little on their succession planning strategy. It is an important task of every leader to develop the next line of leadership in their organization and thus plan for their successors. Developing a second line of leaders is not only important for keeping employees engaged and motivated but is also necessary if the organization is keen to grow and create a greater impact. The fact that all three founders of SELCO were planning to move away from the management of SELCO is indicative that the founders had done a good job of developing their successors and, therefore, had the confidence that the work that they started would be continued and even done better by the new team. Founder transition is an important challenge of any entrepreneurial organization and many entrepreneurs do not find the time to develop the next line of leaders, leading to over-dependence of the organization on the founders. While only time can tell whether SELCO would be able to overcome this challenge, they seemed to be well prepared to deal with it.

EPILOGUE

SELCO has been continuing its efforts in providing low-cost energy solutions to the poor. In August of 2011, Harish won the prestigious Ramon Magsaysay Award, often considered the Nobel Prize of Asia, for SELCO's efforts to put solar technology in the hands of the poor. By 2020, SELCO's interventions had impacted more than 800,000 poor households across six Indian states (Murafa 2020). SELCO, meanwhile, evolved into a family of four initiatives. While SELCO India continued to be a social business, SELCO Foundation, a not-for-profit, was set up to create solar energy-based innovative solutions that could be implemented to reduce poverty. Some of its products, such as portable solar water pumps, head lamps, paddy thrashers and processing mills, improved efficiency, thereby increasing the income of people from underserved communities. SELCO Incubation supported entrepreneurs who provided sustainable energy products and services to underserved communities, while SELCO Fund invested in micro-enterprises that emerged out of their incubation process. Harish was quoted as saying,

> We need to use a decentralized approach to create hundreds of entrepreneurs across the country. Unfortunately, there are barely any investors willing to fund them. Out of frustration, we were forced to create an investment fund for rural entrepreneurs who were not getting private investment or could not speak English to pitch themselves well. But, again, we only got money from foreign investors. (Thaker 2019)

Table 6.6 provides SELCO's financial performance and the number of systems that they sold during 2009–19.

Table 6.6 SELCO India's Financial Performance during 2009–19

Financial Year	Revenue (INR Million)	Profit (INR Million)	Number of Systems Sold*
2009–10	145	2.7	7,268
2010–11	144	4.3	5,957
2011–12	169	5.8	6,804
2012–13	216	2.0	8,248
2013–14	271	6.0	13,197
2014–15	344	3.4	17,316
2015–16	409	7.5	22,230
2016–17	368	3.4	18,309
2017–18	560	11.7	31,068
2018–19	854	33.2	51,033

Source: Provided by SELCO.

Note: *SELCO counts the number of systems sold by the number of invoices. Since an invoice can be for multiple systems sold to a group, the actual number of households impacted will be larger.

CHAPTER LEARNING

Many poor households do not have access to electricity. For them, it is important to get access to low-cost and non-polluting sources of energy, such as solar energy. This will improve their quality of life and enable many of them to increase their income.

While designing and selling products to the poor, such as solar lighting systems, it is necessary to take into consideration their specific needs and be able to customize the product. Only then will such products actually benefit them and enable them to pay for it

Products sold to the poor need to be complemented by suitable credit services that match their cash flows. In many cases, a suitable rental model needs to be created rather than an outright purchase to ensure that the cash outflows are commensurate with cash inflows from income.

The products also need to be provided with prompt service, especially when they are being used for income-generating activities. This will also enable the poor consumers to depend on such products.

Maintaining its inclusive mission will need the organization to make multiple trade-offs at operational and functional levels. Likewise, such organizations need to be careful about how they want to scale because many opportunities for enhancing revenue or profitability might lead to a drift from or dilution of their inclusive mission.

Creating a financially sustainable business model by selling products to the poor is challenging. The organization needs to be committed to it for a long time before they achieve financial viability. Therefore, such organizations also need to choose investors carefully, those who have patience and those who are well aligned with the inclusive mission of the organization

HASIRU DALA INNOVATIONS

Improving Lives of Waste Pickers

India faces a huge challenge in waste management, which is a direct consequence of industrialization and urbanization. Four hundred million urban Indians living in about 8,000 towns and cities generate 62 million tonnes (MT) of municipal solid waste annually. While solid waste management should be one of the basic services provided by municipal authorities in order to keep urban centres clean, almost all such bodies deposit solid waste in dumping grounds within or outside cities haphazardly. Thus, only 43 MT of waste is collected, 12 MT is treated, and 31 MT is dumped in landfill sites (Lahiry 2019). Reports have pointed out that there was potential for recovering at least 15 per cent of the waste generated every day in India, which could provide employment to about 500,000 waste pickers. In many cities, waste collection is done informally where waste pickers collect solid waste from doorsteps, sometimes against a collection fee, and derive income by selling the recyclables. Thus, the informal recycling industry plays a significant role in waste management and ensures that less waste reached the landfills.

However, the economic condition of thousands of waste pickers, who are the foot soldiers of this enormous and critical operation of waste management, is possibly the worst among all professions in the country. They operate in harsh working conditions and are exposed to health hazards, accidents and crises of all kinds. They live in slums, which often lack access to basic infrastructure, such as electricity, clean water and sanitation. They traditionally belong to the lower castes, have low social status and are exploited by contractors and intermediaries. Civil society, municipal authorities and law enforcement agencies view them with hostility, which has prevented them from being integrated with any kind of formal system.[1] Studies indicated that the average life expectancy of a waste picker was 39 years, their income was less than a dollar a day and there was 33 per cent infant mortality among their families.[2]

In this chapter, we discuss about Hasiru Dala Innovations Private Limited (HDI), a social enterprise that offers waste management services primarily to bulk waste generators in the city of Bengaluru. It evolved from its sister organization, Hasiru Dala, which is a not-for-profit focused on providing social justice to waste pickers largely through policy advocacy. While Hasiru Dala operated in Bengaluru from 2011 and as a registered charitable trust from November 2013, HDI was established as a separate entity in November 2015. By 2020, HDI provided its services to 432 residential complexes and corporate establishments, covering about 35,000 households and diverted 900 tonnes of waste per month away from landfills. In the process, it created better livelihood options for the waste pickers and established some of them as entrepreneurs.

HASIRU DALA

Hasiru Dala[3] was founded by Nalini Shekar and Anselm Rosario, both pioneers in working with waste pickers. Nalini had been working for the cause of waste pickers in Pune since 1991 and had co-founded an organization called Kagad Kach Patra Kashtakari Panchayat, which was the first trade union of waste pickers. When she moved to Bengaluru in 2010, she found that waste pickers were not being involved in mainstream dialogues concerning solid waste management and decided to work towards providing recognition to their community. Hasiru Dala started identifying waste pickers and organizing

---

[1] See P. Chandran, N. Shekar, M. Abubaker and A. Yadav's *Informal Waste Workers Contribution Bangalore*, available at https://hasirudala.in/wp-content/uploads/2020/12/Informal-Waste-Workers-Contribution-in-Bangalore.pdf.

[2] See 'I Got Garbage (IGG) – The Technology Platform for Waste Management Is Now Open for Bangalore Citizens', available at https://www.mindtree.com/news/i-got-garbage-igg-technology-platform-waste-management-now-open-bangalore-citizens (accessed 20 May 2020).

[3] *Hasiru dala* means green brigade in Kannada.

them in Bengaluru and had a chance to intervene in a case on solid waste management in the Lok Adalat.[4] The Lok Adalat recognized the contribution of waste pickers in Bengaluru and directed the municipal authority, Bruhat Bengaluru Mahanagara Palike (BBMP), to register waste pickers, itinerant waste buyers and scrap dealers, and issue identity cards to them.

In 2011, the BBMP started issuing identity cards to waste pickers with the logo of the city and the signature of the commissioner, becoming the first city in India to do so. Identity cards made them eligible for benefits through different government schemes. They then, with help from Hasiru Dala, were able to open bank accounts. Children of waste pickers got educational loans from the central government and 1,800 families were able to avail health insurance from government schemes (Arakali 2018).

Hasiru Dala was formally registered as a trust in November 2013. The municipality of Bengaluru is divided into 198 wards, each of which had to construct decentralized dry waste management infrastructure called Dry Waste Collection Centre. These were managed by the waste pickers with whom the BBMP had signed a memorandum of understanding. The BBMP provided them with the infrastructure and the waste pickers operated them like individual businesses. Hasiru Dala worked with 32 of them, helping them manage their relationship with the BBMP as well as enabling them to take advantages of the various government schemes.

FOUNDING OF HDI

It is officially estimated that the city of Bengaluru, with a population of 11 million, produces 4,500 tonnes of waste every day, though unofficial estimates put this figure much higher. A significant part of this waste gets transported to about 10 landfills in the periphery of the city that are estimated to carry 2.5 MTs of mixed waste. The village of Mandur housed one such landfill, which became the face of the city's mismanagement of waste in 2013. Mandur used

---

[4] Lok Adalat, or People's Court, is an alternative dispute resolution mechanism in India that has statutory status. Here, cases pending at a court of law are settled.

to receive 300 truckloads of garbage every day, estimated at 1,800 MTs, from the city, which was much more than the capacity of the waste processing units that were commissioned there. As a result, mountains of unsegregated waste piled up, leading to accumulation of biomethane, posing threats of the garbage dump catching fire as well as leading to severe deterioration of land, air and water quality. The piles attracted vultures, dogs and other animals, while the leachate comprising acids produced from the rotting garbage piles threatened to seep into the groundwater. The plight of the villagers who started to suffer from respiratory and vector-borne diseases attracted the attention of citizen activists and organizations who were able to put pressure on Bengaluru's municipal authorities to seek some long-term solution through regulations and changes in policy.

In 2014, the BBMP passed a rule that they will not service bulk waste generators (BWGs), defined as residential complexes having more than 50 households or commercial establishments that produced more than 10 kilograms of waste per day. It was estimated that BWGs accounted for about 40 per cent of waste generated by the city and they had both the responsibility and financial capacity to manage their waste. Therefore, it was mandated that BWGs had to service their waste on their own or hire service providers empanelled with the BBMP. Several citizen activists who were familiar with Nalini requested her that Hasiru Dala should offer responsible waste management services to the BWGs. Hasiru Dala saw it as an opportunity to provide predictable livelihood to the waste pickers and decided to experiment with a business model within the trust. Their intention was to raise funds, create a business model, provide market access and, thus, enhance the income of the waste pickers. They were one of the first to get empanelled by the BBMP and within one year, Hasiru Dala started servicing 60 apartment complexes and 8,000 households.

Hasiru Dala Innovations stared operating from November 2015, with a capital of INR 1.7 million contributed by Nalini Shekar, her husband Shekar Prabhkar and Marwan, the co-founders. It got empanelled with the BBMP, transferred its clients from the Hasiru Dala Trust and started to operate from April 2016 with 80 clients.

During their experiment, they realized that it was a scalable and financially viable business and decided to take it forward. The choices before them were to create a cooperative society,[5] something that Nalini had experience of running during her days in Pune, a Section 8[6] company or a private limited company. After considerable debate, they decided to incorporate HDI as a private limited company. Shekar noted,

> Private limited companies seemed to be best suited for scaling and could easily access human and financial capital. Not-for-profits that are usually focused on human rights and social justice may find it hard to attract risk capital and, therefore, they struggle to scale.

From the beginning, they ensured a Chinese wall between the two organizations and ensured that there was no cross-utilization of resources or service providers between Hasiru Dala Trust (HDT) and HDI, except for sharing of the brand name, for which HDI was to pay a royalty of INR 2.5 million over three years. The objective of both these organizations remained promoting the welfare of the waste picker. While HDT worked towards providing social justice to the waste picker, HDI worked towards providing them with economic justice by giving them access to markets and creating opportunities for entrepreneurship and livelihood. Table 7.1 provides revenue earned by HDI over the period 2015–19.

Table 7.1 Revenue of HDI

Year	FY 15–16	FY 16–17	FY 17–18	FY 18–19
Revenue (USD thousand)	18	368	576	1,280

Source: From HDI.

---

[5] They did not find the cooperative laws in Karnataka very progressive. There were instances of cooperatives becoming politicized because they represent vote banks and Nalini and Shekar had to deal with some officials during their discussions who expected bribes from them.

[6] Section 8 companies do not allow giving returns to investors and, therefore, find it difficult to raise funds.

FUNDING

HDI received a capability building grant of INR 3 million from Millennium Alliance,[7] INR 5 million seed capital from Social Alpha[8] and INR 7.5 million from Ennovent,[9] with INR 50 million post-money valuation. Manoj Kumar from Social Alpha joined their board, while Ennovent is yet to exercise its option of appointing a board member. In 2018, HDI received USD 300,000, to be paid as milestone-based tranches, from Shell Foundation to set up a biogas plant. They also received awards from Bangalore Innovation Challenge – an initiative launched by the University of Chicago and the Government of Karnataka for crowdsourcing innovative ideas for improving air and water quality. In March 2019, they received a grant of GBP 300,000 for expanding their aggregation centre capacity and set up a pilot PET[10] recycling plant.

OPERATIONS

HDI got into an agreement with a BWG, such as an apartment owners' association, typically for one or three years and applied the dual principle of the *polluter pays* and *pay as you throw* in order to arrive at the pricing. The waste generated was classified into *wet waste,* typically organic and biodegradable, *dry waste,* which could be recycled, and *rejects,* which needed to be sent to landfills. HDI estimated that about 50–65 per cent of waste from the households was organic wet waste, 20–25 per cent comprised recyclable,

---

[7] A three-year project grant. Grants received by for-profit entities are taxable.

[8] A not-for-profit supported by Tata Trust that incubates social-impact start-ups. In many of them, Social Alpha makes seed investments in exchange for minority equity stakes.

[9] Ennovent Impact Investment Holding invested in early stage social enterprises in developing countries.

[10] PET, or polyethylene terephthalate, is a type of plastic polymer that is commonly found in bottles and containers used for packaging wide range of food products and consumer goods.

while the rest needed to be sent to landfills. Given India's tropical climate, organic waste degraded rapidly. Therefore, segregation at the source was of utmost importance. Segregation ensured that the waste could be transferred and processed in a manner that caused minimum harm to the environment.

HDI charged the households highest for the rejects, followed by wet waste, and then the dry waste. Anything that was not segregated was considered as rejects. Households in a complex with 50 apartments were charged a fixed fee of INR 75 per month and INR 5, INR 3 and INR 1 per kilogram of rejects, wet and dry waste respectively, per month. When adequately segregated, the charges worked out to be about INR 170 per month per household. According to a study by the University of Chicago, this unique pricing model achieved close to 91 per cent of segregation and was instrumental in creating a culture among the households of being sensitive to the environment and be disciplined about segregating dry and wet waste at the source. HDI provided training to households regarding waste segregation that included children and house-helps and refused to collect waste that was not segregated.

HDI facilitated waste pickers to become franchisees and contracted with them for a fixed monthly service fee and incentives linked to performance. The Waste Picker Franchisee (WPF), on an average, serviced about 1,500 households, owned a commercial vehicle and employed a driver and four waster pickers. It collected wet waste and rejects daily, dry waste one–two times a week, electronic waste once in two–three months and garden and construction waste on an ad-hoc basis depending on truck loads. The waste that was collected by all such WPFs was transferred to a secondary transfer area where five–seven waste pickers were employed as sorters. HDI bought land and created the sorting area because they did not want to do that by the roadside as was done by some of the others. The sorted wet waste was transferred through a tipper for composting and to biogas plants, the rejects were sent to a private landfill operator whom they paid a tipping fee, the dry waste was sent to the godowns of waste picker franchisees for them to sort and sell, the garden waste was sent to farms and the e-waste to authorized recyclers. The waste picker thus had two sources of income – a fixed monthly fee from HDI with incentives for performance against service level agreements and revenue from recyclables.

HDI invested heavily in field operations to ensure reliable services. It appointed field supervisors, almost one for every three vehicles deployed in the field by the waste pickers. HDI learnt that while many citizens had the enthusiasm to segregate and dispose waste responsibly, their dominant need was a reliable service to minimize their own involvement in terms of time and attention. Therefore, HDI needed to operate like a utility service provider with high standards of quality. HDI installed a customer care helpline operating seven days a week, from 6 a.m. to 10 p.m., that was geared to resolving problems quickly. HDI was able to achieve a collection coverage of 99 per cent[11] and even with 410 clients, they had less than two calls per day. Customers who had left their services because they had found a cheaper service provider came back to them, bearing testimony to their reliability and credibility.

CREATING ENTREPRENEURS

It was estimated that India had 1.5 million waste pickers who were at the bottom of the economic pyramid, fighting day to day for survival. The city of Bengaluru had about 30,000 waste pickers, many of whom were migrants from other states. HDI's mission was to enhance livelihood opportunities for them, so that they could break out from the vicious cycle of poverty. Shekar believed that entrepreneurship was an innate ability among the waste pickers, and they should be provided the opportunity to bring it to fruition by setting up their own businesses. Therefore, they were keen to develop entrepreneurs among the waste pickers, rather than engage them as employees of HDI. To enable this, they adopted a franchisee model for the primary collection of waste.

During the first year of the contract, HDI built connections and did contracting with the clients on behalf of the entrepreneurs. Subsequently, the entrepreneurs assumed charge. The entrepreneur functioned like a franchisee, employed four waste pickers and a driver, and operated a truck.

---

[11] On rare occasions, all the houses may not be covered because of time or capacity overruns, or the dry waste collection, which was twice or thrice a week, was missed by mistake.

HDI sometimes helped them finance their trucks, while others like scrap dealers already owned their trucks. Some of them could also run multiple such franchisees if they had the ambition to scale their business. After four years, they got ownership of their trucks and could choose either to continue with the business or do something else (Ray 2016).

By January 2020, HDI had developed 26 entrepreneurs who collectively employed about 300 waste pickers as full-time wage-earning staff members and operated 32 trucks. Decentralization successfully addressed two other challenges, those of absenteeism, which was endemic in physically demanding work such as waste collection, and fleet maintenance. The waste picker had a greater ability to source labour locally, typically from nearby slums. They also took greater care of the vehicles that they owned, compared to if they had to maintain vehicles that were owned by HDI.

Their experience taught HDI that many of the waste pickers were not ready to join a formal organization because they preferred to be masters of their own time. The informal economy of garbage collection worked on a piece rate system, which implied that the waste pickers could earn more if they worked harder. Shekar commented,

> The idea is to first professionalize the sector, before trying to formalize it. How does one make the waste picker understand the notions of service level agreements, meeting expectations of customers, the importance of being punctual or to leave the pick-up point clean? Their lives revolve around earning their day-to-day living. To think of future consequences is often a luxury for them. We can achieve this only by working with them as partners, treating them as one of us and involving them in decisions about the enterprise. We need to enhance their income as well as bring in more predictability to their earnings.

HDI devised a couple of training modules with the objective of enabling the waste pickers to run successful businesses or act as service providers within a franchisee model. Scrap dealers who ran trading businesses were provided training on managing a business and how to become profitable. Shekar held meetings with the waster picker entrepreneurs every month, discussing with them the challenges and arriving at decisions democratically. These meetings were typically held at the HDI office and attended by 60–100 waste pickers. Many of the attendees talked about what they learnt from these trainings and interactions when they met their families and friends and encouraged some of them to take advantage of the opportunities that existed in this domain. As a result of these meetings, a family-like bond existed between HDI and the waste pickers. There was hardly any attrition among the waste pickers, except in cases of termination because of non-performance.

In parallel, the Hasiru Dala Trust worked closely with the waste pickers to raise funds to take care of their health expenses and to ensure that they were not harassed by the police. They enabled children of waste pickers to procure educational scholarships and collaborated with organizations such as Mindtree[12] to raise funds for providing scholarships, books, uniforms as well as hostel accommodation. Shekar believed that to break the cycle of poverty that waste pickers perennially found themselves locked in, their children needed school education and thus the ability to choose their own destiny.

HDI ensured that most of their 26 waste picker entrepreneurs filed their income tax returns. The possibility of witnessing quantum changes in the lives of the waste pickers acted as a great motivator for the HDI team. For example, Lotfar had joined HDI in 2014 and was one of the first three workers in the organization. In 2010, he had moved from Delhi to Bengaluru and tried to make ends meet through a small garbage business that he owned. He had joined HDI based on a friend's recommendation and had struggled through the initial days of the organization when the basic processes were being established and relationships with stakeholders were being built. Five years hence, he owned two trucks, a scooter and employed 22 workers in his franchisee. Annamma, an operator of a Dry Waste Collection Centre, improved her financial condition substantially with support from the

---

[12]   Mindtree is an information technology company based in Bengaluru that partnered with social enterprises working in the waste management space like HDI with the objective of improving the lives and working conditions of waste pickers. In 2014, they launched a technology platform called I Got Garbage that had various service capabilities for management of waste and engagement of stakeholders.

Hasiru Dala Trust. Apart from buying her own truck, she built a house and was able to send both her daughters to college.[13]

ENGAGING WITH MULTIPLE STAKEHOLDERS

Apart from empowering waste pickers and delivering a high quality of service, successful operations for an organization like HDI were also dependent on their constant engagement with multiple other stakeholders, such as elected representatives, urban local bodies, bureaucrats, officials and policy makers at the centre and the state levels. When HDI started their operations, they faced considerable pushback at multiple levels from people with vested interest in the status quo. However, over a period of time they were able to overcome such resistance. Shekar reflected,

> They probably realized that we were not going to go anywhere. Moreover, we were also able to garner support from many people within the system, such as the solid waste management group at BBMP. Several corporators and Members of Legislative Assembly appreciated our efforts publicly and that certainly helped. When you work in this sector, you will have to engage with the government if you want to bring about change.

When asked about the key attributes that enabled HDI to work with multiple stakeholders, Shekar noted,

> We were able to demonstrate an authenticity of purpose regarding the environmental and social impact, which convinced the stakeholders that we were not there just to make money. We have been transparent in our dealings. For example, we give monthly reports to the BBMP, zone wise,

---

[13] Adapted from https://yourstory.com/socialstory/2019/03/hasiru-dala-innovations-waste-pickers-entrepreneurs-bmatxxvdbf (accessed 18 November 2020). In case of DWCC operators, the BBMP directly signed contracts with them. Therefore, they were supported by the Hasiru Dala Trust rather than HDI.

about the multiple dimensions of our service, which enables them to hold us accountable. And we have always stuck to our value of integrity in a steadfast manner and never shown any intension to cut corners even if that means losing money in the short run.

Over the years, HDI was also pleased to note a gradual change in the attitude of citizens towards waste pickers. In the past, waste picking was viewed as an unclean occupation and the majority of the waste pickers were from the Dalit community, traditionally viewed as a lower caste in India. They were, therefore, shunned by the rest of society and had limited interactions with people outside their own caste. Even in the slums where they lived, they were relegated to the periphery. The government-recognized identity card that Hasiru Dala was able to procure for them was an important first step towards recognizing them and their profession. Subsequently, HDI found that some of their clients provided the waste pickers with tea when they visited their houses and, on another occasion, a client threw a dinner party for them.

EXPANDING BUSINESS

HDI expanded its scope of business to include the management of waste that was generated at large events, such as celebrity shows, corporate events, weddings and marathons. On an average, they cleaned up 100 such venues annually and generated an income of INR 550 per day for waste pickers. The waste pickers also enjoyed working in such events because it not only provided them with additional income but also an opportunity to interact with different kinds of people. Inspired by HDI's efforts, a trend of eco-friendly weddings started in the city. They also won a tender from ELCITA,[14] which gave them the contract to process the waste of 84 companies in Electronics City, including e-waste. Rama, the CEO of ELCITA, noted,

---

[14] Electronics City Industrial Township Authority. Electronics City is an industrial estate on the outskirts of Bengaluru that houses several electronics and software organizations along with residential complexes and educational institutes.

Four years ago, there was no waste management facility at Electronics City. Today, almost 10 tonnes of waste is processed by us, from private companies and hotels. We have benefitted from engaging with Hasiru Dala Innovations, which has demonstrated both technical and commercial strength over the past one year. (TheCityFix Labs India 2019)

HDI produced 'product compost kits', which were delivered to individual households by waste pickers, who explained to the customer how to set up and use the product. This process had the social dimension of empowering the waste picker and making them confident because of their ability to interact with the household and educate them about this aspect of sustainability (Ray 2016). But it has since closed this line of business because being a product company demanded different competencies than services, which was HDI's forte.

SOCIAL PLASTICS

Thanks largely to the efforts of the waste pickers, India has one of the largest rates of plastics recycling (Chatterjee 2017). At 90 per cent, the PET bottle recycling rate in India is above those of Japan (78 per cent), USA (29 per cent) and Europe (48 per cent). The price of plastics, both virgin and recycled, follow global oil prices, which implies that when oil prices fall, the price of recycled plastics also fall. Most of this fall in price is passed on to the waste pickers, which pushes them further into poverty. HDI wanted to prevent this and create a model where they were able to provide them a floor price so that they were protected to some extent from the risks. Thus, Shekar and his team started to approach private organizations who used PET-based plastics as packaging material with the proposal of supplying them with recycled plastics that would be ethically sourced. While usage of recycled plastics would be a sustainable practice for the organization and enhance the appeal of their brands, it would provide a steady source of income for the waste pickers.

HDI collaborated with Plastics for Change, a multinational fair-trade organization, and signed a contract with The Body Shop to supply them with food-grade PET that they would use for packaging their product. It was a fixed price contract and The Body Shop agreed to pay a premium price because the plastic was creating a positive impact in the lives of the waste pickers. As a result of these contracts, HDI exported 114 tonnes of PET at a social impact premium in 2019–20 and in May 2019, The Body Shop[15] launched their Ginger Shampoo product with 100 per cent food-grade PET packaging, 15 per cent of which was sourced from India, mostly through HDI.

HDI also secured funding of GBP 300,000 from Unilever under their Transform initiative to increase the capacity of their waste aggregation centre and create a washing and palletization line for PET. This would increase their current capacity of aggregation from 1.5 MT to 5 MT, delivering economies of scale, and create a PET processing capacity of 3.5–4 MT. Shekar explained,

> We wanted to integrate forward because in recycling, the highest margins are towards the end of the process. With these capacities, we will be able to earn more and pass it down the value chain to enhance the income of the waste pickers.

CHALLENGES

HDI turned earnings before depreciation, interest and taxes (EBDIT) positive within 23 months of its operations and expected to have a small profit by 2020. It reported a revenue of INR 90 million in March 2019, which was 70 per cent more than that of the previous financial year. Their engagement with ELCITA turned profitable within the first year of its operation. They were confident about the financial viability of the model, despite having no subsidies or financial support from the government. However, what they have covered so far was only a small part of the total market. Of the 5,000 bulk generators in Bengaluru, HDI was able to cover about 250. The BBMP spent INR 7–10 billion annually for solid waste management, of which 70 per cent was handled

---

[15] The Body Shop International Limited is a UK-based cosmetics, skin care and perfume company. It is a subsidiary of the Brazilian cosmetics company Natura & Co. and had a turnover of the USD 1.4 billion in 2017. Available at https://en.wikipedia.org/wiki/The_Body_Shop (accessed 18 June 2020).

by private contractors. Thus, Shekar and his team felt a compelling need for scaling.

Client behaviour remained the biggest hurdle to scaling because many apartment owners, despite being financially well-off, were still unwilling to pay even INR 170 per month for the waste they generated. Shekar noted,

> Obviously, it is not their inability to pay. It is their unwillingness. Part of the reason for this is the wrong narrative of 'wealth from waste' that has permeated this space. People wrongly think that this is a lucrative business, money can be easily made from waste, when in actuality, it is a negative value system. The only way out is to make the waste generator ('polluter pays' principle) and the producer of the product whose consumption led to the waste pay (principle of extended producer responsibility, or EPR)[16] and to design products so that they generated less waste in the first place and whatever they generated could be reused or refurbished.

Despite efforts put in by organizations like HDI, when it came to managing waste for the city of Bengaluru, a lot needed to be done. The seven waste treatment plants had a capacity of processing 2,100 MT, which was less than half of the waste that the city generated. Therefore, the remaining mix of dry and wet waste was dumped into the city's ever-growing landfills. While the BBMP spent INR 70 billion for waste management during 2015–20, residents around the landfills continued to suffer and authorities were in search of new places to dump the city's garbage. Most plans for setting up compost development units, waste-to-energy units and other waste treatment methods were either yet to take off or have had a premature termination because of poor estimation, maintenance and commitment. While the site at Mandur was closed in 2013, nothing much was done to restore its environment.

---

[16] Extended producer responsibility (EPR), first introduced formally in Sweden in 1990, is the policy of adding the environmental costs associated with a product to the market price of the product. This made the manufacturer of the product responsible for the entire lifecycle of the product, especially take-back, recovery and disposal, and created incentives for the producer to design products that had minimal environmental impact.

A report by the Comptroller and Auditor General noted failure at multiple levels, such as low utilization and diversion of funds for works other than solid waste management, discrepancies in awarding of work and including conditions in tender documents to favour particular bidders. Activists noted that the authorities deliberately chose to ignore the recommendations of several studies and state policies for the involvement of communities because a large part of the waste management was controlled by garbage contractors who benefitted from the status quo (Sharma 2019).

Notwithstanding such challenges in the ecosystem, HDI was moving steadily towards their mission of integrating waste pickers into the mainstream circular economy by fostering entrepreneurship and creating better livelihood opportunities for them, as well as inculcating sustainable practices among customers and producers. They were hopeful that things would change and twenty years hence, the organization should no longer exist for the reasons that they existed at present. Rather, they should evolve into a global waste management company that was owned by waste pickers and employees.

DISCUSSION

THE NATURE OF SOCIAL ENTREPRENEURS

What are the factors that make waste management such an intractable problem in India? This is because of a variety of reasons. Urban India generates waste in excess of the capacity available to treat it in a sustainable manner. Different actors in the production supply chain, such as the producers, the distributers and the retailers, do not use packaging material that are either biodegradable or can be disposed of in a responsible manner. This happens because of a combination of ignorance, apathy and negligence. As we learnt from the case, consumers do not take the responsibility for segregation of waste, which puts an additional burden of separation and processing on the waste management functions downstream, neither are they, even those who are financially well-off, willing to pay a modest amount that is necessary for processing household waste in a sustainable manner. Finally, there is corruption in municipalities that prevents adoption of best practices and encourages opportunistic behaviour among garbage traders and contractors of waste pickers, who manage to gain from lack of accountability in the supply chain of waste management. A related tragedy of the system is widespread exploitation of waste pickers, who are at the bottom of the economic and social hierarchy, do not have voice or power and are perennially caught in a vicious cycle of poverty. Some authors have argued that inadequate waste management in India stems from a deep-rooted Indian cultural belief where high importance is given to keeping private places, such as one's house clean, but very little importance is given to keeping public places clean. All of these imply that there is no silver bullet or one effective solution to the problem of waste management.

Despite the popular narrative that wealth can be made from waste management, the experience of people working on the ground indicates that it is far from reality, at least in countries such as India. Waste management is not just a matter of creating an efficient supply chain for sustainable disposal of waste. In order or create a sustainable solution, there need to be changes at multiple levels of society, such as change in behaviour of individuals, to creating incentives for businesses for behaving responsibly, and breaking the nexus that seems to exist between policy makers, corporators and traders who benefit from the present situation. This is seemingly beyond the scope of an individual organization, more so if it intends to be profitable. This is a domain where markets cannot function smoothly because of information asymmetry, institutional voids and poorly developed infrastructure. Organizations that want to operate in such a domain need to make a lot of investment in changing the various elements that hinder proper functioning of the market. Such efforts intended towards change are bound to be time-consuming and expensive, making any business model financially unsustainable. Therefore, this domain needs social enterprises whose primary motive is to solve the problem of waste management and who may not have the need to show much or any amount of financial profitability.

Given that there is no easy or well-defined path towards solving this problem, it is likely that such social enterprises will adopt different strategies to deal with the problem. This is what is being witnessed in India. For example, Daily Dump promotes the recycling of waste by households themselves that results in savings of 50 tonnes of organic waste every day and reduces the daily garbage output from homes by nearly 80 per cent. Help Us Green, a for-profit social enterprise, collects 2.4 tonnes of waste flowers daily from Indian temples to make organic fertilizer and biodegradable packaging material, waste that is otherwise dumped in rivers and water bodies near such temples. Apart from preventing such dumping of chemical-ridden floral waste and recycling them, Help Us Green enhances the income for about 100 waste pickers (Gulati 2018). Sahaas Zero Waste, a for-profit organization in Bengaluru, works with BWGs like HDI does, but sets up waste management units within campuses of BWGs and converts recyclables into useful products, such as roofing sheets and T-shirts.

Given the complex nature of the problem and the various possible ways of dealing with it, a social entrepreneur like Shekar has to make choices about the scale and scope of their activities. One option for him would have been to focus on improving the efficiency of the supply chain, beginning with better segregation at source and recycling of wet and dry waste in a manner that not only retrieved maximum value from them but also ensured minimum waste being sent to landfills. That per se would have been a very useful way of dealing with the problem. But in addition to doing all of that, HDI went beyond and tried to ensure that there was systemic change in the life of the waste pickers. This is probably because HDI emerged from Hasiru Dala Trust whose focus has been the welfare of the waste picker. Therefore, the importance of improving the lives of the waste picker always stayed with HDI even while it chartered a different course for itself.

Shekar and Nalini believed that to break the vicious cycle of poverty the waste pickers are trapped into, it was absolutely important to provide education to their children, which, in turn, was only possible provided the parents had a steady source of income. That is why Hasiru Dala Trust made efforts to secure scholarships and other necessary support to admit them in schools. This is the true characteristic of a social entrepreneur who is not only trying to solve the immediate problem but also thinking of the changes that can reduce or eliminate the source of the problem itself. If we apply this lens to the work that Help Us Green is doing, one would expect them to start thinking about reducing the floral waste over and above the work that they have been doing in recycling them. Flowers per se are not very harmful as waste because they are biodegradable. The real problem in this case is the usage of pesticides and inorganic fertilizers by flower growers. Often, such chemically treated flowers end up in rivers and water bodies that are close to the temples, giving rise to several waterborne diseases. Therefore, the elimination of the problem would require Help Us Green to work with flower growers and ensure that they did not use harmful or inorganic pesticides and fertilizers, something that would require a completely different kind of effort to bring about behaviour change.

Social entrepreneur Bill Drayton, the founder of Ashoka, said, 'Social entrepreneurs are not content just to give a fish or teach how to fish. They will not rest unless they have revolutionized the fishing industry.' They want to change the social order by challenging the status quo and creating new patterns of behaviour and transactions for society and the community. In Shekar and Nalini, we find such examples of social entrepreneurs.

DUAL ENTITY ORGANIZATION

As an organization, Hasiru Dala was involved with two sets of activities concerning the waste pickers – improving their income and livelihood opportunities as well as helping them find a voice, enabling them to get benefits that they deserve and those that are provided by the government. The first set of activities that are linked to income or livelihood generation were dealt with HDI, the private entity. The second set of activities was handled by Hasiru Dala Trust, the not-for-profit. In India, many social enterprises follow this dual-organization structure, where one entity is structured as a private company, while the other is a not-for-profit. This is primarily because Indian laws are yet to provide a legal structure that is suitable for a social enterprise or an inclusive business that enables an organization to maximize social impact while achieving financial sustainability. For example, an organization structured as a not-for-profit in India cannot attract investments and, therefore, needs to raise grants and donations to meet its financial objectives. However, American laws allows for legal entities, such as the low-profit limited liability company (L3C), for socially oriented for-profit ventures that can attract financial investments from private investors as well as from foundations.[17] Likewise, in the UK, organizations that want to focus on social

---

[17]   Another organization form that social enterprises can adopt in the USA is that of benefit corporation. Similar to L3C, they are structured to pursue

objectives as the primary mission instead of maximizing shareholders' wealth can be structured as community interest companies (CICs).[18]

In the absence of a legal structure, Indian social enterprises need to choose between being a not-for-profit or a for-profit entity. While the not-for-profit can be registered in different forms, such as a trust, society or a Section 8 company, none of them can raise investments and have restrictions on the kind of activities that they can carry out and how they can distribute profits. For example, a Section 8 company can carry out commercial activities, but the income needs to be reinvested in the company and cannot be distributed among its members. This restricts such companies from accessing capital markets and constrains their growth. If HDI was structured as a trust, society or a Section 8 company, it would have been very difficult for them to create the franchisee waste picker model that they have established. But, most importantly, it would have created significant constraints on their growth because they would not have been able to attract the kind of investments that are needed to set up and scale their operations.

Therefore, the only option available before them was to be structured as a for-profit private entity, where the existing regulations do not have any provision for the primacy of their social mission. This implies that they do not have access to funds from foundations or charities and the tax laws of the country treat them the same as for-profit entities that have purely commercial motives. However, because HDI is working with an underserved vulnerable community like the waste pickers, they need to make a lot of investment in developing the market structures, which typically do not exist in such a domain. They also would like to maximize their social objective and not shareholders' wealth, which might make many investors turn away, even

---

social benefits ahead of profits and their management is expected to make every operating, financing and investment decision giving primacy to the social cause. They, however, do not have such broad capital market access as an L3C.

[18] CICs attract investments and can issue shares. While CICs can accept grants, unlike charities, their main source of income is expected to come from sales or from trade. CICs do not get any tax exemptions even though their objectives are expected to be entirely charitable.

though that is the only route available to HDI to raise investment. This is why social enterprises try to raise funds from a special category of investors, called the impact investor, whose mission is aligned with the social objective of the enterprise. This implies that such investors do not expect a high rate of return, but are investing their money to create positive social impact. While the category of social or impact investors is increasing, which is a very positive development for the social sector, in reality, some of them are not as patient with their investments as they claim to be and they put pressure on the social enterprise to scale and turn profitable, so that they can increase their exit multiple. However, given the present scenario, entities such as HDI do not have any other option but to be structured as a for-profit entity and thereby deal with the challenges of being clubbed with commercial entities by several stakeholders.

While HDI's intention is to establish a financially sustainable business model, there are several activities that they would like to do for the welfare of the waste pickers that will not generate any revenue and increase their costs. All such activities that are necessary for their mission, if conducted by the for-profit entity, will further reduce their chances of being financially sustainable. Therefore, such activities that are essential for the betterment of waste pickers' lives are conducted by the not-for-profit entity, Hasiru Dala Trust. Being structured as a trust, it can raise grant money without any expectation of returns or payback. Free from the pressure of investors, they can focus only on their social objective even while living with the constraints of the quantum of funds that they can raise. Such not-for-profit entities that complement the activities of the for-profit social enterprise can also be found in other examples described in the book, namely LaborNet and SELCO. In the case of Rang De (discussed in Chapter 4), they were forced to make a transition from a not-for-profit entity to a for-profit because of regulatory changes.

CHAPTER LEARNING

Waste pickers play a very important role in collecting, segregating and recycling waste that is generated every day in urban India. Yet they remain extremely poor and are shunned by society.

Since waste management has revenue streams in the form of fees from waste generators and income from recycling, an inclusive business model can be created that benefits the waste pickers by enhancing their income.

A franchisee model involving the waste pickers rather than employing them may work better because it allows the waste pickers to remain independent and leverage their entrepreneurial spirit in getting things done. However, waste pickers need to be trained to professionally deliver acceptable levels of service quality.

Revenue earned from recycling alone is not sufficient to make the business model financially viable. It is important to charge fees from households and institutions that generate waste as well as make manufacturers pay for the waste that they generate. Forward integration through investments in suitable infrastructure is another means to enhance the income and profitability for the business.

Such waste management businesses need to work closely with the local government and municipal authorities, despite the usual constraints and challenges that exist in managing such alliances.

Apart from enhancing the income of waste pickers, there is need for complementary services such as policy advocacy and linking them to beneficial government schemes that would improve the quality of their lives. Since such activities are not easy to monetize, they are best done by a not-for-profit that complements the activities of the inclusive business.

8

RELIANCE RETAIL

Creating Inclusive Supply Chain

One of the key problems besetting the Indian agricultural sector is inefficiency in the supply chain. Poor connectivity between the source of production, the villages and important markets in urban India, inadequate storage facilities and the inability of the farmers to have market information on time – all result in a high degree of intermediation and significant wastage. While some degree of intermediation is necessary for the functioning of complex supply chains, excessive intermediation as witnessed in the Indian agricultural supply chain results in the farmer receiving only a small share of the price at which the products are sold to the final consumer. Anecdotal evidence indicates that farmers growing a fruit like kinnow,[1] which retails for INR 70 per kilogram in the urban market of Bengaluru, does not realize more than INR 7 per kilogram, which sometimes make it unviable for them to grow the fruit. This is paradoxical because kinnow has a high demand in the urban markets and is considered a premium product, which ideally should provide high returns to the producer.

In 2006, Reliance Industries Limited, the Indian multinational conglomerate, entered the organized retail sector with an investment of USD 5.6 billion. Prior to 2006, Reliance invested primarily in the textile, petrochemicals and telecommunication sectors. But by the turn of the century, Reliance started to express interest in the agricultural and retail sectors, which were considered to have significant but unrealized business potential. In his speeches to stakeholders, the chairman, Mukesh Ambani, explained that the Indian agricultural sector not only presented a USD 500 billion business

---

[1]   A hybrid citrus fruit cultivated in India and Pakistan.

opportunity but also had the potential of creating employment for millions of Indians. By investing in the agriculture and retail sectors, Reliance would address a significant social need of the country, which would be his way of acknowledging the opportunity that the country provided him with by allowing him to create an enterprise with limited liability.

As part of their retail operations, Reliance decided to create dedicated supply chains for fruits and vegetables that would source products from villages and deliver to hundreds of Reliance Retail stores that were planned to be set up across the country. Bananas were chosen first among the fruits because they had almost unlimited demand and supply in India; they were available throughout the year and Reliance assessed that there was considerable scope of value addition by an organized player, given the existing state of the supply chain. Reliance thus became the first organized retailer in India who undertook development of supply chain for bananas.

However, things did not go as planned. Reliance's foray into organized retail was met with stiff resistance from the existing unorganized retail sector who were afraid that corporations would drive the traditional mom-and-pop retail stores[2] out of business. This was compounded by an economic downturn, slump in demand and delay in the delivery of properties. Reliance Retail was forced to scale back its expansion in terms of its retail outlets. But it did not want to scale down its supply chain operations and decided instead to supply the excess bananas to other retailers, both in the organized and unorganized sectors. While this would result in a loss of competitive advantage, the team at Reliance Retail reasoned that they were not into the retail business or development of the rural supply chain with the sole intention of making money. Rather, they were driving the transformative potential that organized retail had for India by creating employment, enhancing the income of the farmers and delivering better quality to the consumer.

This changed the way Reliance looked at the supply chain of bananas. While earlier it was conceptualized as an essential backend process for its own retail operations, they realized that an organized banana supply chain had much larger potential. Since India is the largest producer of bananas,

---

[2]   Known as *kirana* stores in India.

producing 25 per cent of the world's produce,[3] Reliance could get into exports in a big way if efficiencies earned from the supply chain could be leveraged to deliver bananas of global standards. Moreover, the experience earned from developing the banana supply chain as well as the infrastructure that was set up could be leveraged to source other fruits from the Indian hinterland that could be retailed in India and abroad. And all of these would finally benefit the farmer through enhanced income and greater livelihood opportunities mostly for people living in Indian villages. Reliance's entry into the supply chain of bananas promised to be an important first step in solving one of the more intractable problems of the Indian agricultural sector.

CHALLENGES IN TRADITIONAL SUPPLY CHAIN

Believing that banana was no longer a 'poor-man's fruit' and that it represented a USD 1-billion opportunity, Reliance created a dedicated team that would understand the various challenges of the supply chain and figure out the best ways of solving them. The team realized that a significant amount of losses was happening in the supply chain because of the unhygienic manner in which it was ripened and the unscientific way in which the fruit was harvested and transported. Moreover, the presence of monopolistic intermediaries, who did not maintain any transparency in financial dealings, resulted in a low price realization for the farmer. This, in turn, was discouraging the farmer from growing bananas for his livelihood even while making the fruit expensive for the customer. Therefore, interventions were necessary at multiple points in the supply chain to ensure that the customer got high quality fruit at a reasonable

---

[3] Global production of bananas is estimated to be 114 million tonnes with India being the largest producer at 29 million tonnes (2017). Almost all its production serves the local market. Globally, the largest exporters of bananas are Ecuador, Philippines and Costa Rica. See 'Banana Facts and Figures', Food and Agriculture Organization of the United Nations, available at http://www.fao.org/economic/est/est-commodities/bananas/bananafacts/en/#.XvQvGtjis2w (accessed 24 June 2020).

price and the banana grower got a higher share of the retail price such that growing bananas became financially attractive.

The process of buying and selling farm produce was highly regulated in India, through the state Agriculture Product Market Committee (APMC) Act that mandated that all fruits and vegetables be sold to licensed traders at designated auction markets, known as *mandi*s. This system, as it was envisaged, would provide maximum benefit to the small farmers by providing them the highest price through competitive bidding among the licensed traders. However, in practice, the system was riddled with problems. The APMC licence holders often formed cartels. They lent money to the farmers, who were perennially short of cash, obligating them to sell their harvest only through the money lenders, thereby forming local monopolies. The auctioneer also provided credit to the buyer and lent money to the farmer for personal consumption, and often his financial business took precedence over the trading of fruits and vegetables. Thus, there was little or no concern about productivity and quality. Most of the times, the 'bid price' at the auction had little relevance because the auctioneer would deduct money from it for his handling charges and for the alleged poor quality of the output. Farmers who were financially dependent on him were not in a position to negotiate or demand transparency. The net result was a vicious cycle of low productivity and indebtedness among the farmers.

Subsequently, some of the Indian states amended the APMC Act[4] to allow retailers to procure directly from the farmers. Thus, Reliance and several other organized retailers, such as the Tatas, Godrej Agrovet and Aditya Birla Retail, procured licences to buy directly from the farmers. This provided the farmers with a choice at the farm-gate and created competition among the retailers. Moreover, when retailers procured directly from the farmers, the farmers did not need to pay transportation and handling charges[5] that they incurred when they sold through the *mandi*s. Because of that, the big farmer with large outputs no longer needed to go to the *mandi*s but directly did business with organized retailers and exporters from his farm. Small farmers still needed to go to the *mandi*s because it was often not viable for large companies to deal with them directly.

---

[4]   APMC Model Act 2003.

[5]   Estimated to be INR 1 per kilogram for transport and INR 5 per kilogram for handling and loading.

DEVELOPING INTERMEDIARIES

The Agricultural Land Ceiling Act in India prevented Reliance from buying large tracts of land and cultivating banana as an organization. Reliance did not find contract farming suitable for banana cultivation because of the price volatility and also because it would be difficult for it to enforce any kind of contract on the banana farmers, given the socio-economic realities of rural India. Reliance, therefore, decided to source bananas from individual farmers without having any exclusive contracts with them. The average farm size in India is only 3.3 acres and large farms, defined as those greater than 25 acres, account for less than 1 per cent of India's 120 million farms.[6] This meant that Reliance had to deal with a large number of small-landholding farmers, something that was very difficult for an organization to do in a cost-effective manner. Moreover, being a large corporate entity, it would have been difficult for Reliance to earn the trust of small farmers who were used to dealing with local traders and auctioneers with whom they had long-standing relationships.

Therefore, Reliance decided to develop intermediaries, someone from the local community who would act as a go-between with them and the farmer community. The vendors, as they are called by Reliance, were often banana farmers themselves who worked closely with its field executives in planning and monitoring farm-level activities of a large group of banana growers. Known as *hundikari*s in the local language, they performed multiple roles of consolidating supply, trading, operations management as well as convincing farmers to adopt better farming practices. Reliance's field executives communicated to them the market demand, which they equated with the volume that they could procure from different farmers. Overall, the vendor was responsible for organizing farm labour for harvesting and transporting the produce to Reliance's processing centres known as city processing centres (CPCs). The Reliance executive would explain to the vendor its standards and expectations about the quality of the fruit and paid him on the basis of his

---

[6] 'India – Agricultural Economy and Policy Report', January 2009, available at www.fas.usda.gov (accessed 14 September 2011).

weekly supplies.[7] The vendor, in turn, paid the farmers and the field labourers who were employed for harvesting.

Dadasahib Patil was one such vendor who worked with Reliance in Solapur[8] who sent about 300 truckloads of bananas to the company every year. On a given day, he typically employed 20 farm labourers for loading a truck of bananas and sent two to three trucks a day to Reliance CPCs during the harvesting season. He owned 80 acres of land across four villages, of which 20 acres was dedicated to banana cultivation. His annual income from the banana business was estimated to be about half a million rupees. Thanks to Reliance, he transformed into an entrepreneur, handling labourers and transporters, and developing insights into modern farming techniques and supply chain management. Over a period of time, vendors like Dadasahib Patil grew in prestige within their communities because of their ability to generate employment and being seen as working with a large company like Reliance.

Reliance's field executives worked closely with vendors like Dadasahib, setting expectations and advising them in running the field operations as well as assessing the quality of fruits. If any farmer approached the executive directly, he redirected the farmer to the local vendor. The field executive thus played an important part in developing Reliance's relationship with the local community and it was expected that he would have a good command over local languages and possess a high degree of familiarity with local traditions, customs and politics. Parag Shah, Banana Value Chain Manager of Western India, explained,

> It has been always Reliance's intention to work with the system and to enable the local farmers to grow. At the same time, we have to make sure that we are sourcing the desirable quality and quantity, which can only be achieved if the farmers adopt modern practices. It is a fine balance that can only be achieved by building a trustworthy relationship. Thus, we are in

---

[7] The vendor was paid a commission of 25 paise per kilogram and the labourers 45 paise per kilogram. There was an acceptable loss of 8 per cent by weight, which was factored in while making the payment to him.

[8] Solapur city is the district headquarters in the Indian state of Maharashtra. Dadasahib Patil hailed from one of the villages in Solapur district.

constant discussion with the farmers, explaining to them our expectations as well as trying to understand their constraints, even if we are not directly dealing with the individual farmer.

ORGANIZING AT THE FARM

Reliance had to intervene at multiple points of the supply chain to reduce wastage, increase yield and improve quality. Its farm-level intervention started with advising farmers on sourcing of banana saplings. Reliance's Life Sciences Division conducted research on the high-yield variety of bananas and came up with tissues that were sold at INR 12 per plant to the farmers. While this was much more expensive compared to saplings that farmers could buy from the open market at about INR 3, plants grown out of banana tissues had higher output, needed shorter time to mature and provided greater predictability in terms of timing and quality. Reliance left the final choice to the individual grower. But it was usually their experience that once the farmer bought tissues from Reliance, he came back for it next year because of the enhanced income that it produced, sometimes as high as INR 125,000 per acre annually.

Bananas that are needed to be transported before they can be sold are not allowed to ripen on the plants. Green, mature bananas are cut from the plants and transported to be artificially ripened. The thick stem where bananas grow is known as a loom. Each loom comprises 10–11 'hands' or subsidiary stems that grow about 130 bananas or 'fingers'. Reliance provided farmers with bags, known as sleeves, to cover banana looms while on plants to avoid exposing the fruit to direct sun rays and to prevent attacks of pests. Sleeves also enabled farmers to harvest plants that were at the border of the farms, which were otherwise wasted. Farmers were charged for the sleeves but were paid back the money during the harvesting time when they brought them back. This ensured that the bags were not re-used. Reliance used them as packing material during transportation. Reliance provided farm labourers with handling pads, so that they could carry the looms on their shoulders instead of their heads, as was the traditional practice.

Reliance taught the labourers to 'de-hand' the bananas using nylon threads instead of their bare hands to reduce damage and wastage. De-handing at the farm-gate enabled early identification of low-quality bananas. After de-handing, each of the bananas was washed in water that contained fungicide. Subsequently, they were dried, oiled, sorted, graded and carefully packed in crates. During the entire process, it was ensured that the fruit never touched the ground so as to minimize spots or damage marks. Transporting bananas in crates instead of looms reduced the handling and transportation losses and minimized damage to the bananas in transit.[9] While traditionally, the collection and distribution centres were separate even at the field or village level, Reliance decided to do away with collection centres. They became necessary where the production per field was low and there was a need to aggregate output from various fields before the minimum economic quantity for transportation was achieved. Reliance ensured that an entire truck could be filled with the output from one farm or a cluster of farms in the same location, thereby eliminating one step in handling the fruit. Similarly, the distribution centres were co-located with ripening centres, which reduced another set of unloading and loading. This reduction was very important because the maximum damage to bananas happened while loading and unloading, and minimizing such activities directly added to the quality and shelf life of the fruit.

Reliance estimated that in the traditional way of handling and transportation, there was about 20 per cent loss from damage and another 10 per cent loss due to poor quality. It was difficult to sell those bananas at a premium in the markets. However, with the methods practised by Reliance, the losses due to damage were minimized and it was possible for the farmers to get average prices of INR 9.5–10 per kilogram from Reliance. The landed price for Reliance averaged between INR 12 and 12.5 per kilogram.

One of the critical challenges for Reliance was to ensure a steady supply of bananas throughout the year. Usually, there was very high production between December and March, resulting in shortage of labour and support infrastructure for taking the product to the market. This was followed by a period of two to three months when there was absolutely no fruit available for selling. Farmers had their own beliefs and intuition about banana markets.

---

[9] Almost all retailers in unorganized markets sell bananas from looms and de-handing in traditional supply chains happen at the point of sales, sometimes even by the customers. This leads to a lot of wastage.

For example, many farmers believed that bananas would not sell if other fruits such as mangoes were available in the market. Therefore, they tried to avoid a planting cycle that would coincide banana harvesting with the availability of mangoes. Over a period of time, by educating the farmers and assuring them about markets, Reliance was able to extend the growing season from three months to nine months. Their final objective was to stretch it further to twelve months by convincing the farmers to take some risks and plant off-season. A twelve-month growing season was necessary for Reliance to maintain continuity in their operations.

Banana trees consume a significant amount of water. The typical input costs, including fertilizers and pesticides, were about INR 20,000 per acre. It was possible to get three crops from one sapling in two-and-a-half years, at intervals of twelve, eight and six months respectively, and farmer profitability was about INR 50,000 per acre in the first year and INR 100,000 per acre in the second and third years. After three crops, the plant needed to be uprooted and the soil enriched by means of crop rotation for four to five months. However, many farmers did not like to uproot the mother plant even after three crop cycles because they believed that nutrients were passed on to the baby plants from the mother plant. Reliance advised but did not enforce uprooting of the mother plant. It believed that if it could provide an economic incentive to the farmer to get rid of the mother plant, he might get convinced. Therefore, Reliance was in discussion with Gujarat University to develop technology that could make fibres out of old banana plants, which could be used for making bags.

Reliance endeavoured to develop new sourcing locations and not rely on traditional sources, such as Jalgaon.[10] However, each of the locations had unique challenges of their own. For example, Solapur, one of the areas

---

[10] Jalgaon, a city in the western Indian state of Maharashtra, has the nickname of 'banana city'. In 2018, it produced 3.4 million tonnes of bananas, accounting for about half of Maharashtra's banana production and 16 per cent of the total bananas produced by India. See 'How Jalgaon, "Banana City of India", Is Fast Becoming the "Banana Republic"', *Financial Express*, available at https://www.financialexpress.com/india-news/how-jalgaon-banana-city-of-india-is-fast-becoming-the-banana-republic/1210358/ (accessed 23 March 2020).

which Reliance was developing, had suitable climatic and soil conditions to grow bananas. Moreover, its proximity to Ujjani Dam[11] provided farmers with plenty of water that was essential for growing bananas. The challenge in Solapur was to convince the farmers about the utility of banana farming, since most of them had been traditional growers of sugarcane. Sugarcane farming was less labour intensive and since farmers sold their entire output to farmer cooperatives, they did not have to worry about markets or fairness in pricing. Farmers typically earned about INR 25,000 per acre from sugarcane over a 14–16-month crop cycle. Gradually, Reliance was able to convince the farmers to diversify into bananas, which, because of steady increase in market prices, generated more income. Unlike sugarcane, the price of bananas was not controlled by the government, which implied that if farmers could improve the quality of bananas, it would translate into higher prices and enhanced income. Jatinder Patil, *sarpanch* of Kandar village, said,

> We were in the sugarcane business because the market was steady. If we get a steady buyer, proper rates and payment on time, we can grow bananas. Banana traders from Delhi visit us only for a few months. They do not give us fair prices. We do not trust them. With Reliance, there is transparency.

The challenges in Osmanabad, another location that Reliance was developing, were different. The climate there was dry, the farmers were dependent entirely on rainfall and the average yield per acre was less than the yield in other locations such as Solapur. The average farm size was smaller and the farms were dispersed. No big trader or organized retailer went to Osmanabad to source banana. Banana prices there were cheaper by about INR 0.5 per kilogram and Osmanabad was close to Hyderabad, a large market. In Osmanabad, Reliance advised the farmers to use drip irrigation for banana cultivation and helped them procure state subsidies that were available for

---

[11] Ujjani Dam, also known as Bhima Dam or Bhima Irrigation Project, on the Bhima River, a tributary of the Krishna River, is an earthfill-cum-masonry gravity dam located near Ujjani village of Madha *taluk* in Solapur district of the state of Maharashtra.

drip irrigation.[12] Reliance was developing alternate sources, realizing that they might not be able to get an alternative supply from Osmanabad. Reliance estimated that they sourced close to 50 per cent of the total produce of Osmanabad at a rate of about 75–80 metric tonnes per month.

Typically, 1,200 banana plants were grown per acre and 300 plants were harvested every week from an acre of plantation. The output of about 7–7.5 tonnes[13] was carried every week in a truck to CPCs and the whole farm was harvested over a month. Reliance used a particular variety of foldable 'honeycomb' crates, which ensured that a maximum number of them could be packed within a given space without damaging the bananas in any way. It took a truck about 16 hours to cover the distance between a sourcing centre at Solapur and Mumbai, the nearest CPC, and the journey resulted in 2 per cent weight loss of the fruit. However, if transportation was made using refrigerated trucks, known as reefer vehicles, there was no weight loss. Reefer vehicles cost 30 per cent more and handled marginally a greater number of crates.[14] But the biggest gain was realized from better quality of the product. Therefore, Reliance planned to tie up with transporters who could provide them with refrigerated vehicles to transport the bananas.

BUILDING PARTNERSHIPS

The Reliance supply chain team realized that it was not possible for them to do everything on their own and they needed input from specialists. They, therefore, embarked on building partnerships with companies within the Reliance Group as well as outside. They tied up with Yara International, a Norwegian company that manufactured specialized crop specific fertilizers, BASF India, which specialized in fungal and bacterial disease control, and Swal Corporation for pest control. Demonstration plots were laid, where

---

[12]   The government subsidizes the cost of drip irrigation to the extent of 50 per cent and provides an additional amount of INR 40,000 per hectare.

[13]   Twenty-five kilograms of output per plant, taken in 385 crates, each with about 18 kilograms of bananas.

[14]   Reefer vehicles can carry 420 crates.

the three companies carried out their recommended practices for the entire crop cycle at their own cost to demonstrate to the farmers the benefits of best practices. Such demonstration plots were laid in different sourcing locations in north, central, west and south India to establish suitability of the recommended practices for all agro-climatic zones as well as to understand how such practices needed to be customized to suit different environments.

Banana growers were able to notice the difference in growth of fruit in the demonstration plots after the first month and started enquiring about specialized fertilizers and sprays. This enabled the agro-input companies to sell their products and establish their efficacy across different locations for banana crops. It resulted in a substantial improvement in the quality and yield of fruit, which was beneficial both for the growers and for Reliance. Reliance also engaged qualified agriculturists from the local population to work as Technical Facilitators in each of the locations. It was, however, not binding on any of the farmers who adopted Reliance-recommended practices to sell to the company.

Reliance Retail derived benefits from products developed by other companies within their group. For example, the Polymer division of Reliance Industries developed the polypropylene material that was used to make bags that acted as fruit cover. These bags had special properties to exchange gas and moisture and were expected to last for more than two years. Reliance conducted trials with these bags and it was expected that the new bags would reduce the cost of the fruit bunch cover by 30 per cent.

RIPENING AND DISTRIBUTION

Upon their arrival at the CPCs, the bananas were sorted according to size, girth and visual attributes. Subsequently, the fruit were taken to the ripening chambers. Reliance considered ripening to be one of its major value additions in the banana supply chain. In order to keep a tight control over quality and hygiene, Reliance owned all its ripening facilities. Ripening was done in ethylene gas chambers that were located within its CPCs. A typical ripening centre was set up at a cost of about INR 70 million. It processed 100 metric tonnes of fruits and vegetables daily of which about 12–13 metric tonnes were bananas. About 5.5 metric tonnes were shipped to Reliance Fresh stores and 7.5 metric tonnes to other retailers.

Banana required one day of pre-cooling and four days of cooling to ripen. At an optimized basis, that is, when the full capacity was being used, there was an insignificant difference in the ripening costs vis-à-vis those followed by the unorganized sector, which typically used carbide-based chemicals for ripening fruits.[15]

A typical collection centre dealt with 25–30 farmers daily and more than 50 per cent of Reliance's total procurement was taken directly from the farmers. This ensured that the benefits of disintermediation were passed on directly to either the farmers or to the customers. Ninety per cent of the payments were made directly to farmers' bank accounts, which made them familiar with banking methods. Overall, Reliance was able to achieve 50 per cent reduction in wastage in fruits and vegetables compared to the traditional supply chains. The quality of bananas available in the market went up and there was enough indication that customers were willing to pay higher prices for better quality.

After ripening, bananas were distributed from the CPCs to the markets through three channels. About 45 per cent of the output was delivered to Reliance Fresh outlets. Of the remaining, a significant portion was sold through semi-wholesalers in the open market, while the rest was sold to other organized retailers. All organized retailers who were competitors of Reliance Retail with the exception of Big Bazaar sourced their bananas from Reliance. The organized retailers often had internal quality control systems, which resulted in some amount of fruit being rejected. Therefore, the price to them included transportation losses, transportation price and Reliance's margins. The semi-wholesalers picked up the entire mix, that is, bananas of various qualities, and paid Reliance directly. They incurred their own transportation

---

[15] Carbide-based chemicals are highly toxic and using them to ripen fruits is banned in India. Carbide has been found to have harmful effects on the human brain, liver and kidneys, and is especially dangerous for children. Industrial-grade calcium carbide can contain traces of arsenic and phosphorus, both of which are harmful.

costs and delivered fruits to the open market retailers. Realizing that some of the semi-wholesalers might have cash flow problems, Reliance started working with financial institutions to extend credit facilities to them.

Organized retailers operated on fixed volume contracts, while Reliance asked its distributers to provide weekly demand estimates. This demand was aggregated from across the markets and passed on to the central sourcing information centre in Mumbai. There, a weekly sourcing plan was created, which was communicated back to the field. On the field, this demand was broken down into a daily plan and Reliance field executives, along with the vendors, decided the sourcing clusters. Consistency in supply was critical, since stock-outs weakened the trust that retailers had developed in Reliance. The retailer had the option of purchasing fruit from the *mandi* (a marketplace for agricultural commodities) to meet the demand, in case Reliance was unable to supply to them. However, they started to depend on Reliance because of the quality of fruit that the company supplied them with.

Since it took one day to transport the harvested bananas and one day for pre-cooling before the fruit were put in the ripening chambers where they stayed for four days, there was two days of buffer stock that was built in the operations. This was usually enough to deal with variations in demand and supply. Thus, any anticipated shortfall could be communicated to the retailer four days in advance. In rare cases, Reliance bought bananas from the open market to make up for the shortfall. If the increase in demand could be anticipated, such as during a religious festival, Reliance was able to adjust its supply chain to meet the greater demand.

Traditionally, semi-wholesalers had a stranglehold over small retailers who sold bananas from push carts or small shops in wet markets. They tied up the retailers through multiple financial obligations and were not eager to follow transparent practices that Reliance wanted them to adopt. Reliance thus decided to develop new semi-wholesalers, often people who were earlier auto-rickshaw drivers. Twenty-two-year-old Satyanarayan, one of Reliance's distributers in Hyderabad, was a case in point. He started by delivering bananas to the market in his auto-rickshaw, earning INR 1 per kilogram. A few months later, Reliance gave him the additional responsibility of bringing back the delivery crates as well as payment from the retailers. Finally, he became a distributer for Reliance, paying the company to buy fruit, distributing them to 13 push-cart retailers in the city and collecting money from them at the end of the day. On a daily turnover of INR 800, he earned a monthly income of INR 7,000. Likewise, Ramesh, who used to earn INR 4,000 per month as a personal driver, earned INR 7,000–10,000 per month after becoming a Reliance distributer. Only two out of nine distributers in Hyderabad were formerly semi-wholesalers, while the rest were developed by Reliance to become micro-entrepreneurs.

Muhammad Ali, who owned a fruit and vegetable chain in Hyderabad called Fresh and Crunchy, was one of Reliance's customers. He bought 1 tonne of bananas daily from Reliance and sold them at INR 22–24 per kilogram, which, he claimed, commanded a premium of 33 per cent. He owned five stores that sold 600 kilograms and three push carts that sold 400 kilograms of Reliance bananas. He said,

> Even if the local fruits are cheaper by INR 10/dozen, customers demand Reliance fruits. I have the capacity to double the intake from Reliance, since I have 15 stores and can even put more pushcarts on the streets.

Likewise, Wahid, who owned a fresh fruit outlet called New Golden Fruits in upmarket Secunderabad, said,

> Customers come here from long distances and pay higher prices because they appreciate the better quality of Reliance bananas. These bananas have a better shine and longer shelf lives. The chemicals used by Reliance (for ripening) are better, giving the fruits a good appearance and taste.

Wahid wanted Reliance to supply him with more B-grade bananas, possibly because he made higher margins on them and because he sold fruit salads that did not need the A-grade ones.

Interventions by Reliance at multiple points of the supply chain started to yield substantial results within the first three years of its operation. Reliance Retail sold 13,000 metric tonnes[16] of bananas – the trademark big yellow ones[17] – through Reliance Fresh outlets and a larger quantity through other

---

[16]   One metric tonne is equivalent to 1,000 kilograms.

[17]   Reliance sold the Robusta variety of bananas – one of the common varieties available in the Indian market, typically large and green in colour even when

retailers. Their efforts at developing an organized supply chain for bananas created livelihood for more than 2,000 farmers, 150 intermediaries and 100 distributors across India and generated employment for 500 labourers daily. The farmers' share of consumer price went up from 28 per cent to 42 per cent and wastages in the supply chain reduced from 30 per cent to 15 per cent. This is schematically shown in Figure 8.1 where the prices and margins of Reliance's banana value chain is compared with the traditional banana value chain. Reliance's best practices also had a positive impact on how its competitors conducted business. Following Reliance, some of them also started to employ better methods of ripening and transporting the fruit in crates – practices that improved industry standards.

OPTIONS FOR GROWTH

Having significantly developed the supply chain for bananas, the team started to consider options for growth. They were already sourcing much more bananas than what could be sold through their own retail outlets. Continuing to supply high quality bananas to their competitors was not a sustainable strategy for the long term. Therefore, the first option they started to consider was exports. Banana is one of the most widely traded commodities in the world. Global trade in bananas occurs from Central America and the Philippines to Europe, Middle East, Japan, Singapore and Taiwan. In Central America and the Philippines, climatic conditions are suitable for growing banana and farmers have come together to provide large fields for cultivation. Governments in many of these countries have provided implicit subsidies for banana exports.

However, bananas from Central American countries, such as Honduras and Ecuador, were becoming more expensive and the Philippines did not have any more land that could be brought under cultivation. Therefore, large banana

---

fully ripe. The other common variety is Yelakki, which is smaller in size and yellow in colour when ripe. Apart from Robusta and Yelakki, there are about 200 other varieties of bananas available in the Indian markets.

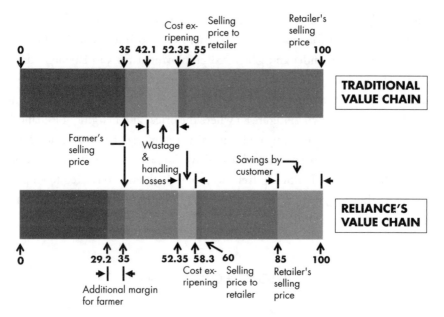

Figure 8.1 Comparing Reliance's Banana Value Chain with Traditional Banana Supply Chain (Cost/Price per Kilogram Indexed to 100)

Source: Author's analysis based on information received from the company.

Note: 1. Data represents typical instances and is illustrative only.

    2. Retailer is buying higher and selling lower per kilogram in the instance of Reliance because of greater longevity of fruit and lesser wastage.

    3. 'Wastage and handling losses' comprise moisture loss, ripening loss, de-handing loss and other wastages.

    4. Source of 'Additional margin for farmer' comprises harvesting, loading, transportation, unloading charges and agent commission, which the farmers do not have to bear in the instance of Reliance because they are either not applicable (for instance, agent commission) or borne by Reliance.

    5. The retailer's selling price in the Reliance value chain is applicable to Reliance Retail stores.

companies, such as Chiquita and Dole,[18] were in search of new sources. India and Sri Lanka were potentially new sources. India could become a big hub

---

[18]   Dole Foods was the world's largest in this domain with a turnover of USD 6 billion. They owned 70 ships used for exports. About 60–70 per cent of their revenue was earned from bananas and pineapples.

because it was well connected on the east to Singapore and Taiwan and on the west to Europe. However, India lacked the quality as well as the kind of infrastructure necessary for a quick turnaround that is essential for bananas. India was also a large banana-consumption country. It was dominated by local traders and one could not do business in India unless companies tied up with local traders. Fragmentation of sources was also the reason why international export companies did not operate in India. Abroad, where farming was corporatized, exporters worked with large farmers who owned 1,000–3,000 acres of land. China, however, followed a different model, where farmers created large agricultural cooperatives.[19] Individual farmers leased out their own land to the cooperatives while continuing to work on them. Thus, there was aggregation of output, enabling them to be linked to the markets.

The Head of Reliance's Retail business said,

Banana can be a billion-dollar opportunity and we can have an equivalent of Operations Flood[20] in bananas. However, we need to evolve a model that is suitable to Indian conditions. It is important to realize that only 20–30 per cent of a farmer's produce can be exported, while the rest will have to be consumed locally. Thus, one's export strategy needs to be complemented by what one does in the domestic market, both with better- and not-so-good-quality bananas. This is where some of the existing exporters went wrong – they only focused on export quality bananas and left the farmers in the lurch when the fruit quality was not up to the mark. The farmers naturally

---

[19] Chinese Agricultural Cooperative (CHAODA) was listed in Hong Kong Stock Exchange.

[20] Operation Flood was a rural development programme started by India's National Dairy Development Board in 1970. One of the largest of its kind, the programme's objective was to create a nationwide milk grid. It resulted in making India the largest producer of milk and milk products in the world. It reduced malpractices by milk traders and merchants and helped in alleviating poverty and famine levels from their dangerous proportions in India during the era. At the heart of Operation Flood were village milk producers' cooperatives.

felt cheated. Someone will have to get the three elements together – proper genetics (of the fruit), farmer engagement and link to international markets. Since one cannot have corporatization, cooperatives are possibly the way to go. One needs to form farmer cooperatives and provide them with the best international practices. One needs aggregation, even while maintaining the sanctity of the individual farmer.

The other growth option before the team was to develop a supply chain for other fruits, such as papaya. India produces 2.6 million tonnes of papaya per annum, with Andhra Pradesh, Karnataka, Maharashtra, Gujarat, Madhya Pradesh, Chattisgarh and Jharkhand being the major production belts. Papaya is available throughout the year, has significant therapeutic value and is very popular among the consumers. But similar to many other tropical fruits, it is difficult to handle.

Papaya is normally cultivated on smaller plots, unlike banana, which requires large acreage. Papaya is highly disease-prone, mainly to viral attacks. At the fruiting stage, the papaya grower usually contracts the entire field to middlemen for a fixed amount. The major markets for papaya are located in the north Indian states of Jammu & Kashmir, Punjab, Haryana, Delhi, Uttar Pradesh and Rajasthan.

Traditionally, papaya is harvested when it is green. The green papaya, being quite hard, is easy to transport. It is ripened at the destination using calcium carbide. It takes about 3–7 days to ripen them. About 25 per cent of the fruit is usually lost in the process because of multiple handling and the vulnerability of papayas to fungal infection.

After studying the existing supply chain, Reliance realized that in order to improve the quality of the fruit, it had to be harvested when it was mature and not when it was green. However, the mature fruit was soft and could not be handled and packed loose. Therefore, they developed Styrofoam net packing in which the whole papaya could be inserted, which provided a cushion and prevented fruit from rubbing against one another. An Indian supplier was identified for Styrofoam nets and farmers were advised to allow the fruit to fully mature on the tree. They also trained vendors to identify fruit with the right maturity and for harvesting, treatment, grading and packing. As in the case of bananas, vendors were responsible for fruit procurement, engaging farm labour and transportation to CPCs. At the CPC, fruit were kept in a ripening chamber and ripened to full colour in 2–3 days.

The new process had several benefits. The farmer obtained a higher yield with a fully matured fruit. Styrofoam packaging provided visibility of the entire fruit to the customer unlike paper wraps that were used traditionally. It also reduced the fruit damage to less than 5 per cent. The fruit had a better shelf life at the consumer's end and they appreciated the better taste that was a consequence of harvesting the fruit when it was mature.

However, the new process had its own set of challenges. Styrofoam packaging added an extra cost of INR 1.20 per kilogram. The transportation cost increased by 30 per cent because fewer fruit could be loaded per crate. The chances of papayas acquiring viral diseases at the farm were higher because the fruit were allowed to mature before harvesting. In the winter, because of low night temperatures, the fruit took more time to mature while its vegetative growth continued. This resulted in heavier fruit, about 2 kilograms, which was often unacceptable to the retail customer, who typically favoured weights below 1.5 kilograms.

Therefore, the Reliance team started to work on two aspects. First, they needed to help farmers control viral attacks and promote new areas that were virus-free. Second, in order to reduce the cost of packaging they decided to import Styrofoam nets from China, which was 10–15 per cent cheaper. Reliance linked the farmers with agri-input companies who could assist growers by providing good planting material and controlling diseases. Farmers were advised on ways to control the fruit size in winter.

Totally, around 450 acres of papaya cultivation were being monitored in Andhra Pradesh and a supply chain was set up to cater to the Hyderabad market. Reliance started similar work in other states and eventually expected to cover all major locations.

DISCUSSION: CORPORATE INTERVENTION IN INDIAN AGRICULTURAL SUPPLY CHAIN

Reliance Retail's intervention in improving the supply chain of bananas is an important case study to evaluate the impact that large corporations can create if they try to organize the hitherto unorganized supply chains of fruits and vegetables that originate in rural India. As this case indicates, such interventions hold the promise of enhancing the income of small farmers and creating livelihood opportunities for traders and intermediaries even while meeting business objectives of for-profit enterprises like Reliance. Therefore, they can be good examples of inclusive business models. In this section, we take a critical look at how Reliance created value, what lessons can be learnt from Reliance's experience and finally we explore the possible options that Reliance has if it wants to scale its business.

VALUE ADDITION

The different ways in which Reliance was creating value can be summarized as follows:

Reliance improved the productivity of the banana farmers through farm-level interventions, such as by providing them with better saplings and teaching them better ways of planting and harvesting bananas. Overall, this ensured that farmers could gain a higher yield of better-quality bananas and there was less damage and wastage related to transportation and improper handling.

Reliance reduced intermediaries in the supply chain by directly sourcing from the banana growers rather than buying from the wholesale markets. There was a strong nexus among the wholesalers and other intermediaries who also performed the role of creditors, ensuring that the farmers had a weak bargaining position. This resulted in a lower price realization for the farmers. Moreover, because the intermediaries were involved in the financing business, they rarely focused on improving the quality of bananas. Removing these intermediaries resulted in a greater price realization for the farmers as well as more focus on the quality of fruit and its yield. Likewise, when it came to distributing the ripe fruit to the retailers, Reliance created its own intermediaries who doubled up as transporters and collectors.

Reliance introduced greater efficiency in the logistics and ripening operations. This was possible probably because Reliance could take an integrated view of the supply chain and then decide how to improve overall efficiency. Thus, they introduced better methods of transporting and ripening the fruit and ensured greater shelf life. Being an aggregator, it was possible for Reliance to derive economies of scale as well as achieve stability in the supply chain. By taking an integrated view of the supply chain, Reliance could reduce the number of centres that existed earlier (Reliance eliminated separate collection centres and co-located ripening chambers with distribution centres), which, in turn, reduced the number of times the fruits were loaded and unloaded and the probability of damage.

Since Reliance ripened the fruits with ethylene gas, it was safer than traditional methods that used carbide-based products. While this is a good example of value creation, one is not sure how this is being captured by any player in the value chain, given that it is difficult for the end-customer to distinguish between a banana that has been ripened by ethylene gas and the one by a carbide-based product. Anecdotal evidence from some of the fruit retailers suggested a customer preference for bananas supplied by Reliance, though there could be a host of reasons behind it.

One can also argue that Reliance has created employment and provided livelihood options to the intermediaries and farm labourers. However, this is likely to be substitution rather than creating additional employment. While Reliance had appointed new intermediaries, such jobs had possibly been created at the cost of the traditional intermediaries. Since Reliance had improved the overall efficiency of the supply chain, it is likely that more jobs had been lost than created. This raises the question of how one measures 'value addition' in the context of inclusive business models. Can improvement in levels of efficiency that enhances income for some but result in loss of employment for others count for value addition? Should the notion of value addition be viewed differently in different contexts?

UNINTENDED CONSEQUENCES

Let us now consider what might be some of the downsides of Reliance's business model. The answer flows directly from the last point in the previous discussion. While in India, the traditional supply chains in fruits and vegetables are very inefficient, they provide employment to a large number of people. According to the Economic Census of India (2005), nearly 42 per cent of employment in rural India is generated from trading and intermediation activities. Thus, any kind of intervention by organizations such as Reliance that is oriented towards increasing efficiency through reduction in intermediation will result in loss of livelihood for several thousands. Harper (2009) noted that modernization of retail in India would result in a loss of 1 million jobs over a period of 10 years, while only about 200,000 (one-fifth) new jobs would be created. Many of these people who would lose their jobs are themselves very poor, and the dominant notion that intermediaries are rich traders who exploit the farmers possibly refers to a few of the thousands. Thus, loss of employment could be a downside of Reliance's business model, at least in the near term. In the long run, the enhanced income of the farmers and, consequently, the greater cash that is injected in the rural economy can lead to the creation of more jobs and facilitate greater economic activities, which might more than compensate for the job losses.

It is not fair to hold Reliance responsible for such job losses of the intermediaries. As a commercial enterprise, it is necessary for them to improve efficiency and maximize profitability. However, it is the policy maker who needs to worry about such unintended consequences of organizing rural supply chains and making them efficient, especially given the fact that India is a populous country where more than 60 per cent of its citizens reside in villages and intermediation is a key source of their employment.

It is also important to note that Reliance does not directly deal with the small farmers, nor does it play any part in facilitating the formation of farmer cooperatives, as is the practice in China. Reliance, instead, chose to create vendors (*hundikaris*) who acted as intermediaries between them and the small farmers. This was sensible from the business perspective because it reduced Reliance's transaction costs and enabled it to leverage local knowledge and relationships. However, the vendors themselves were economically well-off and influential farmers whose powers were likely to get enhanced because of their relationship with Reliance. There is a danger that they themselves might start exploiting the poor farmer because it was unlikely that Reliance as an organization would either have the ability or willingness to intervene in such cases. Thus, it can be argued that while Reliance's intervention has increased the efficiency of the supply chain, it remains to be seen what percentage of such improvement is actually benefitting the poor farmer, or whether there is a possibility that the benefits are being captured by the new set of intermediaries they have created.

CREATING SHARED VALUE

Porter and Kramer (2011) argued that in a capitalist system, organizations are perceived to maximize the wealth of their shareholders at the expense of other stakeholders. This has to be replaced by the notion of value-sharing, which overcomes the traditional trade-off between economic efficiency and social welfare by addressing the needs and challenges of society. Sharing value is not about redistribution of wealth, but about creating enhanced wealth for multiple stakeholders. Reliance, being a public limited company, will need to have a strong focus on creating a business that is commercially profitable. However, it is clear from the case facts that their initiative was creating additional value for stakeholders, such as the producers and customers. Therefore, one can argue that it is indeed possible for organizations to create value for the society at large even while they are focused on creating a profitable business.

What are the critical levers of Reliance's business that enabled them to create 'shared value'? The following might be identified.

The activity that provided a significant social benefit, namely sourcing bananas directly from the farmers, was completely aligned with the core business objective of Reliance. The farmer was possibly the most important element of their value chain and this was not a fringe activity that the organization undertook to discharge its corporate social responsibilities. This implied that integrating the impoverished farmer as the producer was the primary focus of Reliance even as they were constantly investing resources as well as engaging the best talent to ensure that they could achieve the integration. Reliance was also clear that unless they were able to create a financially viable business model, their efforts would not be sustainable. It did not intend to have any dependence on charity or subsidies and spent a significant amount of effort first in linking the product to markets and then to be able to compete successfully in those markets. Reliance Retail was operating in fiercely competitive markets, not only with other big retailers but also with local suppliers who had fewer overheads and did not have to follow some of the good practices. They were sure that while the customer would appreciate good-quality fruits, they were unlikely to pay too high a premium for the same. Thus, it becomes evident that for Reliance, this initiative was a critical business endeavour and even while it was providing better livelihood options to the poor, the businesses had to sustain themselves in highly competitive markets that did not give them any advantage because of the social significance of their business model. For them, it was very important to relentlessly focus on operational efficiencies and innovative means of overcoming the various business challenges that they confronted.

The key personnel involved in shaping Reliance's supply chain model had extensive domain knowledge and experience of managing similar business ventures. Ram Swamy, head of Reliance's banana supply chain initiative, had worked for more than 25 years with rural supply chains for a wide variety of products. His deep insight and a high degree of familiarity with the context not only enabled him to recruit the right kind of team members and intermediaries but also made him comfortable talking to the farmers, advising and thus dispelling some of the apprehensions that farmers had while dealing with a large corporation such as Reliance.

Despite their experience and business acumen, Reliance realized that they needed to work with local partners at the grassroots level to overcome last-mile problems that might stymie such initiatives. It identified intermediaries from villages – typically farmers themselves – who would serve as a critical link between them and the small farmers. Intermediaries served as a two-way communication link, keeping Reliance abreast of the local complexities as well as translating the company's way of doing business to the farmers. Being aware of local demand-and-supply situations, they recruited local labourers and made payments to them and the farmers. Intermediaries were literate and had bank accounts, which enabled Reliance to do financial transactions with them, who, in turn, dealt with the labourers and small farmers who did not have bank accounts and needed to be paid in cash. Over a period of time, intermediaries grew in stature and became opinion makers in the villages, which was leveraged by Reliance to earn the confidence of the local community. Without such intermediaries, it would have been very difficult for a large organization such as Reliance to deal with the diverse local complexities that are typical of Indian villages.

Reliance was acutely aware that socio-economic conditions in Indian villages were very different from urban India where they used to operate before creating rural supply chains. As they wanted to build long-term relationships with local communities, they did not do anything that might be seen as an aberration or disruption in traditions or belief systems of the community. They, therefore, adopted a light-touch model that blended with local practices rather than trying to change them. Reliance wanted to introduce several good farming practices that would increase the quality and yield of bananas. However, farmer beliefs about such practices were deeply entrenched and while Reliance explained and showed them the benefits that might accrue if the farmers changed their mind, it was finally left to the farmers to choose whether they would continue with their old practice or adopt the new one. Reliance was also open to working with the farmers and modifying its own practices if they were found to be more suitable for local conditions.

Given a history of exploitation and the wide disparities that have existed between urban and rural India for decades, it is conceivable that villagers will have deep apprehensions about organizations from cities, especially if they wanted to introduce changes in their lives for the sake of economic development. Therefore, Reliance understood that they had to gain the trust of the local community before they would be able to convince them to change, if at all, for the better. Thus, instead of chasing rapid growth, they focused on building sustainable relationships with the local community – something they considered as essential if they had to integrate the villagers within their value chain.

We will find this as a recurring theme in many of the cases we discuss in this book. While social entrepreneurs and enterprises might have the best of intentions, their 'solution' needs to be context-sensitive to gain acceptability. Target communities, despite the challenges they face, will be apprehensive at the outset of any product or service that is thrust upon them in the name of development. Therefore, an incremental approach that earns the trust of the community is a prerequisite for acceptance and long-term sustainability.

GROWTH OPTIONS FOR RELIANCE

Growth is an essential element of Reliance's business model for two reasons. First, they had made tremendous investments in establishing a viable business model where none existed. The returns on such investments will only be realized if they could replicate their model such that it enabled them to derive scale economies for centralized functions. Second, Reliance had a corporate objective of creating social value. Having seen first-hand the positive impact that its business was having on the lives of the poor banana growers, as well as knowing the magnitude of rural poverty, they were keen to grow their business so that they could create livelihood for tens of thousands rather than the few thousands that they had created so far.

The first option before them was to replicate their banana supply chain in a greater number of locations and thus procure bananas in larger volumes. While this option would provide Reliance the benefits of experience – they would be able to replicate their success and even do better – it would result in the creation of surplus that the organization would need to sell through other retailers in the organized and unorganized sectors. Even in the absence of numbers, one can guess that it does not make much business sense to sell their bananas through retail outlets that belonged to their competitors. The decision to sell to competitors was a contingency measure taken as a consequence of a fewer number of their retail outlets being opened than planned. In the long run, Reliance should not continue with the practice of being a supplier to other retailers, unless they felt that it was the only way to benefit a large number of banana farmers. Thus, if Reliance wanted to increase the procurement of bananas, they needed to consider exporting them. In the export market, Reliance would face formidable competitors from Chiquita and Dole as well as from countries that had a more suitable regulatory environment for exports of fruits compared to India. Moreover, Reliance also had no experience in exporting fruits or vegetables, as its foray into these areas was relatively new.

On the other hand, Reliance seemed to have done its homework for establishing a value chain for papayas. While there were some challenges to be overcome, Reliance could leverage almost similar sourcing channels as well as its relationship with the farmers to procure papayas. These could be sold through Reliance's retail outlets, creating greater opportunity for value capture by Reliance as well as resulting in portfolio diversification for the farmers, which would create greater value and lesser risk for them. Thus, growth by means of procuring a greater variety of fruits and possibly vegetables by leveraging the existing supply chain infrastructure seems to be the most viable option for growth before Reliance.

CHAPTER LEARNING

For-profit, commercial enterprises can make their businesses inclusive through impact sourcing, that is, involving the poor in their supply chain. The supply chains of fruits and vegetables are characterized by inefficiencies, wastages and exploitative intermediaries – all contributing to low income for the farmers.

A resource-rich commercial enterprise can create considerable value in the agricultural supply chain by investing in suitable storage and transportation infrastructure, introducing modern practices and removing exploitative intermediaries. All these would increase productivity, improve quality and translate into enhanced income for the farmer and profitability for the organization.

Such enterprises, when sourcing from the farmers, need to be sensitive to local farming practices and customs to earn their trust. They might find it difficult to enforce legal contracts and, therefore, it is important for them to build long-term relationships with the farmers.

Large enterprises might find it difficult to deal with individual marginal or small farmers. Therefore, to reduce their transaction costs, they need to appoint credible intermediaries and work closely with them to ensure that they meet the expectations of the enterprise, especially in terms of inclusion.

Inclusive business models incubated by large enterprises that enhance farmer income by reducing intermediaries may lead to unemployment of erstwhile intermediaries, some of whom are themselves poor and would struggle to find alternative sources of employment.

9

INTERNATIONAL DEVELOPMENT ENTERPRISE (IDE) NEPAL

Developing Smallholder Ecosystem

In this chapter, we talk about the evolution of International Development Enterprise (IDE), a not-for-profit organization working in rural Nepal, and the impact that its various development initiatives have had in improving the socio-economic conditions of smallholder farmers. IDE raises funds from donor and philanthropic agencies and utilizes them to develop smallholder communities by creating livelihood opportunities.

IDE in Nepal evolved from being a supplier of technology for irrigation and water storage to becoming a critical enabler of a smallholder ecosystem that was sustainable and scalable. While the context of this case is rural Nepal, the socio-economic conditions of smallholder farmers are not very different from that of India and many other emerging nations where the lessons learnt from this case can be replicated. The advantages of developing and empowering economically underprivileged communities are well known. This case demonstrates the process of creating such communities and making them self-sustainable. It also highlights the critical role that various stakeholders, such as the government and development organizations, can play in enabling such communities to overcome their vulnerabilities.

IDE Nepal is one of the few cases in this book dealing with a not-for-profit organization. IDE by itself is not an example of an inclusive business model unlike most other cases described here. However, it enables the creation of inclusive businesses that is essential for developing and sustaining the smallholder ecosystem. IDE's case also helps us to understand the different ways in which a not-for-profit can create value for economically underprivileged communities when compared to inclusive business models. This is a theme that we will visit in greater detail in the concluding chapter of the book.

EVOLUTION OF IDE NEPAL

International Development Enterprise (IDE) is an organization that operates in 11 countries worldwide with the aim of creating income opportunities for poor, rural households in developing countries. Established in 1981 by a group of North American social entrepreneurs, IDE provides the rural poor in Asian and African countries with low-cost access to water for agricultural use and links them to markets so that their agricultural products can be sold profitably. In their 39 years of operation, IDE has worked with 7 million households, increasing their aggregate income by over USD 1 billion, thereby enabling 35 million poor people improve their economic status significantly.[1]

IDE Nepal is an affiliate of IDE, registered with the Social Welfare Council of the Nepal government. It was established in 1992 with the aim of developing low-cost irrigation technologies suitable for smallholders in the rural areas of the country and increasing their income. More than 80 per cent people in Nepal are engaged in agriculture and a significant number of them have smallholdings.[2] Typically, smallholder farmers are economically impoverished and often belong to the disadvantaged classes of society. Along with increasing farm productivity, this would also have the secondary effect of empowering the marginalized, such as women and farmers from lower castes, and bring them into the mainstream of economic activities.

In its initial days, IDE in Nepal experimented with rower pumps. Subsequently, it developed low-cost human-operated treadle pumps suitable

---

[1]   See https://www.ideglobal.org/what-we-do (accessed 17 October 2009). By 2020, IDE impacted 34.6 million individuals in 6.8 million households by improving their annual average income by USD 276; see https://www.ideglobal.org/impact (accessed 24 June 2020).

[2]   K. K. Bhattarai (2009), 'An Overview of Micro Irrigation in Nepal', Department of Agriculture (unpublished report). According to Agricultural Census 1991, 44.7 per cent of Nepalese families involved in agriculture have small holdings, which together comprises 11.3 per cent of the total cultivable area in Nepal.

for irrigation in the Terai[3] region. This was followed by the development of low-cost drip irrigation systems. Subsequently, IDE developed micro sprinkler systems which, along with drip systems, were promoted to farmers in the middle hills of Nepal. IDE also developed low-cost water storage tanks, designed and promoted multiple use water systems (MUS) so that water, a scarce resource in the hilly regions, could be stored and used efficiently for domestic and agricultural use. Often, such MUS were used in conjunction with low-cost irrigation systems to cultivate high-value crops, such as off-season vegetables, in the hilly areas.

The year 2003 was an inflection point in IDE Nepal's evolution when it realized that supply-side interventions, such as technology for irrigation and water storage, needed to be coupled with demand-side interventions so that farmers could be linked to markets. This would enable farmers to sell their products profitably, resulting in increased income. Thus, IDE developed a comprehensive framework of developmental intervention at the input, process and output stages of the agricultural value chain targeted towards improving lives and livelihood of smallholder farmers and disadvantaged groups. Today, IDE Nepal operates in 22 districts, having reached more than 1.4 million poor farmers in 240,000 households. Their programmes have resulted in the sale of 200,000 treadle pumps and 40,000 drip irrigation systems. It is estimated that IDE interventions have generated an additional income of USD 150 per year for each of the 240,000 households they have reached.[4]

IDE'S MODE OF OPERATION

A large number of farmers in Nepal are smallholders,[5] while there are several others, mainly from the disadvantaged castes, who are landless. These farmers

---

[3]   The country of Nepal can be roughly divided into three horizontal areas, namely the northern high mountains, the middle mountains or Siwalik and the southern plains, the Terai.

[4]   See https://www.idenepal.org/Projects.html (accessed 24 June 2020).

[5]   While definitions vary, smallholders are defined as farmers who own less than half hectare of land.

are usually engaged in growing a limited amount of cereals using water that is available during the rainy season. Since their farm income is not enough for livelihood, they supplement their income by working as daily wage labourers or migrate to cities and even to the neighbouring country of India in search of work.[6] IDE realized that smallholdings of these poor farmers could be effectively utilized for growing vegetables if the farmers were provided with suitable technology for irrigation and water management and knowledge input for managing the vegetable farming process. With proper linkages to markets, farmers would be able to sell these vegetables profitably, leading to a substantial increase in income and an improvement in their quality of life.

IDE intended to leverage the comparative advantage of smallholders in order to engage them in profitable farming activities. Smallholders often have an advantage in labour-intensive farming activities because agricultural labour suffers from a 'moral hazard' problem in case of organized farming that employs wage labour. It is difficult to assess or monitor the quality of labour input because the output of such labour can only be measured on longer time horizons, usually when the crop or commodity is harvested or sold. A smallholding that is typically owned and managed by members of a family does not face such 'agency problems' and is thus better off in labour-intensive production processes that require constant monitoring. IDE thus identified the cultivation of vegetables as an activity that was ideally suited for smallholders because vegetable farming was labour-intensive, had a relatively

---

[6] According to the World Food Programme's Comprehensive Food Security and Vulnerability Analysis (September 2005), migration is widespread in Nepal, involving 25 per cent of the adult male population. Even during the harvesting period, 44 per cent of the households have one or more members away to pursue labour opportunities. Migration is a common livelihood strategy for those living in poor Terai communities as well as in Far and Mid-Western hills and mountains. The most popular destination for labour migration is India (40 per cent), followed by cities in Nepal (30 per cent) and other countries (22 per cent). While migration has economic benefits in terms of poverty reduction, it has significant negative consequences, such as severe health risk, widespread violation of human and labour rights and disruption in family lives ('Passage to India', WFP Publication, November 2008)

simple production process and did not require a high level of skills. Moreover, Nepal was deficient in vegetable production and a significant part of its vegetables was imported from India. Thus, if farmers in Nepal were able to grow vegetables, they would find a ready market close to their homes, thereby obviating the need for developing a complex storage, distribution and logistics infrastructure for sending their produce to distant markets.[7]

IDE started off in Nepal by developing and refining micro-irrigation technologies (MITs) that were low-cost and appropriate for smallholders. Such technologies were rarely developed by organizations operating in the private sector because it was difficult for them to enforce patents and thereby recover the investment that they make in research and development, especially those that were targeted at the smallholders. IDE, therefore, invested in the design and initial promotion of MITs. Once the design was stabilized and markets for such equipment were identified, it was possible for private entrepreneurs to start manufacturing and selling MITs as a sustainable commercial venture. The case of Thapa Mould and Die described in a later section was one such example. Apart from MITs, IDE also developed appropriate agricultural equipment for coffee processing, oil distillation from forest products and other high-value agricultural products.

IDE, in its early days received support from MISEREOR, the German Catholic Bishops' Organisation for Development Cooperation, for development of MITs, such as drip systems, micro sprinklers, treadle pumps and water storage and distribution systems. IDE bid for project grants from donor organizations, often in partnership with other development organizations, as and when it identified an opportunity that could lead to an improvement in the economic conditions of the rural poor. IDE received significant financial support from USAID for their Smallholder Irrigation Market Initiative (SIMI) and Education for Income Generation (EIG) projects in partnership with Winrock International. Their Rural Prosperity Initiative (RPI) was supported by the Bill and Melinda Gates Foundation. Other organizations and institutions that financially supported them included

---

[7]   Legally, India did not import fruits or vegetables from Nepal. However, borders were porous and given the small quantities from a macro-economic perspective, such cross-border trade happened.

the UK government's Department for International Development (DFID), the Manitoba State Government (Canada) and the Dutch government, while they have had partnerships with the Center for Environmental and Agricultural Policy Research, Extension and Development (CEAPRED), Support Activities for Poor Producers of Nepal (SAPPROS), Agro Enterprise Center (AEC) and the Government of Nepal in implementing their various projects.

DEVELOPING AGRICULTURAL SUPPLY CHAIN SUITABLE FOR SMALLHOLDERS

IDE figured out that in order to enable the smallholder and landless farmers to become profitable vegetable growers, they needed support that went beyond MITs or superior water management systems. The farmers needed to be linked with several other players, such as suppliers of agricultural inputs (for example, seeds), technologies (for instance, those needed for irrigation, water management) and distributors and sellers of agricultural output. Farmers also needed to be provided timely information about the demand–supply conditions existing in the markets, which, in turn, could determine when and what kind of products they should be cultivating in their farms to maximize their returns on efforts and investment. With this in mind, IDE created an integrated framework named Poverty Reduction through Irrigation and Smallholder Markets (PRISM) and adopted it in Nepal to develop an agriculture supply chain suited to the needs of smallholders.

As part of this programme, IDE aimed to create networks of small enterprises that would provide agricultural supplies needed by farmers and link them to markets so that they could get the best possible price for their farm output. While IDE would continue to work with the farmers and provide them with knowledge input for farm management and productivity improvement, IDE's role was to become an enabler of a self-sustaining system that would continue on its own even after the organization completed its specific projects. Luke Colavito, Country Director of IDE Nepal, explained,

What is unique about the value chain approach is its focus on all enterprises and stakeholders involved in the production, processing and marketing of a commodity. It identifies points of market failures and constraints in availability of appropriate input, processing and access to markets and designs interventions to overcome these constraints. These interventions include building the capacity of enterprises and service providers, establishing linkages between enterprises and institutions, developing and introducing appropriate technologies and working with the government for investing in public goods. Above all, we want to ensure that all services and input providers are profitable and sustainable by themselves – that is the only way in which we can create sustainable livelihood opportunities for smallholders and poor farmers.

IDE's interventions can be broadly divided into three stages, namely input, process and output. At the input stage, IDE worked with manufacturers of MITs, retailers and distributors of technology and other farm input as well as with masons who provide installation and maintenance services of basic farm infrastructure. IDE provided initial support in terms of technology design to entrepreneurs who manufactured farm equipment, such as drip irrigation systems or treadle pumps, ensuring that they were suited to the specific needs of the smallholders. It also provided continuous support in terms of quality control and design improvement and linked these manufacturers with distributers and retailers. IDE kept an informal control over the prices that these manufacturers and retailers charged the end customer, which ensured that the products were affordable. At the same time, they also balanced the profitability needs of the various actors in the supply chain so that the business remained attractive and sustainable for the entrepreneurs. IDE's various interventions with manufacturers are explained in a later section in detail through the case of Thapa Mould and Die.

On the input side, IDE also worked closely with 'agrovets' – entrepreneurs who supplied agricultural input, such as seeds or saplings, to the farmers. IDE trained the input suppliers so that they could also offer information on planting methods and timing, pest management and production of different crop varieties.[8] Such technical knowledge needed to be offered as embedded services

---

[8] IDE offered training to various players in different modules. The organization did not charge the participants for such training. The training

since the farmers had limited access to other means of getting information that was critical for managing the crop production process. Narayan Adhikary was the proprietor of Ahdikary Agrovet in the town of Kohalpur, Nepalgunj. He had started his business with a meagre investment of NR[9] 3,200. After 12 years of business, his shop had an annual turnover of NR 5–6 million from the sale of seeds, saplings and embedded services to vegetable farmers who have benefitted from IDE's interventions. He proclaimed proudly,

> When I started, I had very little knowledge of agriculture. IDE gave me training about various varieties of high-quality seeds, planting and farming methods as well as how to build a nursery that enabled me to provide essential services to the farmers. With IDE's help, I have also created a document that lays down best practices in vegetable cultivation. Till date, I have sold about 1,000 copies of the document.

This indicated the high demand for knowledge input from the farmers. IDE's on-farm or process interventions included providing information to the farmers about the right kind of crops and the timing of cultivation, enabling multilevel cropping and crop diversification to spread and reduce risks as well as providing knowledge input about the right technology for farming and irrigation. Over a period of time, the farmers started receiving such knowledge either from the input suppliers or from the traders with whom IDE linked the farmers. IDE also provided training to some of the farmers so that they, in turn, could become trainers and disseminate the necessary knowledge within the farmer community. However, IDE field workers kept in constant touch with the farmers, informally monitoring their progress as well as helping them in case of some unexpected problems. The field personnel also acted as important linkages between project sites and the IDE head office, both in terms of providing project information as well as seeking help if necessary.

---

cost was recovered from project budgets. IDE trained 10,000–12,000 people every year.

[9] Nepalese rupee, the national currency. USD 1 = NR 75 approximately.

The focus of IDE's output side intervention was to link the smallholders with the markets so that they could realize maximum returns by selling the farm output. IDE decided to organize the smallholders into communities and created Marketing and Planning Committees (MPCs) who would collectively look after the interests of the farmer communities. Creating such communities helped farmers to coordinate their production process, participate in joint training, benefit from the knowledge being imparted to them by IDE and input suppliers as well as produce output suited to market specification such that the downstream processes of transportation and investment in marketing infrastructure could derive scale economies from aggregation. Sooner or later, such communities matured into self-help groups, empowering the rural poor to collectively bargain for their interests and rights. IDE linked these communities with financial institutions to enable a credit model where the community could jointly provide guarantee to loans made to the individual members.

SOCIAL MOBILIZATION

From 2003, social mobilization became a critical part of IDE's activities targeted towards developing the agricultural value chain for the smallholders. The poor farmers, IDE's target group, were either owners of small plots of land or were landless, earning their livelihood through daily wage labour. Using micro irrigation (drip and sprinkler irrigation) to cultivate vegetables was a new concept for them, who, for centuries, had been accustomed to cultivating rice through conventional irrigation methods. However, IDE assessed that there was a large demand for vegetables in Nepal, a significant part of which was met through imports from India. If the farmers were given proper input and information about markets, it would be possible for them not only to meet the local demand but also export their vegetables to India by taking advantage of seasonal shortfalls.[10] However, it was a challenging task to identify these marginalized farmers and convince them about the utility of

---

[10] Because of differences in climatic conditions, seasonal vegetables in Nepal became off-season vegetables for India.

growing a non-traditional product, such as vegetables or fish, using unfamiliar techniques of irrigation.

IDE started their community-building initiatives through a survey or a feasibility study to identify a suitable location and communities that could be engaged. The required data was sometimes obtained from district officials or other agencies like the United Nations that had experience of working in those areas through initiatives such as the World Food Programme. After deciding on the community and a suitable intervention, be it vegetable farming or fishery in micro ponds, IDE identified opinion makers and influencers of these communities and conducted a series of discussions with them, explaining the proposed intervention and the possible benefits that could accrue to the marginalized members of the community. Often, such opinion makers were not poor farmers themselves. However, discussions with them enabled IDE personnel to understand the social situation and concerns of various stakeholders.

Once IDE was able to convince the opinion makers, it took their help to identify the disadvantaged members – the poor, the landless and those belonging to the backward castes. IDE members held a series of discussions, explaining to them the proposed programme, its benefits and what the members needed to do to make it a success. It was from this point that IDE encouraged the community to develop norms of governance among themselves, such as identifying subgroups, team leaders and laying down rules of engagement in collaborative efforts. The focus was on making those communities as self-sufficient as possible with IDE taking the role of providing them the necessary technical input as well as linking the community with input providers, traders and government institutions. IDE also identified local resource persons who were provided further training so that they, in turn, could train other members of the communities on a continuous basis. The communities and local resource persons were assisted by the IDE field personnel, who were capable of providing technical support to these communities. The IDE field personnel also kept a watch on the development and progress of the community and were able to ask for assistance from the organization when the community needed. As a result, the IDE field personnel developed deep relationships with the communities, related to their context, understood their specific problems and provided the essential continuity in IDE interventions even as it transited from one development programme, such as SIMI, to another, such as EIG.[11]

When farmers were formed into communities, it enabled them to get credits from the suppliers because in the absence of any collateral from individual farmers, the suppliers were willing to trust the commitment of the collective towards the repayment of loans. IDE introduced the concept of revolving credit among different communities where community pressures ensured efficient utilization and faster repayment of loans.

THE MPC AT GULARIYA

IDE realized that it was important to establish collection centres for aggregating vegetable production so that smallholders could be linked to traders and regional markets. It, therefore, enabled farmer communities to set up MPCs that could manage collection centres by developing cooperatives, selecting traders who could act as agents for the producers as well as provide supporting services to the farmers, such as the sale of agricultural input, credit, technical assistance, crop planning for marketing opportunities and representing farmers at government and development programmes.

Prema Kumari was the local service provider at the Gulariya MPC in Bardiya district. She also belonged to the executive body of the MPC. Prior to IDE intervention, most farmers in this area were involved in growing paddy, which provided them with an annual income of not more than NR 3,000. They needed to supplement this with daily wage labour, often migrating to distant places, even to India, in search of employment. With training and input received from IDE (under the SIMI project), an average farmer in Gulariya was able to produce 10 quintals of vegetables, such as chilies, ladyfinger and pointed bottle gourd per year and earned NR 45,000. With the additional income, Prema Kumari could purchase a motorcycle and learnt to drive it. She said,

---

[11] Education for Income Generation was a USAID and Winrock sponsored programme between 2008 and 2013 for promoting micro-irrigation.

Now we can send our children to good schools, have highly nutritious food, and use cellular phones to communicate. The best impact of this additional income is peace in the household. When there is no money, there is tension every day. Now people can do what they want and we, the womenfolk, get a lot more say in household matters.

While earlier it was almost unthinkable for women to take a lead in community activities, the Gulariya MPC had almost equal representation of women in its apex decision-making body. Dinanath, who was actively involved in the governance of the MPC since its inception, said,

Today, we have 315 farmers as members of this cooperative, making it one of the largest in the district, with an average vegetable collection of 2 metric tonnes[12] per day. It is our aim to bring all farmers within our fold – this results in price stabilization in the market. Farmers have the assurance that there will be buyers for their produce and customers are assured of a good product at a fair price. Most importantly, the MPC has given a voice to the farmer. We have convinced the district agricultural office to invest NR 600,000 in basic infrastructure necessary for running this collection centre. We realize how much we can gain by working as a collective – there has been a social change of some sort.

MICRO FISHPONDS

At Tepri, another small village under Gulariya municipality, IDE, as part of the EIG programme, created 105 fishponds and helped the local villagers, most of whom were landless, to have a viable source of livelihood. Based on advice from their fisheries expert, IDE provided technical support for constructing the ponds while the United Nations World Food Programme (UN-WFP)

---

[12] One metric tonne = 1,000 kilograms.

provided food to the villagers (100 metric tonnes of rice),[13] who were involved in the excavation and pond construction. Land for the site was leased from the local municipality at a rate of NR 700 per pond per year, which also provided shallow boring pumps necessary for the construction. The villagers spent NR 500 in purchasing the fingerlings, three or more varieties of carp and some chemicals necessary for maintaining water quality. After eight–nine months, each of the ponds yielded about 25 kilograms of fish that could be sold at NR 150 per kilogram. IDE tied up with fish traders who agreed to purchase the output. Prior to the creation of fishponds, those villagers were primarily involved in daily wage labour. Since fish maintenance did not take more than two hours per day and had little or no expenses, income from these ponds doubled or tripled the household income, resulting in considerable improvement in their economic condition. IDE trained a few of the villagers with the techniques of fish production, pond management, maintaining water quality and control of diseases. While there were successful fish maintenance programmes elsewhere, most of those involved constructions of larger ponds. At Tepri and nearby locations, IDE created smaller ponds such that every household had a pond for themselves and results indicated that the micro-pond model was viable and well suited to the local context. Luke said,

> Farmers will cooperate when there is compelling need to do so – and nothing can be more compelling than economic benefit. There is administrative simplicity in keeping the production process individualistic and decentralized, wherever possible. The advantages of centralization are best felt at the market and input stages.

With the construction of nearly 2,000 fishponds, IDE ran the largest fisheries project in Nepal.

---

[13] Under the WFP, 1,120 kilograms of rice was provided to villagers for constructing a 300 square metre fishpond at the rate of 4 kilogram per day per person. It was assumed that it would take a group of seven villagers 40 days to construct a pond. This rice was valued at approximately NR 30 per kilogram in the market.

DRIP IRRIGATION SYSTEMS MANUFACTURER

IDE worked closely with entrepreneurs who manufactured micro-irrigation equipment, which was an essential input for developing the supply chain. Thapa Mould and Die, located in Lalitpur on the outskirts of Kathmandu, was owned and run by Chandu Thapa, who proudly called himself a 'Die Specialist'. And he had every reason to be proud because the constant innovations that he made with his dies, machines and equipment on his factory shop floor made IDE Nepal appoint him the exclusive manufacturer of drip irrigation systems.

Chandu started working with IDE around 1998 and manufactured close to 7,000 drip irrigation systems annually, of which more than 70 per cent were deployed in IDE projects. Drip irrigation systems came in five different sizes, ranging from coverage of 90 square metres costing NR 1,600 to 1,000 square metres costing NR 6,750. Since IDE worked mostly with smallholders, 90 per cent of the demand was for the smallest system. At a price of NR 1,600, Chandu provided a 10–15 per cent retailer margin, spent 4–5 per cent for the transportation cost and was left with a margin of 10 per cent. He said,

> We manufacture the entire annual demand in three months flat, so that we can concentrate on other jobs for the rest of the year. The margins are not very high, but I do this for the sake of reputation. It helps to be associated with IDE and the projects that they do.

IDE provided constant support to Chandu, starting from the finance needed to set up his manufacturing facility, investing in moulds and dies, to providing training necessary for consistent quality in output. IDE fixed the upper limit of prices that Chandu could charge his customer. However, IDE was open to considering the impact of increasing costs and investments so that Thapa Mould and Die remained profitable. After working with two other assemblers in Pokhran and Surkhet, IDE decided to have Thapa Mould and Die as their only manufacturer and assembler. This, they analysed, would reduce costs and increase consistency in output. It also ensured faster delivery of systems to the farmers because, unlike Thapa Mould, the assemblers were unwilling to stock products, which used to result in delays in supply. Since the crops that IDE encouraged smallholders to cultivate had short crop cycles, such delays could result in a loss of critical opportunities.

IDE's design team worked with Thapa Moulds for product innovation. They evaluated flat tubes of larger volumes (12 to 20 millimetres in diameter) being used by IDE India in their drip irrigation system, which had the advantage of being customized for the use of the farmer. However, these tubes were made of LLDP,[14] which was cheaper but made the tubes cumbersome. IDE decided to create such flat tubes with PVC,[15] which they had been using for manufacturing smaller (8 millimetres) round pipes. Chandu experimented on his shop floor and invented a unique way of using his existing machines to produce the 16 millimetre flat tubes even though the machines were originally designed to produce only 8 millimetre round tubes. IDE's design engineers were pleasantly surprised because this, coupled with other innovations that they had introduced, resulted in significant cost savings – as much as 20 per cent for larger drip irrigation systems.

Unlike drip irrigation systems, IDE had five manufacturers for treadle pumps. They were technologically much simpler to manufacture and IDE recognized that a decentralized system of assembly by multiple suppliers was more suitable for their operations.

PARTNERSHIPS WITH THE GOVERNMENT

IDE believed that it had to work closely with government institutions for the long-term sustainability of their initiatives. It leveraged the resources available with the government, such as finance, infrastructure and field personnel, to implement its programmes as well as focused on the developing capacity of government institutions, so that the government could continue with the development initiatives even after the completion of an IDE project. This resulted in a trust-based relationship of interdependence between IDE and the Nepal government, which was quite remarkable, given the usual perception of bureaucracy that is associated with government

---

[14] Commercial plastic derived from linear low-density copolymer of ethylene.

[15] Commercial plastic derived from polyvinyl chloride polymer of ethylene.

institutions. Dr B. K. P. Shaha, Secretary in the Ministry of Agriculture and Cooperatives (MOAC), noted,

> The root cause of political turmoil in Nepal is social inequity and poor condition of many of our farmers. We can significantly improve the situation if we can generate employment and increase income of the poor farmers. And IDE initiatives help to address this fundamental issue. We need rural transformation in Nepal, and we see institutions like IDE as important enablers of government efforts to increase farm income and reduce rural poverty.

Social mobilization, development of market linkages and ensuring continuity were the key reasons that endeared IDE to the Nepal government and resulted in successful implementation of programmes in a partnership model between the government and IDE. According to Dr P. P. Manali, Joint Secretary in the Planning Division of Ministry of Agriculture, Government of Nepal,

> The government and international NGOs (INGOs) have complementary skills. With IDE partnerships, the result has been to get the best of both. The government can provide funds for developing infrastructure and it has a team of officials in the field who can implement various initiatives. However, we are not good at social mobilization, neither are our skills and expertise updated so that they can be used to address field-level concerns on a dynamic basis. This is what IDE is good at. They supplement our resources, provide training and education to our personnel and increase our effectiveness. Above all, they are able to create vibrant communities out of the marginalized farmer groups.

Government officials felt that most international NGOs operated on a project basis. They employed external consultants, who did important work during the duration of the project. However, they moved on as soon as the projects got over, resulting in discontinuity of their initiatives. It was not very long before that all the good work got undone. However, with IDE, there was continuity even across their programmes. Because IDE worked in a partnership mode with the government, the bureaucrats were able to maintain continuity of the programmes even after a specific project got over.

Kamal K. Jha, senior agricultural development officer in Banke district, who was closely associated with IDE projects since 2004, felt that the organization's approach brought about changes in the thought process of policy makers.

> Earlier, our efforts (in the department of Agriculture) were only focused on production. IDE introduced us to the concept of value chain, which is to look at the entire set of activities, that is, inputs for agriculture, water management, irrigation, farm processing and marketing. With this approach, the economic conditions of poor farmers improved significantly, because not only are we helping them to produce, we are ensuring that they are able to sell their produce and get the best possible price. With increased income, the farmers are able to build assets, get better quality nutrition, and have access to healthcare. We can see the transformation happening very fast, even though its full impact might take several years to unravel. Programmes like SIMI have thus created the base on which the government can build its efforts. Unlike other training programmes in government organizations, the training that IDE provided to our department was very focused, addressing the specific needs of the farmer. Thus, our field level staff has become knowledgeable – they can carry on the work that IDE started.

FINANCIAL ASSISTANCE

One of the key challenges for IDE in implementing its programmes was to raise funds. While IDE received significant support from donor agencies, such as USAID, and other developmental organizations, such as the UN-WFP, those funds were never enough to meet all the necessities of the poor farmers. Funds from donor agencies were received for specific periods,[16] which created

---

[16] USAID fund for SIMI was initially planned for two years, beyond which it was renewed three times. Despite the significant positive impact of the programme, further renewal was against USAID policy and, therefore, the SIMI programme had to be terminated.

problems for sustaining the interventions. Likewise, aid agencies had their own objectives, which did not completely converge with that of IDE. For example, while IDE was been able to run a successful partnership with UN-WFP, the latter was a very mobile organization focusing on areas suffering from acute food shortages. And unlike IDE, its primary goal was not income generation. However, they acknowledged that linking their Food For Work programme with IDE's programmes of income generation, as in the case for micro-ponds, led to a long-term improvement in the economic conditions of the target population, over and above helping them tide over a crisis situation.

Thus, IDE made constant efforts to tap sources that could provide financial assistance to the poor farmers and smallholders, so that they could buy input and build infrastructure that was necessary for farming and ensuring the farm output reaches the markets. The banking sector did not provide loans to small farmers because of high transactions costs[17] and lack of any guarantee that the poor could provide. Microfinance institutions were not well developed in Nepal, neither was the microfinance model suited for agricultural loans.[18] Therefore, IDE worked with the government at various levels such that block development and other grants could be used to provide finance to the farmers. Luke said,

---

[17] High transaction costs arise because the loan amounts needed by poor farmers are small and they do not possess any assets that can be provided as collaterals. Therefore, lending institutions have to spend additional efforts in evaluation, monitoring and verification of the credit worthiness and how the loaned amount is being utilized. This additional effort needed for servicing small amounts of loan makes lending financially unviable for commercial banks. Microfinance institutes specialize in lending small amounts. However, the high transaction costs that they incur result in very high interest charges, ranging from 24 to 32 per cent.

[18] Typical microfinance models involve weekly collections, with loan repayments starting from one week after the loan has been disbursed. Thus, they are suitable for activities that generate constant cash flows, rather than for agriculture where cash inflow is lumpy and happens towards the end of the harvesting season.

Vegetable farming with the right set of input and marketing information results in significant profits for the farmers – our model has shown this time and again. The paradox of the situation is that despite the potential of such profitability, the farmer today is starved of funds. With financing, he can buy more good quality seeds, get better agricultural equipment and cultivate greater areas. But there is nobody who is willing to lend him the initial capital.

The Government of Nepal launched the Youth Self Employment Fund (YSEF) programme where commercial banks needed to allocate one-third of their 'deprived loan' portfolio for providing loans to young entrepreneurs at 10–12 per cent rates of interest without collaterals.[19] Those seeking loans needed to get certified skills training from institutions such as the Federation of Nepal Chamber of Commerce and Industries (FNCCI) and put forth a proposal before the bank about their venture that was based on their acquired skills. IDE signed a memorandum of understanding with the Ministry of Finance and commercial banks that it would provide skills training to poor farmers and certify the successful completion of such training, which the farmers could then use to get loans. IDE helped the farmers write business plans for procuring loans that could be used to finance the purchase, installation and usage of MITs and MUS.

Under instruction from the Central Bank of Nepal, nearly NR 3 billion was kept aside by the commercial banks for financing this initiative and there were close to 700,000 loan applications. Dealing with such large numbers was a big challenge for the banks, who were quite apprehensive of these loans without collaterals. However, given IDE's record of working successfully with poor farmers, the banks reposed a lot of faith in candidates who were trained by IDE and whom the organization had helped to write the proposals. To minimize the perception of risk, IDE encouraged the farmers to apply in groups such that the MPCs could provide some kind of guarantee to the banks about the authenticity of the endeavour. IDE also provided adequate information to the bank officials about their projects and took them for field

---

[19] The government would provide 60 per cent subsidy on interests charged if the loans were repaid on time.

visits so that the bank officials could see first-hand where and how the money they lent would be put to use. That was the first time that formal linkages were established between the MPCs and financial service providers.

CHALLENGES AHEAD

It has been argued that when markets and institutions are not well developed, organizations need to undertake a diverse set of activities (Khanna et al. 2005). This explains why IDE had to take on the mantle of acting as a facilitator for developing the agricultural value chain. However, several challenges remained. Given its lack of infrastructure, especially in rural areas, the transaction costs of any business activity in Nepal, be it financial services or supply chain of farm outputs, were very high. Thus, IDE needed to continuously work with the government and other institutions to improve access of poor farmers to complementary services, such as micro-credit, insurance, post-harvest facilities, transportation and timely information about demand and prices. Only then would the potential of rural Nepal be fully realized.

Nepal is a small country with open borders. This implies that it is unlikely to have tight control over the prices of its agricultural output. At relatively small levels of production, the farmers could take opportunities of local variations in demand–supply conditions and command good prices in the market. However, with a substantial increase in farm output, Nepalese farmers needed to compete in global markets, implying the necessity for creating some kind of competitive differentiation. Else, the small farmers would remain 'price takers' subjected to the vicissitudes of global commodity pricings, rendering the linkages between farm productivity and increased income tenuous. IDE Nepal would, therefore, need to find ways of creating differentiation for Nepalese farm output and monitor global price trends to decide on crop diversification.

Finally, convincing international donors and raising finance for their interventions remained IDE's continuous challenge. Luke said,

> Some donor agencies have grown short-term these days. While they have their governance reasons for keeping the project durations short, it does not work well for agricultural projects. It makes planning difficult and increases

project uncertainty. Projects need to be of a minimum duration of five years to make and sustain the impact.

DISCUSSION: THE DIFFERENT DIMENSIONS OF VALUE CREATION BY IDE

Nepal is one of the poorest countries of the world, where about 25 per cent of the population survives under a dollar a day. While 85 per cent of Nepal's population is dependent on agriculture, food prices are high, farming methods are outdated and there is limited expenditure on public systems. Nepal is landlocked and mountainous, making development and transportation of resources difficult. Nepal has also been a victim of numerous natural disasters, such as earthquakes that have displaced millions and destroyed property and assets. The annual growth rate of agriculture in Nepal remains lower than its population growth, resulting in the country importing food grains. There were several constraints before agricultural growth in Nepal, primarily because being a mountainous country, only 18 per cent of Nepal's total land is cultivated, of which only 44 per cent is irrigated.[20] Moreover, agriculture in Nepal has remained traditional, with limited diversification or commercialization, resulting in low farm income and close to 40 per cent of people living below the poverty line.[21] Political uncertainty has further contributed to poor economic development, with Nepal receiving an insignificant amount of foreign direct investment (FDI).[22] A majority of farmers in Nepal are smallholders who are poor, earning their living from 1-acre farms. Polak (2008) argues that the root

---

[20] C. Pokarel (2007), 'Agricultural Diversification in Nepal: Status, Constraints and Opportunities', in *Agricultural Diversification and Smallholders in South Asia*, ed. P. K. Joshi, A. Gulati and R. W. Cummings, 271–95 (New Delhi: Academic Foundation).

[21] As estimated in Nepal's 10th Five-Year Plan (2002–06).

[22] FDI in Nepal has been respectively USD 7, 0, 2 and 7 million between 2003 and 2006, according to the Least Developed Countries Report 2008. Unofficial estimates suggest that FDI in 2008 was USD 6 million, while international aid was close to USD 1 billion.

cause of poverty of such smallholder farmers was their lack of access to low-cost tools for irrigation, good seeds, fertilizers, access to markets as well as having the knowledge about what kind of crops to grow and what not to grow. In the following sections, we analyse how IDE Nepal helped in solving the problems of the smallholder farmers and what insights can be drawn from their interventions. We end by discussing the advantages that IDE had for being structured as a not-for-profit enterprise.

MARKET MAKER FOR LOW-COST IRRIGATION TOOLS

Smallholder farmers face a set of adverse conditions that perpetuate their poverty. Since their farm sizes are small, they are not amenable to mechanization. Their farming methods remain antiquated, resulting in low productivity, barely crossing subsistence levels. They represent unattractive markets for farm input providers and their meagre produce prevents them from directly accessing output markets, forcing them to go through a series of intermediaries. Smallholder farmers typically have little crop diversification and grains such as rice, wheat and corn remain their primary output. However, even in developed nations, where farmers have access to the latest technology and modern agricultural practices, not many large acreage farms can manage to earn more than USD 200 per acre by growing grains, which only becomes economically viable when farm sizes are very large, typically in excess of 2,000 acres (Polak 2008). Growing grains is unviable for farm-family enterprises with limited acreage. On the other hand, smallholder farmers have an advantage in simple labour intensive processes because they can deliver labour at a very low cost and, being family-owned, they incur little or no agency costs, unlike in large-scale agriculture. It was, therefore, attractive for them to grow high-value labour-intensive crops, such as fruits and vegetables, provided they had access to irrigation.

This is where IDE started its interventions in Nepal. It invested in research to create low-cost tools, such as treadle pumps and drip irrigation systems, which could be used in small farms to grow off-season fruits and vegetables. Being an international not-for-profit organization, its practice was to make all its innovations open source. As a result, its products were priced lower compared to those that were patented and it also enabled them to freely source technical knowledge from its international network. While patents create strong incentives for invention, they also increase the price of the final product, putting such products beyond the reach of poor customers. The pharmaceutical industry is a good example of it. Therefore, the open source model of invention is more suited for inclusive markets and IDE acted as an enabler of it.

After having developed the products, it was important for IDE to ensure that costs were kept low during the production and distribution process, so that the final price to the customer was affordable. IDE did not want to get into production themselves because they saw this as an opportunity for developing local entrepreneurs. However, they wanted to maintain control over the final price and assumed the role of a market regulator by restricting the number of producers as well as keeping the producers dependent on them by providing them training and advising them on process and technology improvement. Markets such as these have the potential problem of becoming monopolistic. While IDE ensured that the entrepreneurs made enough profit to be financially sustainable, they prevented the entrepreneurs from being opportunistic and raising prices to the extent where it would have become unaffordable for poor farmers. IDE also ensured that farmers were made aware of the advantage of using such irrigation tools. Therefore, they took on the task of disseminating information and provided the farmers with necessary training, so that they made the right choices of crops and could use these products to improve their farm productivity.

To summarize, IDE played the role of a market maker, absorbing many of the costs of reaching technology to impoverished markets. Scholars have pointed out that it is difficult to develop sustainable business models selling products to the poor because in such markets sellers need to incur a lot of hidden costs arising from institutional voids. In this case, IDE was performing the important role of filling up such institutional voids, so that the small entrepreneurs could establish a viable business model that was beneficial for all concerned stakeholders.

INTERVENTION ACROSS THE AGRICULTURAL VALUE CHAIN

Despite all this, IDE realized that only developing farm productivity was not enough to improve the income of the smallholders. Being small and disintegrated was a disadvantage in both upstream and downstream processes of the value chain. Therefore, to improve their income, intervention was required both in the input and output markets. While the smallholders have an advantage in farming labour-intensive crops because of their disaggregated nature, the same disaggregation makes them unattractive customers in their input markets, that is, for anyone who sells them products or services. Likewise, their disaggregated nature gives them poor bargaining power in their output markets. Therefore, IDE intervened to aggregate their demand in their input markets and their supply in their output markets. Apart from irrigation equipment manufacturers, IDE liaised with sellers of other farm input, such as seeds and fertilizers, as well as service providers like installers and masons, so that the suppliers got a proper demand estimation and derived scale economies and the farmers received the necessary input at a fair price. In well-functioning markets, such coordination between demand and supply happens automatically because of price and competition. However, in markets such as those of smallholder farmers, such an 'invisible hand' rarely works and IDE had to step in to establish these important connections. IDE's intervention was similar in the output markets, where aggregation of the farm produce and timely availability of information provided the farmers with greater bargaining power and the ability to match the demand with supplies. However, IDE wanted to make their interventions sustainable, which led them to their next stage of evolution, namely getting involved in social mobilization.

SOCIAL MOBILIZATION FOR CREATING EMPOWERED COMMUNITIES

As a development organization, IDE's purpose was to improve the capabilities of the smallholder communities, so that the improvements they brought about could be sustained even when they moved away after the completion of their project. An important aspect of such capability-building was developing inclusive, democratic and fair norms of governance. A well-governed community would be able to look after its own welfare, be able to strike fair bargains with all external stakeholders as well as ensure that there was no exploitation within the community that could fracture their solidarity and weaken them. Thus, even while they did not get involved in governance, IDE facilitated the formation of MPCs and guided them to establish norms. This resulted in a greater representation of women and lower castes in the MPCs as well as the emergence of leaders on the basis of demonstrated competence and ability to work for the community.

The other important dimension of IDE's activity was linking the communities with the government and administrative bureaucracy. Typically, national and state governments have several schemes to help the economically underprivileged and minority communities. However, the communities themselves are often unaware of such schemes and are hence not able to derive much benefit from them. Such lack of awareness also creates conditions for corruption where intermediaries divert resources from the intended beneficiaries. When communities become aware and united, they can demand services that they deserve. Apart from establishing such linkages, IDE also acted as a benevolent intermediary by helping farmers write loan applications and business proposals as well as by providing implicit guarantee to the loan-granting institutions. Lending to a large number of small farmers is a challenge for any institution because of high transaction costs and the risks involved because of lack of collateral. However, the lending institutes were willing to trust IDE because they were seen as working closely with the farmers for their welfare and financial sustainability.

Thus, starting with the relatively simple intervention of providing low-cost irrigation and water management tools, IDE evolved into playing a much greater role in developing the ecosystem of smallholder farmers. The case already described the visible and the invisible positive impact that they could create through their interventions. In the next section, we discuss some of the generic lessons that we can derive for organizations working in the development sector.

CRITICAL FACTORS FOR CREATING POSITIVE IMPACT

The most important factor behind IDE's success in creating long-lasting impact at scale was its ability to extend the scope of its activities. Even while it focused on the smallholder farmer, it became the enabler of an ecosystem of the agricultural value chain. It understood that there were deficiencies at multiple points in the supply chain and for the smallholder farmer to realize the gains of enhanced farm productivity, multiple interventions were needed.

In the process, IDE exhibited remarkable ability as an organization to deal with a diverse set of stakeholders. It had no doubts that the government had the maximum resources and ability at their disposal that were essential to bring about change on a large scale. Therefore, through their credible efforts, they earned the trust of the government and were able to remove the supply side constraints that usually prevent government aid from being deployed for the welfare of the poor. IDE was also quite flexible in strengthening the market forces in some parts of the supply chain even while acting as a regulator, where they foresaw that market forces would have adverse consequences for the smallholder farmers.

The second important factor, which has come up in some of our discussions about other inclusive business models such as those of RuralShores and Vaatsalya, is IDE's deep understanding of the context and, subsequently, making interventions that did not disrupt the socio-cultural set-up of the communities. In this respect, possibly led by the rich experience that IDE had from their interventions in different parts of the world, the organization had a well-structured process where, prior to any intervention, they systematically collected information about local communities through their own employees as well as from the government and other development organizations. They talked to opinion leaders of the communities to get a first-hand understanding of the social and political power structure. Most of IDE's interventions were participatory in nature, where they worked with local community members as service providers. Therefore, they were not seen as foreigners imposing their solutions on the community, but as partners working with the community to evolve solutions from the ground up. In the process, they were able to earn the trust of the community that enabled them to understand their needs and aspirations even better.

ADVANTAGES OF BEING A NOT-FOR-PROFIT

We close this chapter by discussing the advantages that IDE had by being a not-for-profit. This issue is salient because IDE Nepal could become an inclusive business if it wanted to since it worked closely with income-generation activities. IDE could have taken up the task of selling low-cost irrigation equipment themselves and the profit from such sales could have made them financially viable. They could have also generated other revenue streams, such as by providing advisory services to the farmers on agricultural practices or taking commission from the traders in the input and output markets for aggregating demand and supply. There are many such inclusive business models that have been set up by private entities in and around the agricultural supply chain in India and other nations, and IDE in India is a social enterprise structured as a for-profit engaged in the sales of low-cost irrigation equipment. What then are the advantages of IDE being a not-for-profit?

First, by being a not-for-profit, IDE could take a longer-term view of markets and make investments in areas that had no market-linked benefits, such as research and development of farm equipment for the poor. It could also open source such innovations and use other similar ones, which enabled it to keep the prices low. Second, by being a donor-driven model, it could reach the poorest of the poor and not worry about whether their customers had the ability to pay them for their products or services. Most inclusive businesses struggle to address the bottom-most markets where the intended beneficiaries have little or no capacity to pay. Third, it enabled IDE to get involved in activities that were important for the development of the community but had no income-generation opportunities for the organization. IDE's involvement in facilitating the establishment of MPCs and strengthening the governance of the communities is an example. An inclusive business, even if it has noble intentions, will not be able to justify its involvement in development activities unless they have a direct bearing on their business and income opportunity. Finally, it is probably easier to establish credibility with the government if one is structured as a not-for-profit rather than a social enterprise that has private investors. Being a not-for-profit provides some kind of social legitimacy, which is not accorded to inclusive businesses because of the duality of their mission where external stakeholders might not be sure about the balance they intend to have between their profitability and development objectives.

CHAPTER LEARNING

Not-for-profit (NFP) organizations can play an important role in incubating inclusive business models. In the domain of agriculture, they can create sustainable communities of marginal farmers.

NFPs need to make interventions at multiple stages of the farm value chain if they want to make a long-term impact on the lives of marginal farmers. Interventions that lead to an increase in productivity can only translate into increased income, provided farmers are linked to markets that have enough demand for their products.

As an ecosystem builder, NFPs need to play multiple roles. They can leverage market mechanisms to encourage entrepreneurship and price-based competition in the input markets. However, they also need to regulate such markets to ensure that prices are kept at a level that can be afforded by marginal farmers.

NFPs should link communities with the government and educate them about how to access funds from various schemes that might have been introduced for helping the economically underprivileged.

Since donors provide grants for a specific number of years, NFPs are compelled to operate on a project basis. Therefore, they need to ensure that beneficiary communities become self-sufficient before the project gets completed. Otherwise, the positive impact of the intervention will not sustain itself beyond the life of the project.

For creating self-reliant communities, NFPs need to educate marginal farmers about fair and equitable norms of governance and self-administration. Before such interventions, they need to earn the trust of the community.

In the absence of any pressure to make profits, NFPs have some inherent advantages, such as being able to get involved in non-income generating activities, being able to reach the absolute poor as well as having greater credibility with the government and society about their social mission.

10

RURALSHORES

Delivering Inclusive Service

While close to 62 per cent of India's 1.3 billion population lives in villages,[1] agriculture contributes to only about 15 per cent of India's gross development product (GDP) (Plecher 2020). Even though a significant part of the rural workforce is involved in non-agricultural activities, such as services and trading, rural India is unable to generate adequate employment opportunities for its workforce, resulting in high rates of unemployment as well as disguised unemployment. Any such adverse statistics are more unfavourable for the female population than the male. For example, while the employment-to-population ratio for rural male was 51.7 per cent in 2018, it was a mere 14.2 per cent for women.[2] This results in large-scale migration of the youth from villages to cities in search of jobs. Given the conservative nature of India's villages, it is very unlikely that parents of young women would allow their daughters to go to cities on their own in search of jobs. Therefore, while educated men from Indian villages often have the option to migrate, educated women can only search for employment opportunities within their villages until they get married. Their inability to find suitable livelihood opportunities not only acts as a dampener for parents to educate their girl child but also perpetuates the idea that the only responsibility of the parents of girl child is to get her prepared for marriage, which, therefore, should be conducted as early as possible.

---

[1]   As per the 2011 census, 68.8 per cent of India's (then) 1.21 billion population lived in villages.

[2]   Rural Job Data, 1 April 2019, *Mint*.

With a total revenue of USD 28 billion, India has a thriving business process outsourcing (BPO)[3] industry that employs about 1.1 million people (Talgeri and Singh 2018). Almost all such BPO organizations are located in big cities, such as Bengaluru, Gurugram or Pune. Apart from the ready availability of English-speaking educated youth, these cities provide the suitable physical infrastructure that is essential for running such a business.

RuralShores is a BPO organization that wanted to change this urban-centric model and set up operations in rural India. It intended to create employment opportunities for the rural youth close to their villages to prevent their migration to cities. It was established in 2008 and three years later, it operated 10 centres across seven India states and provided employment to over 1,000 rural youth. The following sections describe how it established its business, the impact that it created and the challenges that it confronted on its way.

EVOLUTION

Murali Vullaganti got the idea of creating a rural BPO when he was spearheading rapid expansion plans of Xansa[4] as the head of its Indian operations. In order to fulfil its ambition of scaling from 500 to 5,000 employees in 2003–04, Xansa's recruitment team went about searching for employees in smaller cities and villages. Although adequate talent was available in those places and many of them readily joined urban BPO organizations, such as Xansa, the remuneration that they received[5] was just enough for them to eke

---

[3] Business process outsourcing refers to contracting out a business function such as payroll processing or customer call-centre by an organization to a third party. The interaction between the organization and the third-party contractor or the organization's customer usually happens by leveraging information technology. By leveraging information technology, such services can be provided remotely. India emerged as a hub for such outsourcing because of the availability of English-speaking youth at a low cost

[4] Xansa Plc was a British outsourcing and technology company that was acquired by Steria in 2007.

[5] Entry-level salaries were approximately INR 10,000 per month.

out a living in a city such as Bengaluru. The employees could not save any money to send back home. Hence, they were prone to changing jobs if another company offered them a marginally higher salary. High employee attrition was an endemic problem for the entire BPO industry. Yet, despite such frequent job changes, the employees were rarely receiving the income or quality of life that they desired. Murali said,

> We could not get sufficient candidates from Tier I cities, so we started tapping into Tier II and III markets. Many of them were performing better than their urban counterparts. But the downside was that with a salary of INR 10,000 per month, they were stuck in the cities unable to provide their families with any moral or financial support. I thought when they are already doing so well, why do they have to come to cities? Why cannot jobs go to them? (Vitta 2016)

Murali thought that one way to break out of this lose–lose scenario was to move jobs to the villages rather than compelling the youth to migrate to urban centres. He, however, realized that the business model of a rural BPO needed to be significantly different from urban ones. Rural BPOs needed to be much smaller in size, having not more than 100 to 200 seats, for them to be viably established in villages that had a population of less than 20,000 people. In contrast, urban BPOs typically aimed to employ at least 5,000 people to gain economies of scale.

In 2005, Murali, along with a fellow devotee of Satya Sai Baba,[6] Sujata Raju, set up a proof-of-concept centre at Puttaparthi.[7] Initially, they received some work from a livelihood promotion organization, BASIX. This was followed by work from HDFC Bank (one of India's leading private sector banks) that involved opening accounts for the bank's retail operations. It was not long before the number of employees at the centre increased to 100, which gave Murali enough confidence about the viability of a BPO business

---

[6] Satya Sai Baba (1926–2011) was a spiritual leader and philanthropist with wide following in India and abroad.

[7] Puttaparthi is a town in the Ananthpur district of the Indian state of Andhra Pradesh with a population of less than 10,000.

model based in rural India. He decided to develop a business plan to scout for investments and put together a team of promoters who would help him set up the business. Although their initial plans were to start 12 centres, potential investors encouraged Murali to be aggressive and develop a plan for 500 centres. In May 2008, after Murali and his team made a presentation to Deepak Parekh, Chairman of HDFC, the financial institution decided to invest INR 10 million for a 26 per cent stake. RuralShores was incorporated soon after and formal operations started in October 2008. By then, Murali had put together the founding team comprising Sudhakar Ram (Chairman of Mastek), G. Srinivasan (Vice President of Wipro Finance), V. V. Ranganathan (Ernst & Young), C. N. Ram (Head of Operations at HDFC Bank) apart from Sujata Raju. The promoters together put in INR 10 million and even though RuralShores was incorporated as a private company, the promoters conceptualized it as a social enterprise. It was agreed that none of them would derive any personal gains from their investments and commercial surplus would be used to fund social projects. RuralShores Foundation was subsequently set up as a Section 25 company for the purpose of doing developmental work. RuralShores received an additional financing from Lok Capital in 2009 and 2011.[8]

SETTING UP THE FIRST CENTRE

RuralShores started its BPO operations from Bagepalli, a small town in Karnataka, with a population of less than 20,000 people. RuralShores did not want to purchase either land or buildings. A trust that ran a school in Bagepalli provided them with part of a building on a long-term lease. This continued to be one of the operating principles of RuralShores and many of its centres set up subsequently were located in government buildings.

---

[8]   While funding from HDFC and Lok Capital in 2008–09 was largely utilized to meet capital expenditure for centres and working capital finance, USD 3 million received from Lok Capital in 2011 was meant for creating management bandwidth and technology infrastructure that would enable RuralShores to scale.

Since RuralShores generated employment for local youth, it usually did not encounter any problem in obtaining buildings on lease from either the government or local organizations. The pilot project at Puttaparthi taught them that the critical infrastructural bottleneck in remote locations would be provisioning of electricity and telecommunication links, and there was need to build adequate redundancies if they wanted to deliver high quality service from rural locations. Even though a town such as Bagepalli was connected to the electricity grid, power supply was erratic. Therefore, an electricity generator was always kept on standby. For telecommunications, RuralShores tied up with two service providers, one acting as a back-up for the other. Most of the times, they were committed to delivering uninterrupted transactional services to their clients and such redundancy was essential to maintain high availability.

Given the lack of employment opportunities in rural India, recruitment was seldom a challenge. Word about RuralShores usually reached the local community as the centre got ready, resulting in a stream of people enquiring about jobs. RuralShores also got in touch with local schools and colleges, requesting them to identify suitable candidates. However, training new recruits took longer because most of them were not familiar either with English as a medium of communication or with computers. They also had to be trained in soft skills that one took for granted in case of employees who grew up in an urban environment, such as the expected standards of grooming and behaviour in a professional environment. Many of them had to be taught about the importance of planning their leaves of absence. In the initial days, sometimes the entire group of employees failed to turn up for work without informing because there was a wedding in their village! Likewise, there would be a lot of absenteeism during the harvesting season because many of the employees had to help their families in the fields. Based on such experiences, RuralShores created a standard manual, which was used for foundation training during the induction period.

RuralShores signed a contract with its first customer, I-Mint,[9] in December 2008. Before that, 40 employees were recruited as process

---

[9] In June 2010, I-Mint was acquired by Payback, the card business arm of German-based Loyalty Partner.

associates and sent to Puttaparthi for training. A few MBA graduates were recruited in June 2008 from the Satya Sai Institute and trained as process leaders for six months in a Chennai-based BPO company that was managed by Sujata Raju. A person with seven–eight years of experience in the BPO industry, wishing to work for a social venture, was appointed as the centre manager. Thus, the entire team was recruited before the commencement of operations for I-Mint in February 2009. Soon after, RuralShores received orders from two other customers and the number of employees at Bagepalli increased to 130. The senior management felt that it was time to set up the second centre, which would increase customer faith in their delivery capabilities. In May 2009, the corporate office was set up in Bengaluru and other senior-level appointments, such as a business development manager and operations head, were made.

GROWTH THROUGH MULTIPLE CENTRES

An educational trust, managing a high school in Rathinagiri in the Vellore district of Tamil Nadu, approached RuralShores and offered to provide them with building and space for setting up a centre. Rathinagiri's proximity to Chennai made it suitable for showcasing it to potential customers and, thus, the second centre was set up in October 2009. In the next two years of operation, RuralShores established 10 centres throughout India and embarked on a path of steady growth.

The choice of location was typically driven by customer requirements. The centres were established in small towns or large villages with a population of less than 40,000, and the employees came from 15–20 villages within a radius of about 10 kilometres. The centres needed to be well-connected by road, if not by trains, have electricity for at least five–six hours a day[10] and the feasibility

---

[10] RuralShores spent close to INR 40,000 per month on electricity charges at the rate of INR 12 per unit. This was an area where they would like government intervention since electricity was supplied at a subsidized rate in rural India by the government for many activities.

for Internet connectivity. Each centre had its own generator for uninterrupted supply of electricity. The work that was carried out in these centres were rule-based transaction processing, local language or dialect voice support, and processes of low to medium complexity. High-end analytics, decision-based work and voice support in English were kept out of scope.

Each centre had 100–120 employees. RuralShores did not want to scale a centre beyond 200 employees because they assessed that the larger size would create the need for superior infrastructure and more managerial hierarchy, thereby making the operations more complex. The employees usually worked in two shifts between 6 a.m. and 10 p.m., with women working only in the morning shift and men in the morning and afternoon shifts. The RuralShores leadership team sometimes held meetings with village elders and parents of potential employees to dispel any apprehensions they might have about the workings of the organization. Unless it was absolutely essential, RuralShores avoided working in night shifts because that often created health problems for employees and disrupted their family lives.

Typically, a centre with 100 employees involved an investment of INR 6 million and took about three to four months to become operational. Even if the centres did not appear fanciful from outside, each of them had the same quality of necessary infrastructure that would be found in an urban BPO. Early in their life cycle, senior management at RuralShores learnt that they could only win customers if they were able to deliver greater value than urban-based BPOs – no customer would outsource its processes because of RuralShores' social mission. Therefore, RuralShores needed to set the same standards of security, confidentiality, responsiveness and quality. Every RuralShores centre had biometric access control, close-circuit televisions, and was ISO 27001 compliant that mandated specific information security requirement, which could be formally audited. The only leeway that RuralShores sought from its customers was a larger gestation period because the employees needed more time for handholding and training. RuralShores expected to reduce this gap in the future with greater process standardization in recruitment, training, transitioning, measuring and monitoring.

However, standardization did not make RuralShores hesitate from taking up assignments that were non-routine in nature. Maharaja Gokulavasan, the Head of Service Delivery, said,

Take the case of email processing that we do from our centre at Tirthahalli.[11] Our employees respond appropriately to email queries that come from our client's customers, who are users of credit cards. First, the emails need to be read and understood. Then the employee needs to look into product features and promotion announcements to determine the validity of customer queries. Finally, the employee needs to respond to the email. Imagine this being done by someone who probably did not even have English as her second language and have no familiarity with the concept of credit cards to recognize terms such as 'points' or 'redemption'. Many aspects of these kinds of operations cannot be standardized, which makes it complex and challenging for us.

In August 2011, a client outsourced to RuralShores the work of abstracting US and Chinese patent documents. Carried out from its Rathinagiri centre, this was a landmark project because it fell squarely within the domain of knowledge process outsourcing, work that could only be delivered by engineers. For the first time, RuralShores recruited engineers from nearby colleges based on tests and technical interviews, and provided 12 weeks of training on customer location. Although it took them some time to ramp up, the team soon reached a size of 60 members and started to outperform other teams whom the client had engaged for similar work.

CENTRE-PARTNER AS A MODEL OF GROWTH

This heterogeneity among available resources at different centres made RuralShores realize that it would be a challenge for them to set up centres on their own in rural locations across India that were completely unfamiliar to them. Activities such as meeting the infrastructure requirements of the centre or recruiting the village youth required local knowledge and influence. Therefore, after setting up the first five centres, RuralShores embarked on a centre-partner (CP) model, whereby a contract was made with a local entrepreneur who would set up the centre and manage the infrastructure. In this

---

[11] Tirthahalli was the third centre of RuralShores, a small town in the Shimoga district of Karnataka with a population of less than 15,000.

model, RuralShores was responsible for service delivery, while the CP ensured availability of all associated services, such as electricity, telecommunication, building infrastructure and housekeeping. RuralShores took the CP's help for recruitment, who was aware of the potential sources. By 2011, four of the ten RuralShores centres were partner-managed, and it was planned that in the steady state, 80 per cent of them would be managed by CPs. RuralShores would retain complete control of centres if the customers insisted on doing so or if they did not find a suitable CP at a particular location.

Since financial investments were made by the CPs (about INR 6–7 million per centre), growing through this model did not put pressure on RuralShores' financial resources. The partners were compensated based on the number of employees at the centre and it was estimated that they would earn an internal rate of return of 12 per cent in the first five years and recover their capital expenditure over 40 months.

RuralShores was pleasantly surprised to find a large number of individuals and organizations eager to become its CPs. Such individuals typically were professionals with roots in the villages who wanted to give back to society. They considered RuralShores as an enabler of their social service. Even if they did not stay in the villages, they knew enough people who would take care of the local infrastructural and administrative issues. Organizations that had large manufacturing operations in rural areas also approached RuralShores to set up centres near their location, in order to provide employment to families of their employees. This, they figured out, would generate goodwill for them and build loyalty among their employees. They were helped by the fact that RuralShores did not require their employees to have high qualifications – they could train a person to be a process associate if he/she had passed the twelfth standard examination.

RuralShores realized the importance of selecting the right kind of partner in order to maintain its social mission. Through personal interactions with potential partners as well as by leveraging its network for reference checks, it ensured that the partner was someone who was looking at an opportunity to do good rather than only seeking high commercial returns. Although partner selection was done in a bespoke mode, RuralShores was keen to evolve a standardized process, so that it could set up a new centre that would become functional in 90 days.

TRAINING

RuralShores preferred to recruit youth from economically challenged backgrounds. The minimum required qualification was completion of twelfth standard. A new employee went through two months of foundation training comprising training in reading and writing English, computer skills and soft skills, and about two months of process training that involved understanding the specifics of client processes. Thus, a new recruit was ready to work on projects in about four months. The corresponding time for urban BPOs was two months. Although the village youth possessed the capabilities, they often lacked confidence and did not have the knowledge of what was expected of them in a professional environment. During training, they were familiarized with items such as credit or ATM card – typical items that RuralShores' customers would use but were often a rarity in rural India. These skills were imparted during the foundation training – something that most urban-based BPOs did not need to do.

Foundation training acted as a funnel, where the trainee was provided with a job after successful completion. Almost 90 per cent of the trainees completed the training successfully and were employed at RuralShores' centres. The remaining 10 per cent were usually given extended training until they acquired the requisite skills and were, subsequently, provided with jobs. It was only a few who did not succeed, primarily because of their unsuitable attitude. A few years later, RuralShores started to leverage third-party training institutes such as NIIT Foundation[12] to train its employees. These institutes provided candidates with a certificate after they successfully completed the training. Although the candidates paid for their training, RuralShores ensured that these institutes did not charge unreasonable prices. If any candidate had financial constraints, RuralShores paid 50 per cent of their training costs upfront, which was subsequently deducted from their salaries once they joined as employees. It was observed that the candidates

---

[12] NIIT Foundation is a not-for-profit set up by NIIT, an Indian technology services organization. NIIT Foundation had the mandate to provide education and skills development training to the economically underprivileged.

felt a certain amount of pride and ownership if they paid for their training and secured a job based on that.

HUMAN RESOURCES

Every RuralShores centre had a three-tier structure comprising associates, process leaders and centre managers. Typically, a process leader looked after 15 associates and a centre manager was in charge of eight such process leaders. Although the associates were recruited locally, the process leaders and centre manager were experienced in working at urban BPOs. Several of the centres reported to a region that was headed by a regional service delivery manager.

There were many reasons for the process leaders and centre managers to be attracted to work for RuralShores. Some of them were keen to create positive social impact and the novel business model of a rural BPO gave them an opportunity to be part of a new experiment. Others were originally from the areas where the centres were set up and were keen to get back to their roots. Govinda Reddy, a devotee of Satya Sai Baba, spent 20 years associated with Satya Sai University in Puttaparthi before he joined RuralShores as Manager of Operations at the behest of his guru. He said,

Before our centres came up, life was very difficult for most of our employees. RuralShores has been able to improve their standard of living dramatically. Personally, I took it as a challenge to recruit a girl from an economically challenged background. She picked up the necessary skills in two months and became a very good performer. With the money that she saved, she bought clothes for her family, furniture for the house. There are innumerable such instances, which shows that with a little help, it is possible to make them self-sustainable, put the smile back on their faces. This makes me contented, my life fulfilled.

Others were attracted by the enhanced responsibility that they would shoulder at a very early stage in their careers. The fact that they were paid salaries comparable to their urban counterparts while the cost of living in rural areas was substantially lower added to the attraction. The steady stream of résumés that RuralShores continued to receive reaffirmed their conviction that there were many individuals who believed in their mission and were passionate to make a difference to society.

GENERATING BUSINESS

RuralShores faced challenges in convincing clients that it could deliver services of requisite quality from rural locations. Murali said,

> Getting to the CXO level was easy but convincing the process manager to outsource work to us is always difficult. They are the ones who are responsible for the process – being on the floor they are on the firing line. Not only do they need to realize the value but they also need to find time to do the transition. Sales cycles are long, close to six months. However, with more centres and more reference clients, we are able to make breakthroughs. Today, we are discussing opportunities that would require 1,500–2,000 people over 12 months operating from multiple centres.

RuralShores appointed business development managers in Mumbai and Delhi to focus on the demand side. It discovered allies among large BPO companies who, being perennially under pressure to reduce costs, started outsourcing work to RuralShores. They also started jointly bidding with RuralShores for business opportunities in the domestic market, where the price points were lower compared to international markets. By 2011, about 30 per cent of RuralShores' business was sourced from large BPOs, which, apart from being a steady source of revenue, provided RuralShores with the experience of working with different processes as well as increased its credibility in the market. RuralShores also started procuring business processing jobs from the government for its various schemes, such as the National Rural Employment Guarantee Scheme (NREGS), and health and life insurance, an opportunity space that it expected to grow significantly in the future. The domestic market remained its prime focus, where RuralShores estimated that rural BPOs could generate 1.5 million jobs.

Other rural BPOs also presented opportunities for partnerships. Several state governments offered incentives to entrepreneurs to start rural BPO centres. This led to the opening of a large number of single-location BPOs, many of which struggled to find business. RuralShores outsourced work to them sometimes to tide over short-term demand spikes. Many of them were also willing to become partners, presenting RuralShores with a readily available growth path in Karnataka and other Indian states. Murali observed,

> If you are a one-off centre, no one will take you seriously. They can give you some short-term project work. But to outsource a core project, the client will have to be confident in your ability to scale and sustain yourself. Ninety per cent of the work that we do is on core client processes, very often on a real time basis. Even though the initial contracts are for three years, they are sure to get renewed.

Although RuralShores had to spend the first few years selling the concept of a rural BPO and convincing customers that it was possible to deliver quality service from rural locations, the degree of difficulty in acquiring customers reduced once they could show the customers their performing centres. They could start bidding even for end-to-end projects,[13] so that they could become an integral part of their client's operations. Internally, RuralShores started to develop specialized service propositions for business verticals, such as insurance, telecommunication, retail and e-governance. During their first two years of operations, the organization had completed small projects for the local state government, such as those pertaining to cattle census and land records. Based on their good performance, they could, subsequently, qualify for larger government projects, justifying the creation of a dedicated vertical for e-governance. Although transaction-intensive verticals, such as telecommunication, were likely to give them more revenue, others demanded bespoke services and improved their bottom line.[14] Since many of

---

[13] For example, acquisition of loyalty customers along with data entry operations for capturing the details of loyalty customers.

[14] RuralShores collected daily sales information from regional sales offices of a reputed fast-moving consumer goods company and sent it to the Head of

RuralShores' clients had semi-urban or rural customers who were themselves not well conversant in English, the organization discovered one unexpected competitive advantage – their employees could interact with such customers combining local language with English. Sometimes, their employees could also understand the customers' problems better, which resulted in fewer number of repeat calls and greater customer satisfaction.

RuralShores developed a workflow application that enabled remote distributed processing. The tool ensured that a piece of work could be executed simultaneously from multiple centres, which not only increased the speed of execution and reliability but also ensured business continuity. Moreover, it enabled RuralShores to deploy additional resources from other centres during a sudden increase in the volume of work. Such a tool, it was envisaged, would provide them with long-term competitive differentiation as well as minimize the initial investment that customers needed to make when they decided to outsource their business processes.

BUSINESS ENABLEMENT SERVICES

Ever since liberalization, there has been a huge rush among Indian and multinational enterprises to tap rural markets. Banks, insurance companies, telecommunication companies and retailers have devised strategies to sell their products and services to nearly 800 million people, who inhabited 620,000 Indian villages. However, except for a few fast-moving consumer goods (FMCG) companies, such as Unilever India, who had been developing their rural distribution channels over several decades, most organizations faced an insurmountable last-mile problem. Given the dispersed and diverse nature of Indian villages, it was difficult for them to reach the end-consumer in a financially sustainable manner. Being located in the Indian hinterland, RuralShores perceived this problem of reach faced by other companies as a business opportunity for themselves. It had the potential to become a critical enabler of business in rural India by acting as a gateway, providing

---

Sales. Such outsourced processes, though small in volume, provided them with higher margins.

complementary services to a variety of organizations – both through its own process capabilities and through the network of field partners that it typically developed for managing its operations. For example, agricultural companies that intended to sell seeds, fertilizers and pesticides to the farmers needed market intelligence to understand which products to sell and identify distribution partners to reach them. RuralShores could utilize its partner network to procure local knowledge and sell products. They could also operate a help desk in the local language for the farmer-clients of the company. Maharaja explained,

> Financial inclusion, a critical challenge in rural India, needs the integration of four elements – feet on the street, field-level automation, back office processing and banking. We are working with a couple of banks to create the infrastructure for small savings, micro-loans and pension. While the final delivery will be done by business correspondents, we can either take end-to-end ownership of the entire model or make selective interventions in training and back-office processing. These might not contribute to our volumes but will be our value-added services.

It was decided that while RuralShores would not be directly involved in cash-based transactions that fell outside the purview of business processes, its business enablement services could provide income opportunities for CPs and career opportunities for many of its process associates. Moreover, its facilitating role would generate backend processing jobs that would directly contribute to the top line. While RuralShores could independently create about 100–150 jobs in each of its locations, they envisaged that acting as a gateway to other companies would create employment for another 200–300 people.

IMPACT

The BPO industry operated under the constant pressure to reduce cost. Reducing the cost of operations was a big challenge for urban BPOs because of the rising cost of living in big cities as well as the increase in salaries resulting from competition for employee acquisition. As a consequence, some segments of the BPO business, such as voice-based call centres, shifted to lower-cost geographies, such as the Philippines. RuralShores, despite its higher costs of training, could offer price points to its clients that were almost 40 per cent lower than its urban counterparts. Operating from remote locations ensured that there was very little employee attrition, as low as 4–5 per cent,[15] which was beneficial both to RuralShores and its clients. RuralShores also felt that compared to its counterparts in urban BPOs, its employees were more dedicated and committed to their jobs, all of which translated into better business results. Therefore, it was not surprising that a steady state centre at RuralShores performed better than a comparable centre of an urban BPO on several parameters, such as customer satisfaction.

RuralShores was one of the few businesses that could generate employment near villages. Owing to the proximity, it could also employ women, most of whom, unlike the men, did not have the option of migrating to cities in search of jobs. This had two significant social consequences. First, it empowered young women and allowed them a greater say in their future. Second, it inspired the village youth to complete their education at least up to Class 12 and encouraged parents to send their children to schools,[16] so that they could join a profession rather than being engaged in farming or associated activities. Keeping an eye on their potential to empower women, RuralShores consciously recruited a significant number of women in its centres. Even though women employees had greater attrition because some of them had to move to other locations after marriage, RuralShores felt that the positive

---

[15] The average attrition rate of urban BPOs was approximately 40 per cent, according to the Monitor Group working paper (June 2011) 'Job Creation through Building the Field of Impact Sourcing'.

[16] Two problems of the Indian educational systems were a high dropout rate, especially after primary classes, and lower enrollment rates among girls ('Indian State Development Scorecard', Indicus Analytics, December 2011). Both were consequences of the fact that parents did not see much value in continuing with their children's education beyond making them literate because more education made the youth unwilling to do farming or menial work, yet with such education, they were unable to procure employment in the cities.

impact on the socio-economic condition of the village would be more if more women were provided livelihood opportunities.

The case of 30-year-old H. N. Punyavati was a typical example. Before she joined RuralShores as a project associate in March 2009, she and her husband were in dire straits – her husband had lost his job while she was expecting their first child. There was absolutely no income opportunity for Punyavati had it not been for her INR 4,000/month job at the Bagepalli centre, which enabled her to restore financial stability in their young family (Sivaramakrishnan 2009). B. Keerthi, another process associate at the Bagepalli centre, felt that RuralShores had encouraged villagers to become more modern in their outlook, created their appreciation of youngsters and improved communication across generations (Magnier 2010). For E. Pushpa, the work gave her independence that she could once only dream of (Fitzgerald 2010). She said,

> My parents wanted me to get married as quickly as possible to a man of their choice. Now, I give half my salary to my parents and use the rest for a correspondence course. I want to become a social worker ... earning money on my own is very liberating.

Finally, setting up a centre resulted in an injection of cash, close to INR 1 million per month, into the village economy, which created additional jobs and positively impacted the economic conditions of the village. The additional income enabled many of the families to send their children to schools as well as to avail better nutrition and healthcare services.

An employment survey conducted by RuralShores indicated that about 65 per cent of their associates helped their families in traditional work, mostly farming, besides working for RuralShores. Prior to joining RuralShores, 40 per cent of them had no annual savings and almost none had access to any kind of insurance. Within three years of its inception, the positive impact of RuralShores on the lives of the people in the villages where they operated was evident. The challenge in front of RuralShores now was to scale this model if they were to achieve their mission of establishing a centre in each of the 500 rural districts in India and provide livelihood to 100,000 people. Most inclusive businesses like RuralShores faced tremendous challenges in scaling their operations because, unlike commercial organizations, they had to simultaneously achieve the objectives of business growth and making social impact. Although their initial success could be ascribed to the experience and commitment of the founding team, it remained to be seen whether the same level of excellence in service could be delivered once the organization expanded. Given the differences in the socio-economic conditions between one Indian state and another, a model that was successful in Karnataka might fail in a state such as Orissa. The task of managing an organization with 1,000 employees was qualitatively different from managing one that had 100,000, especially because RuralShores could not afford to have an elaborate hierarchical structure similar to its urban counterparts. Moreover, until 2012, RuralShores did not have to face any competitive backlash. However, there was no guarantee that if they grew bigger, large players in the IT services and BPO space would not start to compete head-on.

DISCUSSION

Like some of the other cases discussed in this book (Reliance, GNFC), RuralShores is an example of an inclusive business that involves the poor in the value chain. Through this, they create enhanced livelihood opportunities and/or opportunities for income diversification, both of which are critical enablers of poverty alleviation (Krishna 2007). The uniqueness of RuralShores' business model is its ability to use the poor as service providers. When scholars such as C. K. Prahlad introduced the idea of businesses addressing the needs of the poor, they largely talked about creating affordable products and services for the poor. Subsequently, other scholars such as A. Karnani argued that in order to alleviate poverty, it was necessary to enhance the income of the poor. Such businesses should focus on creating sustainable livelihood over and above creating affordable products or services for the poor. This possibly inspired the creation of a number of inclusive business models, which integrated the impoverished producers in an already existing supply chain or created a suitable supply chain to reach products from poor producers to the markets. Although RuralShores creates livelihood for the rural poor, its uniqueness lies in the fact that in its business model, the poor are used to deliver a service rather than create a product. Services are different from manufacturing because, in the case of the former, production and consumption occur almost at the same time and the service provider is exposed to the consumer. Therefore, integrating the rural poor into a service delivery value chain poses unique challenges because, unlike the instance of a producer, such as a village artisan or a vegetable-growing farmer, the service provider (the rural poor here) will have to be trained well enough to directly interact with the customer, who would be expecting high quality service. RuralShores is a pioneering business model because it is possibly the first BPO organization that has been able to successfully integrate the rural poor within its service delivery value chain.

THE SIGNIFICANCE OF RURALSHORES' BUSINESS MODEL FOR RURAL INDIA

Livelihood options are limited in Indian villages, home to about 65 per cent of its population. This results in large-scale migration from rural to urban India. Rural migrants get employed in a variety of occupations, ranging from construction labour to employment in call centres. Given the poor levels of literacy in rural India, most of the jobs that migrants secure are often in the unorganized sector that are low-paying and provide inadequate benefits or social security to the employees. Moreover, most migrants find the urban environment unfamiliar and hostile, which results in their leading a poor quality of life. Such large-scale migration also creates high pressure on the infrastructure of cities, and the poor significantly bear its brunt in terms of inadequate housing, sanitation, electricity and water. Thus, there is an urgent need to stem this large-scale migration, which will only happen if adequate livelihood opportunities are created in rural India. The RuralShores business model is a step in this direction because it creates local livelihood opportunities for educated youth, reducing their need to migrate to the cities.

Livelihood opportunities in a knowledge-based enterprise, as created by RuralShores, act as a source of inspiration for the rural youth to get educated. Education often has a paradoxical effect among the youth in rural India. Once they complete their schooling, they are no longer eager to follow the traditional family practice of farming. However, most of them do not have the financial wherewithal to pursue higher education, nor do they have the competence to compete with their economically privileged counterparts from urban India to get jobs. This often results in disillusionment with education, especially among the parents of rural youth, who view education to be inadequate to provide employment opportunities, yet adequate enough to embarrass their children about the family profession. Since RuralShores employs rural youth who have completed high school and makes them financially self-reliant, it acts as a great motivator for rural parents and children who realize the value of education and its importance in securing jobs, thereby improving their financial condition.

While rural men have the option of migrating to cities in search of jobs, such options are not available to rural women because of security concerns and apprehensions that conservative parents have about urban lifestyles. Thus, the educated rural woman has little or no opportunities for livelihood that is commensurate with her education. In the absence of jobs, they are forced to get married early, and consigned to the life of a homemaker, financially dependent on their husbands with little or no empowerment. RuralShores' ability to create local livelihood opportunities provides rural women with high school education an option for being financially independent. This acts as a critical lever of empowerment with the potential of bringing about significant transformation in the outlook of rural societies that is typically male-dominated. Women who are financially independent can decide about their personal and professional lives as well as take care of their dependent parents, a role that rural India never thought could be discharged by women. Sociologists and development economists have argued that education and empowerment of women is important for the overall socio-economic development of a society and RuralShores acts as a critical link between education and empowerment of young women in rural India. Let us now look at some of the innovations in RuralShores' business model that were necessary to overcome the challenges of its unique context.

INNOVATIONS IN RURALSHORES' BUSINESS MODEL

RuralShores was establishing a new business model – of carrying out business process outsourcing operations from rural India, which was typically deficient in resources, such as infrastructure and high quality talent. Therefore, it had to innovate on multiple fronts to establish a business that was viable and sustainable in the longer run. These innovations pertain to their operating model, their being sensitive to local context and their way of dealing with potential competitors.

INNOVATIONS IN THE OPERATING MODEL

RuralShores realized that they needed to operate a large number of small centres as opposed to a few large centres because, given the dispersed nature of its employees, it was unviable to build large BPOs in rural India. This implied that they had to forgo many of the advantages of a large centre, such as scale economies. The advantage of having small centres was a relatively flat organization with reduced management hierarchy. Moreover, multiple small centres minimized risks that might be associated with a few large locations and created options of redundancy across centres, especially in an environment that might face difficulties because of infrastructural inadequacies.

For its customer, the biggest advantage was RuralShores' ability to provide services at a price that was significantly lower than what was being offered by urban-based BPO organizations. The biggest risk was the quality of such services – whether RuralShores could be trusted with conducting key processes that required high reliability and security. Therefore, RuralShores had to ensure that it could deliver high quality secured services even while retaining its low-cost advantage. In order to reduce its cost, RuralShores decided not to purchase either land or building, but to creatively use existing rural infrastructure. Thus, the organization leased buildings from schools and government organizations and refurbished them to set up its operations. Since it was generating employment for local youth, it did not have much difficulty in securing these places. This is an important advantage – if RuralShores was able to earn the trust of the local community, it would be able to leverage certain local assets and infrastructure that might not be possible for commercial organizations whose costs of acquisition were likely to be much higher.

High availability is a primary necessity of a BPO organization because it is engaged with key client processes that cannot afford to have any downtime. Therefore, RuralShores had to create redundancies in its electricity and telecommunication supplies. Since electricity supplies are erratic and intermittent in rural India, RuralShores had to maintain an electric generator as a back-up. Since the centres were remotely located, it was difficult for its telecommunication service providers to ensure a quick turnaround in case of link failures. Therefore, RuralShores decided to procure connections from two service providers, reducing the chances of prolonged interruption in its operations. In order to generate client confidence about its level of security, RuralShores acquired ISO-27001 certification for all its centres.

RuralShores also realized that it needed to provide extensive training to its employees – much more than what was provided by its urban counterparts – because its employees were unfamiliar with business contexts or unaccustomed to behaviour that was expected in a professional environment. Therefore, it devoted significant resources to training and, subsequently, started to use specialized training agencies such as NIIT. The advantages of using third-party training agencies, apart from reducing transactional load on RuralShores, was its contribution to the employability of the potential candidates. With a certificate of successful completion of training, the candidates were no longer tied to RuralShores and had the autonomy of seeking employment elsewhere. From a strategic perspective, did it made sense for RuralShores to outsource training and increase the bargaining power of its employees? While it might result in some attrition, it would have made RuralShores more attractive to its potential employees. The key value proposition of RuralShores was creating employment opportunities close to the homes of its employees. For the employees, even if they were certified by NIIT, they had no other employment opportunity apart from RuralShores unless they were ready to migrate to cities. Therefore, from both the strategic and operational perspective, this seemed to be a good move. Overall, one can conclude that RuralShores innovated to leverage some of the inherent advantages of its rural location, even while ensuring that none of its inherent disadvantages had an adverse effect on its operating model.

INNOVATIONS THAT MADE RURALSHORES SENSITIVE TO LOCAL CONTEXT

Why was it necessary for RuralShores to be sensitive to local context? In order to establish a viable and sustainable business model in rural India, it was important for RuralShores to earn the approval, support and trust of local communities, without which it would have been impossible to attract and retain good quality talent and deliver excellent services. There are two reasons why the local community would be apprehensive of an organization such as RuralShores – their unfamiliarity with the way in which it operated and the conservative outlook that rural India has.

It is likely that rural India will be familiar with businesses that are based on farming or those associated with trading but not much about an organization that provided remote services by using information and communication technology. Hence, they would be reluctant to send their children to work for such an organization. Conservative rural India also frowns upon unsupervised interaction between young boys and girls, let alone allowing them to work in close proximity for long hours that the BPO model demanded. Moreover, it was also not common for any girl to work and become economically independent. It was expected that she would get married at an early age and be a homemaker, helping her husband and raising their children.

Therefore, it was necessary for RuralShores not to disrupt the socio-economic set-up of the villages but to gradually earn credibility and legitimacy in the eyes of the community. RuralShores decided to avoid working in night shifts because it might have adverse health impact on its employees, and women worked only in the morning shift so that they could go back to their homes by mid-day. It also did not insist on close interaction between men and women employees and decided to go with the natural flow of women employees socializing among themselves. This is in stark contrast to the working environment in urban BPOs where young men and women work in three shifts and freely interact with one another. RuralShores organized employee trainings locally because it was difficult for the women employees to travel outside their village or stay overnight in some other locations, even though it might have been economical for them to organize training in centralized locations. On some occasions, RuralShores even talked to the village elders and opinion makers, addressing their apprehensions and explaining to them RuralShores' work practices. It would be interesting to speculate whether RuralShores will be able to maintain these practices as its volume of business grows. For example, if RuralShores faced a choice between having a third shift in the same centre versus opening a new one, what should they do?

Several well-meaning interventions to improve the economic conditions of the rural poor have failed because they were viewed as alien to the village environment and did not receive support from the local community. Rural India has traditionally been the neglected and often exploited part of the Indian community, and individuals or organizations that are seen as outsiders or coming from big cities are likely to face apathy or apprehension, if not hostility, unless they take special care to earn the trust of the local community. RuralShores realized this early, and sensitivity to the local context was an important dimension of its innovative business model.

COMPETITIVE INNOVATION

Acquiring customers in the face of competition from established players is possibly the biggest challenge that any entrepreneurial organization faces. This challenge gets enhanced when the business model of the new organization is unconventional. RuralShores realized that even if potential customers appreciated the 'rural welfare' dimension that was a likely consequence of its business model, it was unlikely to result in securing business. In order to win business, it had to compete on terms that every player in the BPO industry competed on – low cost and high quality of service delivery. The earlier section described how RuralShores managed to create a business model that was able to deliver high quality service at low cost. However, to build a sustainable business, it was important to ensure that large urban-based BPOs did not drive it away from the market or replicated its business model. Given the brand name, scale of operations, experience and customer contacts that large, established BPO players had, it was inconceivable how RuralShores would have competed against them, even if it was able to deliver services at lower costs. It is here that the final innovative dimension of RuralShores' business model comes into play – instead of competing with large, urban BPOs, RuralShores was making efforts to become their trusted ally. RuralShores realized that if it was able to create a niche for itself in the BPO space, it need not compete with urban BPOs. Instead, it can provide them with complementary services.

Therefore, while urban BPOs focused on international clients, RuralShores decided to focus on local ones as well as providing services to local state governments. While urban BPOs provided English voice-based support (call centres) to international clients (among other services), RuralShores focused on transaction processing and providing multilingual support to Indian clients. Thus, RuralShores posed no competitive threat to large, urban BPOs. Instead, large BPO companies outsourced work to RuralShores because of its superior cost structure and involved it in joint bidding. It is possible that as RuralShores grows its business, some of the urban BPOs will start viewing it as a competitor. At that point, RuralShores' embeddedness in the rural context, a critical business attribute that it has been developing over a period of time, which its urban competitors will find extremely difficult to replicate in the short term, can become a source of sustainable competitive advantage.

GROWTH OPTIONS FOR RURALSHORES

Having established a viable business model, the key challenge before RuralShores was to scale it. Apart from creating more impact, scale would also provide RuralShores certain economies as well as enable it to provide its clients more options. The case mentions three possible growth options for RuralShores – setting up centres on its own, setting up centres in a CP model and increasing the scope of activities of each of its centres through business enablement services. While these growth options are not mutually exclusive, each of them has its challenges and advantages.

Establishing multiple centres on its own is expensive and time-consuming for RuralShores. Therefore, while this option provides maximum control over operations, it is likely to be a slow process, given the challenges of securing funds for investments. The benefits of the CP model, as explained in the case, are lower costs as well as being able to navigate the infrastructural challenges in contexts that were unfamiliar to RuralShores. The inherent diversity of India as a country implies that every village is different from the another, especially across states or regions. Thus, a process of managing infrastructure that worked in a village in Karnataka might not work at all in rural Rajasthan and it was necessary to have a partner at a local level to get the operations up and running quickly. The fact that there were several individuals and organizations keen to become its partners presented RuralShores with a significant opportunity for rapid expansion. In the CP model, in order to ensure consistent quality,

RuralShores retained control of the service delivery process while expecting the CP to manage the complexities and uncertainties associated with infrastructural issues. This seemed to be a win–win arrangement where each of the partners was operating from their position of strength. However, the CP model was not without its challenges.

The CP model was premised on the ability to replicate standardized processes. It was akin to a franchisee model though not exactly, because in RuralShores' model, the ownership of service delivery is retained by them. Shukla (2020) calls this model of growth as 'scaling out', where a partner is able to bring in its own resources, share costs and is able to customize the operating model to suit the local context. While this option of growth is cost-efficient, it has its set of challenges. The first challenge in this model is the identification of a suitable partner. The second and more important one is whether the CP model will result in the dilution of the welfare orientation of RuralShores. While the founding members of RuralShores are categorical that they were looking for partners who were not solely motivated by commercial objectives, it would not be easy for RuralShores to identify a CP's motive, especially given the fact that the CP's investment had reasonable financial attraction. Thus, while the CP model could work very well for a commercial organization such as McDonald's, it is doubtful whether a franchisee model would work well for a social enterprise such as RuralShores without diluting its welfare orientation. SELCO, as discussed in Chapter 6, learnt this the hard way when their franchisee model failed because of misalignment between the objectives of the organization and that of the franchise owners.

Going even a step further, did RuralShores need to retain control of the service delivery model as it grew or could it adopt a pure franchisee model where it trained the CP to run the core processes and maintained supervisory and advisory control over the franchisees? Did RuralShores even need to worry about welfare orientation so long as the franchisee generated employment for the rural youth, delivered high quality services and met its financial commitments? RuralShores definitely needed to worry about the welfare orientation of its franchisees because it was primarily a social enterprise and, while financial viability was important for them, their primary objective was positive impact and not profit maximization. This would require them to make difficult trade-offs at multiple stages of operation – something that might be difficult to enforce unless the partner is ideologically aligned with RuralShores. One of the reasons why social enterprises find it so difficult to scale is because, while it is relatively easy to scale processes and formats of operations, scaling ideology is extremely difficult and time-consuming.

The attractiveness of the business enablement model lies in increasing RuralShores' scope of activities. A typical RuralShores centre will create 100–150 jobs within a cluster of villages, which is small compared to the number of jobs that have to be created if one wanted to have a significant impact on the lives of people in those villages. Since its business model did not accommodate an increase in the number of seats, the business enablement model allowed RuralShores to leverage its local connection and knowledge for other kinds of businesses without disrupting its BPO operations. Thus, acting as a gateway to the villages and providing the last-mile connection to other organizations that wanted to target rural customers seems to be an attractive proposition. Moreover, given the flat organization structure of the centres, it will be difficult for RuralShores to offer career options to all its associates after a few years. If business enablement services were able to generate a variety of other livelihood options, it would be easier for RuralShores to outplace some of its senior associates.

However, the challenges in this model of growth are manifold. Investment in business enablement services might lead to a high degree of diversification in RuralShores' operations, something that a fledgling organization with a relatively thin layer of management might not be in a position to handle. RuralShores' various partners might have different objectives in targeting the rural segment, creating conflict of interest. Many of these opportunities involving feet-on-the-street will not be suitable for RuralShores' women employees and if it decided to get into such businesses, it will adversely impact the very nature of its organization. Thus, in a final assessment, the business enablement model, though promising, seems to be too complex at this point for RuralShores. Instead of acting as an end-to-end player, RuralShores should possibly get into businesses that have a significant component of transaction processing or multilingual support – activities where RuralShores has developed competencies.

REALITY CHECK

Where does RuralShores stand today in 2020, 12 years after its inception? It is still going strong, operating from 17 centres across 10 Indian states, employing about 2,500 people and servicing about 45 processes of 30 clients. Cumulatively, it trained close to 30,000 rural youth. However, growth has not been anywhere close to expectation. A discussion with the senior leadership indicated that some of their centres had to be shut down because of inadequate business, while in others it was difficult to attract talent, as the rural youth in those locations were more inclined towards running their own businesses than working for an organization. Moreover, migration to urban India remained aspirational. A significant part of RuralShores' business was dependent on the Indian telecommunication sector. As the growth in the sector reduced, the demand for BPO services also went down. Seeing the promise of a rural BPO, the Indian government launched the Digital India programme in 2014, with an investment commitment of INR 5 billion. It set a target of having 50,000 rural BPO seats and offered a subsidy of INR 100,000 per seat. Despite such subsidies, the uptake was 18,000 seats until March 2018 (Agarwal 2017), mostly from small companies who had either a single or only a few centres. Thus, RuralShores continues to be the leader in this domain, though the numbers indicate that business conditions have not been propitious for the rapid growth that was envisaged during its inception.

CHAPTER LEARNING

One of the ways of dealing with the unemployment problem in rural India is by creating non-farm jobs closer to villages. This will reduce large-scale migration to cities and enhance real income in poor households in rural India, given the low cost of living.

If BPO services can be delivered from semi-urban or rural locations, they can reduce the cost of service delivery as well as create non-farm employment closer to home. This would be beneficial, especially for young rural women who, unlike their male counterparts, find it difficult to migrate to cities for employment.

Compared to urban BPOs, rural BPOs can pay lower salaries to their employees. However, they need to make greater investment in training and for creating redundancies in utility infrastructure, such as electricity and telecommunication, to ensure business continuity.

Rural BPOs need to be sensitive to local traditions and culture in order to earn the trust and support of the local community. Without such support, they will find it difficult to attract or retain employees, most of whom will be unfamiliar with their mode of operations.

Rural BPOs need to innovate across multiple dimensions in their operating model. For example, they need to operate in a highly decentralized mode, keeping each of their centres small in size. This will prevent them from deriving economies of scale when compared to urban BPOs.

Rural BPOs need to deliver high quality services that are comparable to any urban BPO. They are unlikely to get concessions from their customers in service quality because of the inclusive nature of their business.

Rural BPOs should seek ways of collaboration with urban BPOs, rather than competing with them. Collaboration is feasible because of certain unique capabilities that rural BPOs can develop, such as providing voice-based support in vernacular languages.

Rural BPOs can grow through partnerships with local institutions or individuals in a franchisee mode. While the organization still retains control over operations, partners provide them with financial resources and deal with local issues, such as provision of adequate infrastructure and attracting potential employees.

11

GUJARAT NARMADA FERTILIZER COMPANY'S (GNFC) NEEM INITIATIVE

A Social Business

Nobel laureate Muhammad Yunus pioneered the term 'social business', defining it as 'a no-dividend company dedicated to solving human problems' (Yunus 2017). Conceptually, social businesses are very similar to inclusive business models that we have described so far in the book. However, the examples given by Dr Yunus are about social businesses that are incubated as ventures within or by for-profit enterprises, such as Grameen Danone created by Groupe Danone of France. Thus, these inclusive businesses are created in a unique context, where being conceived by a commercial entity results in some advantages as well as some new challenges for them. In this chapter, we will talk about one such initiative undertaken by the Gujarat Narmada Fertilizer Company (GNFC).

GNFC is one of the large chemical and fertilizer companies in India, with a turnover of INR 61 billion in the 2017–18 financial year. GNFC was established in 1976 with the primary purpose of manufacturing urea and nitrogenous fertilizers. By 2017–18, though it had diversified into energy and information technology, 90 per cent of its revenue and profits came from fertilizer and chemicals, with urea being one of its most important products. In India, urea is a government-subsidized commodity, meant to be used by farmers as an essential fertilizer in agriculture.[1] However, significant quantities of subsidized

---

[1] The Government of India regulated both the price and production volumes of urea. Urea was sold at a subsidized price to farmers, with the difference between the selling price and the cost of production reimbursed to farmers by the government. To keep the subsidy bill low, the government imposed limits on production volumes, a process known as reassessed capacity. As

urea used to be diverted from farming for use in chemical factories as low-cost input, often resulting in shortage of urea for agriculture.[2]

A few years ago, a report prepared by the Agricultural Development and Rural Transformation Centre, Bengaluru, suggested that coating urea with neem[3] oil would improve soil health and reduce pests and crop disease, thereby decreasing the need to use pesticides. More significantly, it would also make the urea unusable for non-fertilizer applications, and thus prevent diversion (Ramappa and Manjunatha 2017).

Apart from preventing diversion, the coating of urea with neem oil was expected to increase usage efficiency by preventing the evaporation of urea into the atmosphere and its leaching into the soil and water. It was estimated that more than half of the nitrogen present in urea was not assimilated by crops because of various factors, including ammonia volatilization. Neem had properties that reduced losses by slowing down the process of nitrate formation. All these factors resulted in cost-savings to the farmer, as well as reduced environmental damage otherwise caused by the excessive application of chemicals and fertilizers. It took quite some time for this research to make its way to policy makers, until 2012, when the Government of India issued an advisory that all urea manufacturers were required to coat at least 35 per cent of their production with neem oil. Prime Minister Narendra Modi, the then chief minister of Gujarat, was very keen to prevent the diversion of subsidized urea and had written several letters to the central government asking for an increase in the quantum of neem coating to 100 per cent of production

---

a result, domestic production of urea (about 25 million tonnes per year in 2012) fell short of demand (about 32 million tonnes per year in 2012) and the balance had to be imported. In April 2017, the government relaxed production limits of urea to reduce India's import dependency. In 2016–17, the total subsidy provided by the government was INR 182 billion on domestic production and INR 123 billion on imported urea (Das 2017).

[2] The extent of diversion was estimated at 30–40 per cent (approximately 9 million tonnes), both to chemical factories in India and neighbouring countries of Bangladesh, Nepal and Sri Lanka (Gupta 2016).

[3] Neem, common term for *Azadirachta indica*, is a tree in the mahogany family that is native to the Indian sub-continent.

because it was felt that the 35 per cent coating requirement was neither being implemented by most manufacturers nor was it adequately effective in curbing diversion. Fertilizer was a central subject in India, and thus the states did not have any leeway in implementing an enhanced urea coating policy on their own. Therefore, after Modi became the Prime Minister, it did not take long for the government to mandate that 100 per cent of the urea produced in the country be coated with neem oil. Once the policy was implemented, there was a decline in sales of urea and consequently in imports.

GNFC'S FORAY INTO NEEM SEED COLLECTION

Dr Rajiv K. Gupta, a member of the Gujarat cadre of Indian Administrative Services, took over as the managing director of GNFC in May 2013. Prior to this appointment, Dr Gupta had closely worked with Prime Minister Narendra Modi. Being aware of the emerging policy direction, Dr Gupta began laying the groundwork at GNFC to be ready for 100 per cent neem coating of urea very early in his tenure. Until then, it was the usual practice for urea-producing companies to purchase neem oil from private players in the open market. The neem oil that was sold in the market was often adulterated with rice bran oil or palm oil and then topped up with azadirachtin.[4] Dr Gupta was unhappy when a file came to him seeking approval for the purchase of neem oil at INR 92 per kilogram for coating urea, which, he felt, was much too expensive. He asked his team to explore the possibility of GNFC producing the neem oil it needed in-house. His proposal was not readily accepted by his team, who argued that extraction of neem oil was not a core activity for a large fertilizer and chemical company like GNFC. Dr Gupta, however, persisted and encouraged his people to visit oil mills and study the process of extracting

---

[4] Azadirachtin is a chemical compound found in seeds of the neem tree, *Azadirachta indica*. It fulfils many criteria needed of a good insecticide, is biodegradable and shows very low toxicity to mammals. Oil derived from neem seeds contains other insecticidal and fungicidal components apart from azadirachtin. See https://en.wikipedia.org/wiki/Azadirachtin (accessed 20 February 2018).

oil from neem seeds. They reported that it was indeed possible to set up an oil mill by investing a relatively small sum of INR 6.5–7 million, and that the process and operations involved appeared to be quite simple. Meanwhile, Dr Gupta also started to leverage his connections in the various government departments that he had led as a senior bureaucrat, with a view to ensuring adequate support for the novel initiative that GNFC sought to launch.

It was decided that GNFC would purchase neem seeds from individual collectors and process them to extract oil. While GNFC would start their operations by outsourcing the extraction activity to oil-millers, they would shift to in-house production as soon as they could commission their own expeller plant. It was, however, not easy convincing millers to produce oil from neem seeds because neem oil has a strong odour and was non-edible, and millers were afraid that if they used their mills for extraction of the oil, their machinery would become unusable for other extraction. Finally, after much persuasion, GNFC could identify one miller whose soya extraction plant was lying idle, and he became their steady partner.

The first challenge for GNFC was to establish a network for the collection of neem seeds. Communities had to be persuaded and trained to collect the seeds and a network of entrepreneurs who would be willing to purchase seeds from the collectors and deliver them to GNFC's drying and extraction units had to be established. GNFC already had a well-established fertilizer product distribution network in rural Gujarat, which they decided to leverage to source neem seeds. At the grassroots level, GNFC established Village Level Collection Centres (VLCCs) that were run by rural entrepreneurs. GNFC also appointed Service Provider Partners (SPPs) – another set of entrepreneurs who would transfer the seeds to intermediate drying and storage facilities or directly to the oil extraction mills.

Neem seeds have to be collected during a limited time window of 45 to 60 days prior to the onset of the rains, usually between May and July. Once the rainy season sets in, collection is not feasible, as neem seeds were either washed away or soaked and too soft to be of use. Thus, neem seeds were collected during the peak summer months, making this labour-intensive process even more arduous. Typically, seed collectors came from impoverished backgrounds and were usually women, often from lower castes. Anecdotal evidence suggested that people from the upper castes, even if impoverished, were unwilling to get involved in the collection of neem seeds. GNFC, through their agricultural extension network and sales personnel, was already well-embedded in rural Gujarat. Often, GNFC worked with village-level women's self-help groups (SHGs) – an endemic feature in Gujarat – and development organizations to reach out to agriculturalists as well as landless labourers. The neem team leveraged this existing network first to evangelize the benefits of seed collection and, subsequently, to set up supply-chain operations at the grassroots.

Seed collection operations involved women and, in some instances, men and children, foraging in and around their villages, individually or collectively, to gather as many seeds as possible and to bring them to the VLCC at the end of the day. At the centre, their collection was weighed, and they were paid in cash. The purchase price for neem seeds, which was announced daily, was set by GNFC, which was well above what private aggregators offered.

While the process of collection was reasonably standard across the districts in which they operated, there were some differences at the operation level, depending on the location and norms of the community. For example, at Kesarpura village, women gathered seeds from within the village, as they had to tend to their households as well as farm animals and could, therefore, only sporadically engage in collection activities during the day. In the village of Devkaran-Na-Muvada, collection activity was orchestrated by the SPPs, who owned several tempo travellers – small commercial transport vehicles. During the season, groups of people travelled in these vehicles, sometimes as far as 100 kilometres from their villages, collecting seeds and bringing back their collection to the VLCC at the end of the day, often even as late as midnight. The SPP charged them a daily fixed rate, INR 150 per person, for transportation. The quantity of seeds collected by individuals varied considerably and ranged from 5 to 20 kilograms per day.

Almost none of the seed collectors owned any land and had low levels of education and no lasting means of livelihood. The villages where they lived did not have access to irrigation and were thus growing one crop a year during the rainy season. Apart from their seasonal involvement as labourers during the sowing and harvesting seasons, seed collectors engaged in odd jobs provided by the informal sector, earning on average not more than INR 200 for four hours of labour.

Prior to GNFC's neem initiative, some of them collected seeds that were sold to private players, who paid them not more than INR 1–2 per kilogram.

GNFC's VLCC paid them, on average, INR 6–7 per kilogram; additionally, they felt that they received a fair deal in terms of weights. The dual effect of better rates and a fair weighing process made collectors allegiant to GNFC. For several women, collections and, therefore, their income from neem seeds increased rapidly. A few of them became aggregators, arranging for working capital finance from other sources, and collecting from multiple SHGs. Some of them used the money so earned to get back or buy land, while others became entrepreneurs by purchasing sewing machines or *papad*[5]-making machines.

Laxmiben Ajitsinh Dabhi, a 48-year-old mother of three from Chhipiyal village in Kheda district, was one such entrepreneur who aggregated 30 tonnes of seeds collected by about 100 women and transported them to the Kapadwanj APMC[6] in 2017. That year, while the collectors were paid INR 7.5 per kilogram, Laxmiben earned close to INR 15,000 as commission at the rate of INR 0.5 per kilogram. This substantially added to her annual income of INR 36,000 that she usually earned by sewing clothes and selling milk (Damodaran 2017).

A United National Development Programme (UNDP) study[7] that assessed the impact of GNFC's neem project noted that a significant number of rural women in Gujarat worked as agricultural labourers, were from economically backward families and were illiterate. They faced considerable financial difficulty during the post-harvest lean period. The project increased the annual income of agricultural labourers by as much as INR 7,000, providing an incremental livelihood opportunity during the lean season. This represented an increase of 58 per cent over their annual income of INR 12,000. Anecdotally, this resulted in reduced migration, greater empowerment of women, reduced violence at home and increased their ability to invest in assets, such as livestock and stoves.

---

[5] *Papad* or *papadam* is an Indian food based on seasoned dough made from gram, lentil or rice flour. It is often associated with the empowerment of women because *papad* is mostly produced by individual and unorganized businesses run by women. *Papad*-making requires minimal investment and provides a steady source of income, and is, therefore, a very popular activity across most parts of India.

[6] APMC stands for Agricultural Product Market Committees.

[7] *Assessment of GNFC's Neem Project*, January 2017.

However, it was not a smooth ride for GNFC in several other locations, where, despite all their efforts, they could not convince the villagers to get into the collection of neem seeds. In some villages, they had to adopt innovative means. For example, in Devkarn village, where people were not enthused enough to collect seeds on their own, GNFC decided to hire them as labourers at INR 200 per day for the same activity. At the end of the day, when their collections were weighed, villagers realized that they would have made more money had they opted to collect and sell the seeds themselves, rather than being hired by the company.

Soon, they switched over to becoming independent collectors. In Biliya village, when awareness campaigns did not yield any result, the GNFC team decided to exhibit neem seeds at a prominent place in the village. This attracted the attention of children, who, on enquiry, were told that GNFC would pay them money if they collected neem seeds. The children took to seed collection as a game, and when they started to make some money, it attracted the attention of their parents. Subsequently, the adults were convinced about the potential in seed collection and engaged in this activity.

With each passing year, the villagers gained more confidence that the collection of neem seeds could be an important activity for them, especially in areas where there were limited or no alternative livelihood opportunities. While some of them became more enterprising in identifying areas where they could garner substantial collection, others cleared the ground under the neem trees during the season to ensure that collection was made easy. There were also some indications that villagers were becoming conscious of the economic value of neem seeds and, consequently, restricted others from doing so in areas that they felt belonged to them. However, given that the earning opportunity from neem seed collection spanned only for 1.5–2 months in a year, none of them viewed this as a steady livelihood opportunity, and women in some Sakhi Mandals[8] often requested GNFC to set up manufacturing or processing operations that could employ them and provide income throughout the year.

---

[8] Sakhi Mandal Yojna is a government initiative for the empowerment of women, especially in rural Gujarat. It involved organizing women in groups and providing them necessary assistance, such as training and finance, so that they could earn their livelihood and become financially independent.

The SPPs were the link between the seed collectors and GNFC. Unlike the seed collectors, SPPs were financially sound. Once the seeds were transported and the delivery information recorded, GNFC paid the SPP 80 per cent of the procurement price through RTGS[9] electronic funds transfer system set up by the government. The balance payment was settled after a few days, once the invoice was raised after final valuation. With their turnover from neem seed operations ranging between INR 10 million and 20 million, SPPs were able to make a net profit of INR 200,000–400,000, over and above their income from the sale of other GNFC products. For example, Pankaj Patel, a GNFC fertilizer dealer and SPP at Kapadwanj APMC, sourced 1,200 metric tonnes of seeds from about 3,000 VLCCs (such as Laxmiben), screened, weighed, bagged and transported them to GNFC storage warehouses. He received a commission of INR 0.25 per kilogram (Damodaran 2017). In 2017, it was estimated that GNFC involved 225,000 seed collectors and generated employment for about 125,000 people through this initiative.

FROM UREA COATING TO SOAP MANUFACTURING

Once seed collection and oil production were stabilized, GNFC realized that they were producing more neem oil than they required for the coating of urea. Moreover, the neem oil obtained from cold-press expellers had far higher azadirachtin levels than was necessary for the coating. Therefore, they had to find a way to utilize the excess neem oil, which was of high quality. Dr Gupta suggested that his team should utilize the excess oil to produce soap. He approved an investment of about INR 2 million for setting up a soap manufacturing plant.

The GNFC team visited different manufacturing units, observed the process and set up their own unit in about two months' time. They decided to employ women from economically challenged backgrounds, who were selected from SHGs and trained in soap making. In January 2016, GNFC's soap unit became operational. The research and development team at GNFC was involved in product and process development. While experimenting with

---

[9] Real time gross settlement – a method of transferring funds electronically.

various product options, the team also decided to produce and sell neem oil, which was technically more complex than making soap.

GNFC launched its first products, GNFC Neem Soap and GNFC Neem Oil, in September 2016. With 21 per cent oil content, GNFC's products were far superior to most other herbal products in the market, especially since other products contained neem extracts produced using benzene as a solvent. GNFC's research and development team continued to experiment with different product variants and in April 2017, it launched Neem Hand Wash, then followed it up with an organic pesticide in July and shampoo in September. In the interim, they also launched different variants of soap. In December 2017, GNFC launched Neem Mosquito Repellent. While most other repellents available in the market were based on chemicals such as tansfluthrin that could be harmful to human beings, GNFC's neem oil-based repellent did not have any known harmful effects.

Simultaneously, GNFC started setting up its sales channels. They tied up with commercial retail outlets, such as Big Bazaar and Star Bazaar, as well as with those run by central and state governments, such as Central Police Canteens and Kendriya Bhandars. GNFC also established many exclusive retail outlets in select cities to target health-conscious consumers and procured permission from municipalities to set up Neem Parlours in public gardens across the cities of Ahmedabad and Surat. Starting in the middle of 2017, GNFC's neem products were also made available through popular e-commerce sites, such as Flipkart, Amazon and eBay. GNFC enlisted its fertilizer dealers with retail outlets to carry and sell neem products in rural areas and contemplated ways to utilize their SHG networks to penetrate the rural market. In December 2017, GNFC signed an agreement with the Gujarat State Civil Services Corporation to facilitate the distribution of its neem products through 17,000 fair price shops across 33 districts and 248 *taluka*s in Gujarat. If one considered the 3,000 private retail outlets that also carried its consumer products, GNFC's neem products were thus available in about 21,000 retail outlets by the end of 2017.

GNFC did not resort to advertising, and most of their sales were prompted by word-of-mouth publicity, leveraging the positioning that neem enjoyed as a traditional product, especially in rural India. Plans for the release of advertising campaigns were in the offing, waiting for the time when GNFC would be able to make its products widely available across a national retail network. By the end of the 2017 financial year, neem products gave GNFC revenues of INR 150 million. It was made clear to the team that while losses would be incurred in the early days of such a business, they must break even and create a surplus. All such surplus would, however, be continuously reinvested in the business.

Most of GNFC's marketing efforts were focused on being present in fairs and exhibitions as well as leveraging its existing channels in rural areas. Both neem as a product and GNFC as an organization enjoyed high credibility in rural markets, which resulted in its products commanding a premium price. Given the high neem oil content in its products, GNFC consciously adopted a strategy of positioning its products based on purity and quality rather than price and remained flexible while sharing margins with its trade partners. GNFC realized that product sales opened greater opportunities for them to touch the lives of the poor and the landless. The more they sold, the more neem seeds would be required, which, in turn, would provide income to a larger number of collectors. Moreover, the new production plants and sales outlets would also create livelihood opportunities for them.

GNFC's foray into the FMCG market with neem-based products coincided with a rising wave of interest in natural products and ingredients in the Indian market. The natural product segment in India's personal care market, with estimated revenues of USD 3 billion per annum, was fiercely competed for by well-established players, such as Unilever India, Dabur, the Himalaya Drug Company, Colgate Palmolive and Patanjali. While Colgate Palmolive focused on product innovations to grow its Naturals portfolio, Unilever India acquired the ayurvedic brand Indulekha and Ayush to re-launch its flagship products in this segment. However, it was Patanjali Ayurveda that successfully created a brand around its founder, yoga guru Baba Ramdev, which was considered a trailblazer. Having surpassed a turnover of USD 1 billion within a few years of its inception, Patanjali harboured ambitions to become the number-one FMCG company in India (Sachitanand 2017).

From 2017, GNFC started sourcing neem seeds from other Indian states. The southern state of Karnataka, with close to 30 million neem trees, was potentially a rich source. GNFC reached out to seed collectors there through dairy cooperatives, not-for-profit organizations and health promotion boards. The plan was to send the seeds collected in Karnataka to an extraction unit in

Anantapur, in the neighbouring state of Andhra Pradesh, from where extracted oil would be sold to chemical and fertilizer companies. By the end of 2017, GNFC had collected close to 5,000 metric tonnes of seeds from other states.

GNFC's neem initiative is an interesting case of an inclusive business created by a commercial enterprise. While GNFC started collecting neem seeds to coat urea and prevent its diversion, since neem oil-based products could be sold in the market, it created the possibility of making the initiative a financially sustainable business. As in the case of Grameen Danone described by Dr Yunus, such an initiative not only made a positive impact on the lives of the poor but also created a lot of excitement and enthusiasm among the employees of GNFC, which can be a powerful way of engaging and leveraging their talent. However, it also creates some dilemma for the organization. Let us, therefore, look at the advantages and disadvantages of inclusive businesses that are created by for-profit enterprises.

INCLUSIVE BUSINESS CREATED BY COMMERCIAL ENTERPRISES: ADVANTAGES AND CHALLENGES

The most significant advantage of an inclusive business created by a large for-profit enterprise is its ability to access resources. Entrepreneurial organizations suffer from liability of newness[10] and have high failure rates because they do not have access to adequate human and financial resources. However, if they are incubated by a large establishment, they can leverage its financial and human resources, especially if the inclusive business is well aligned with the business objective of the larger organization and is being driven from the top. In the case of GNFC, both these conditions were fulfilled – neem oil had direct relevance for one of GNFC's key products, urea, and the neem initiative was being driven directly by Dr Gupta, the managing director.

Having been into production and sale of urea for a long time, most employees of GNFC were aware of the problem of subsidized urea being

---

[10] Stinchcombe (1965) introduced the term *liability of newness* to indicate the struggles for survival that young organizations face during the first few years of their lifecycle. For a more current review, see Cafferata et al. (2009).

illegally diverted instead of being sold to the farmers. Neem coating of urea was an effective solution to prevent such diversion, thereby making the collection of neem seeds and extracting oil a necessary upstream activity. Several examples from organizations across the world has shown that when a for-profit commercial enterprise is involved in CSR or developmental activities that are directly relevant for their main line of business (for example, a producer of dairy products involved in making nutrition fortified yoghurt for the economically underprivileged), the chances of success and sustainability of that developmental activity is far higher than when such an activity does not have direct relevance for their main line of business[11] (for instance, the same dairy producer investing in educating the economically underprivileged). In GNFC's case, alignment to their main line of business helped the neem initiative in the following ways.

GNFC had a deep connection to the rural community, which enabled them to understand and establish an operational network both for the sourcing of neem seeds and selling neem oil-based products. They understood the need for the economically underprivileged to have a livelihood and effectively utilized developmental organizations or NGOs to communicate the potential benefits as well as to establish the supply chain comprising the seed-collectors and the service providers. Engaging in commercial transactions, especially with the economically underprivileged, takes considerable time. Such communities who have traditionally been exploited are usually apprehensive about strangers. Since GNFC and their personnel were familiar faces in the villages, and even the grassroots organizations considered the neem initiative as a livelihood opportunity, it was not very difficult for GNFC to earn the trust of the community and enroll them in the collection drive. They were also aware of what the community valued – fairness in pricing and an assurance that their collection would be purchased by GNFC and were thus able to capture the attention and imagination of the community.

---

[11] For example, Porter and Kramer (2011) argued that CSR activities should be integrated with firm strategy and mainstreamed with day-to-day business activities. For a review of CSR's link to business, see Carol and Shabana (2010).

GNFC was able to absorb a significant part of the developmental costs because of its size and access to resources. For example, GNFC's retail outlets in rural Gujarat were used to sell neem oil and neem cake-based products. A considerable part of the same network was used to source neem seeds. If GNFC had to establish this network from scratch, it would have required a lot of investment. However, because they were selling the neem oil-based products to the same customers who bought fertilizers as well as sourcing the neem seeds from the same community, GNFC could utilize economies of scope of their existing distribution network.

Finally, one of their key advantages was that the initiative was being driven by the managing director. Dr Gupta conceptualized and drove the initiative, constantly persuading and encouraging the employees to get it off the ground as well as to make it successful. Being a senior bureaucrat, he was aware of the policy direction and could sense that an initiative such as neem coating would receive enough attention and encouragement from the government if he was able to get it done. He also used his contacts in the industry and bureaucracy to remove hurdles that might have otherwise delayed the initiative. Such a commitment from the top motivated the next level of leaders and thus ensured that the energy percolated throughout the organization. Within the organization, when doubts were raised about whether GNFC should invest time and resources in extracting neem oil when the oil was available in the market from third-party producers, Dr Gupta was able to use his influence, persuasion capacity and conviction to remove such doubts. Nor was there any hesitation on his part to invest financial resources for experimentation that was necessary during the initial phase.

However, this advantage of being driven from the top can become a disadvantage if the enthusiasm is not widely shared by the second line of leaders. Moreover, managing directors in public sector enterprises like GNFC have time-based tenures. Therefore, one is not sure whether a niche initiative such as this will survive once Dr Gupta moves away from GNFC to his next assignment. Will the new managing director be as committed to the neem project, given that its turnover is miniscule compared to GNFC's overall turnover, if she or he feels that the initiative was taking disproportionate time and resources? While GNFC had made some commitment by investing in plant and machinery for the project, it was insignificant compared to their total asset base and it will not be too difficult for the next managing director to write them off as CSR spend. Will there be enough voices in the organization that will support the continuance of the project if someone from the top wanted to reduce the organizational commitment?

The second challenge might be GNFC's ability to provide resources and support to the neem project as it starts to scale up, increasing its demand on GNFC's resources. GNFC seems to have got into the FMCG business almost as an afterthought, to make use of excess oil. The FMCG market in India is extremely competitive with established brands. GNFC was not a pioneer in selling products on the organic or natural platform, neither did it have any particular competitive advantage. As long as they remained a small player in the market, they might be ignored by the established companies. However, if they wanted to scale up their operation, they would start eating into the share of competitors and there was likely to be retaliation. Will GNFC be able to compete in a market where they do not have any experience or competency? Moreover, the products they were selling will possibly have maximum demand in urban areas, while GNFC's experience was in selling to mostly rural customers. Therefore, at this stage, the odds seemed to be stacked heavily against GNFC in becoming successful in the FMCG market at a greater scale of operation.

The other concern about scalability arises from the fact that until date, the neem initiative had enjoyed a considerable degree of internal subsidy across several parts of the value chain, such as sourcing, distribution and research and development. Surplus capacity and existing infrastructure from its main line of business was used to carry out activities for the neem project and some costs were absorbed by its CSR arm, Narmadanagar Rural Development Society (NARDES).[12] While this was feasible for an activity that was reasonably small, it may not be if the demand for time and resources increased because of the increasing scale. Once those costs were computed and allocated to the neem project, as would have been the case if GNFC owned an independent FMCG

---

[12] NARDES was an autonomous GNFC-sponsored not-for-profit that implemented various CSR projects in areas such as education, healthcare, sanitation and skill development.

company, it would become clear whether the initiative could be pursued as an independent business and whether it made sense to be scaled.

Rather than scaling its FMCG business, an option available to GNFC is to sell the excess oil to an existing FMCG company involved in the manufacturing and selling of soaps and shampoos. That approach will not significantly reduce the social impact that GNFC was creating because they will still involve the rural poor in collecting the seeds. However, it will take away the burden of getting into a market GNFC was unfamiliar with and did not seem to be well suited to compete in.

COMPARISON WITH STAND-ALONE INCLUSIVE BUSINESSES

Most other examples discussed in this book are about stand-alone inclusive businesses. How do they compare with GNFC's neem initiative in creating and sustaining an inclusive business? When an inclusive business is incubated by a for-profit enterprise, a lot of questions might be raised by its various stakeholders about the need and legitimacy of the initiative. When such enterprises intend to do some social work, the usual mode of doing it is through CSR. This implies that there is no expectation of generating revenue or creating a business model out of the same. Creating a business model usually would take a lot more effort than doing a CSR activity. Therefore, various stakeholders might question the dedication of additional time and resources to such an activity. We find evidence of this in GNFC in its initial days when some employees and even the senior management questioned its foray into neem seed collection. Since the initiative was driven by Dr Gupta himself, he was able to convince the stakeholders that the initiative should be run as a business rather than a CSR activity.

Once the initiative is started as a social business, the challenge will be to deal with the different logic of social business from for-profit business. While the for-profit business is focused on maximizing profitability, the goal of the social business is to maximize social impact while maintaining financial sustainability. A stand-alone social business does not need to deal with multiplicity of logic. This can lead to confusion, apathy, lack of acceptance, apprehension and resistance towards the social business. It might also have the effect of disproportionate effort being spent on the social business and the for-profit commercial business being neglected. While we do not see evidence of this in GNFC yet, possibly because the neem initiative is still in its early days, the senior management must ensure that it maintains a balance of effort between its fertilizer and chemical business and its neem initiative. A stand-alone social business need not worry about maintaining such a balance between these two kinds of businesses.

The advantages of an existing for-profit enterprise incubating a social business may be many, such as access to financial and human resources as well as existing distribution channels and being able to leverage an existing brand. All of these are evident in the case of GNFC, who has used its sales and relational network in villages for sourcing neem seeds as well as for distributing neem oil-based products. All its investments have been financed from internal resources and GNFC's existing employees, and its senior management have taken the additional responsibility of driving the neem project. Thus, GNFC did not need to make much of the initial investments that a social business starting on its own would have. However, these advantages might disappear as the initiative scales and starts demanding more resources from the parent organization. This can lead to either an inability to scale or dilution of the social mission.

GNFC's social mission is to improve the income of the poor. One of the ways in which this mission can get defeated is if the intermediaries in the value chain, namely the SPPs, become powerful and exploitative, as is often seen in agricultural supply chains in India. The SPPs, who were economically well-off and were making some investments (for example, storage facilities and transportation vehicles) had the maximum bargaining power. They were also the ones who were being paid by GNFC directly and they, in turn, were expected to provide the seed collectors with their share. Given the power differential between the SPPs and the seed collectors, GNFC would have to be careful in monitoring them and ensuring that they did not indulge in exploitative practices. Typically, such monitoring is easier when the scale of operations is small. However, with increasing scale, it would be difficult for GNFC to keep a close watch on transactions at such a micro level, which might result in their social impact getting diluted.

Among the Indian social enterprises, Amul[13] is possibly the most celebrated example of having scaled successfully without diluting its social objective. While there are several reasons for that, important among them was the fact that Amul was structured as a cooperative. Learning from them, GNFC might need to encourage the neem collectors to form a producer cooperative and buy directly from them. This would involve greater involvement from GNFC in dealing with the complexities of establishing such enterprises and it needs to be evaluated whether it makes sense for them to do so from their larger business standpoint. There is no doubt that every stand-alone inclusive business also faces the challenge of dealing with potential dilution of the mission as it scales its organization. The micro-lending businesses described in Chapter 4 were one such example. However, such possibilities are greater for inclusive businesses that are incubated by large commercial enterprises whose basic business logic is structured around scale and profitability rather than social impact. This may be the reason why initiatives such as GNFC's remains an exception till date, even while we find a large number of stand-alone inclusive business models.

---

[13] Amul is the popular brand of Gujarat Cooperative Milk Marketing Federation, India's largest diary organization with a turnover of USD 4.5 billion. See http://www.amul.com/m/organisation (accessed 11 October 2018).

CHAPTER LEARNING

For-profit public enterprises can create or incubate an inclusive business model within its fold by sourcing products from suppliers who are economically underprivileged.

Large public enterprises have an advantage of creating inclusive businesses, given the resources that they already possess, such as access to customers, sourcing and distribution infrastructure and legitimacy to earn trust of various stakeholders and communities necessary to establish the business.

Even if an initiative can generate income for the poor, apprehensions about large enterprises, caste considerations and other local norms might prevent them from taking up such opportunities. Thus, enterprises need to find ways to attract potential suppliers and convince them that they will get a fair deal when they supply to the enterprise.

While generating income even for a short period is beneficial for the poor, enterprises should try to create a stream of predictable income throughout the year for the supplier. Engagements that are sporadic in nature are difficult to sustain.

A well-resourced public enterprise can leverage its internal resources to build an inclusive business model rapidly. However, such internal subsidies can create problems of scaling the business, especially if the inclusive business does not happen to be the main line of business for the enterprise.

For long-term sustainability of the inclusive business, such public enterprises should be careful about getting into unfamiliar business domains for which they may not have the necessary competencies.

12

BRINGING IT ALL TOGETHER

The for-profit model of social enterprises has its share of criticism. For example, Anand Giridharadas (2019) argues that the market-driven capitalistic system is largely responsible for creating the inequality that we see around us. Social enterprises are attempting to solve problems of poverty and inequality by embracing principles of market. However, it is unrealistic to expect that the same market mechanisms will be able to solve the problems of inequality that were created in the first place because of them. Market mechanisms will only ensure status quo of inequality and shift the focus away from the responsibility of the government and regulations. Almost a similar argument was made by Karnani in his criticism of Prahlad's *fortune at the bottom of the pyramid* model, which we discussed in the first chapter. While the social entrepreneurs discussed in this book cannot be blamed for inequalities of the capitalistic system by any stretch of imagination, Giridharadas's argument definitely has a lot of merit. For example, the distress that was witnessed in the Indian microfinance sector, as discussed in Chapter 4, can be viewed as a direct consequence of applying market principles to the sector, which subordinated the social objectives with which microlending was started. Likewise, SELCO's founder Harish Hande has very often spoken about the expectation of markets regarding scale to achieve financial sustainability. In one of the private conversations, he noted that while SELCO was often told to 'scale up to be financially sustainable', a large global bank had to fire 11,000 of its employees across multiple geographies to remain financially viable. Thus, there are multiple examples of organizations needing to 'scale down to be financially sustainable'. One must be careful about the extent one wants to apply market principles to govern social enterprises because, in many cases, wisdom of the markets might do more harm than good.

ROLE OF DIFFERENT ORGANIZATION FORMS

While almost all the case studies discussed in this book are about social enterprises that intend to be financially viable by embracing many market-based principles and·best practices of commercial enterprises, they are by no means the panacea for solving the problems of poverty and inequality. Time and again, we have noticed the limitations of inclusive business models in solving certain kinds of problems. Moreover, the objective of remaining financially viable imposes constraints on these organizations' central mission of helping the poor and making a positive social impact. In extreme cases, this can lead to mission dilution. Therefore, we should not consider them in isolation but understand the roles played by various kinds of organizational forms in the overall business and institutional ecosystem, where inclusive businesses are one kind. If one is able to delineate and discern the advantages and disadvantages of each of these organizational forms, it will be easier for entrepreneurs, organizational leaders and policy makers to understand what each of them will be best suited to doing to add real value to society in general and to the underserved population in particular. With that intention, I propose the following schematic that considers four broad categories of organizations, each of which has an important role to play in society for alleviation of poverty and reduction of inequality. These are government-run organizations, not-for-profits, inclusive businesses and for-profit commercial enterprises.

Many scholars have argued that it is primarily the role of the government to take care of the poor. Some of them have even argued that as an unintended consequence of the development work done by not-for-profits and social enterprises, governments are abdicating their responsibility and not doing what they need to do. Without getting into that debate, let us assume that the government itself is an economic entity that largely gets involved in activities that do not generate a revenue stream commensurate with the costs that are incurred to do those activities. For example, schools that cater to children from poor households are unlikely to make enough revenue to cover their expenses.

Therefore, it is argued that such schools should be run by the government.[1] How does the government finance such expenses? It is through collection of taxes. Thus, taxes imposed by the government are a means of cross-subsidy where a part of the income generated by well-off individuals and profitable businesses are used to subsidize essential public services, such as defence, infrastructure and the needs of the poor. The government's biggest advantage is its scale of operations. It possesses a well-established infrastructure, both hard and soft, for collection of taxes as well as for dispensing of services. There is possibly no other institution or organization that is in a position to create impact at scale like the government.

However, governments, especially in countries like India, have three disadvantages. First, it is perennially under-resourced. The tax revenue that it collects is not enough to meet the various needs of the nation. For example, governments across the globe spend about 6 per cent of their GDP in meeting the healthcare needs of their nations. However, historically, the Indian government has not been able to allocate more than 1 per cent for healthcare, the remaining being done by private providers of healthcare, which has its attendant consequences. Second, the government machinery is often found to be bureaucratic, slow to react to needs and relatively inefficient. While there are a host of reasons for these, for any organization, there is an inverse relationship between its size and adaptability. Larger the organizations, more the rules and regulations they need to operate within, which make them slow and sometimes inefficient. Finally, there is often a trust deficit that exists between the citizens and the government because of instances of corruption. One is not sure how the government will be using the money that one pays as taxes, whether it will be used to purchase anti-submarine guns or to supply food grains to the needy or whether it will be part of the leakage that is characteristic of activities done by the government. Therefore, in general citizens are found to be reluctant to pay taxes and explore means to avoid paying them, legally or even illegally, adding to the first problem of the government being unable to match demand for resources with the tax revenue.

---

[1] There are other ideological reasons advanced for the necessity of education and healthcare to be run by the government, but we do not need to delve into them here.

Not-for-profits have traditionally stepped in to service those needs of the society that the government has not been able to service. They have been involved in various kinds of activities, such as giving voice to the poor, lobbying on their behalf before the government, building communities, enabling them to form organizations of their own that have good governance norms as well as providing services such as education, healthcare and energy access, most of which do not have any revenue model. Even if there is one, it is not enough to cover the expenses of the not-for-profit. In that sense, not-for-profits are perpetually making losses, their expenses being substantially higher than their revenues. Therefore, they raise funds through grants and donations, which is conceptually equivalent to a cross-subsidy, a mechanism to transfer some amount of income from economically well-off individuals and profitable organizations to finance the needs of the poor.

Why are not-for-profits able to raise funds and deliver these services when the government is unable to do it? An important reason is that the not-for-profits are able to close the loop in the mind of the donors because of their focus and smaller size. Most not-for-profits are focused on a specific service, such as education for the girl child or providing employment to persons with disability. It is, therefore, able to attract donations from individuals and organizations[2] that emotionally connect to the cause as well as able to show the positive impact that such a donation is making in the lives of the beneficiary. Given their small size compared to government organizations, they are able to customize both their messages for the donor and their services for the beneficiary, which leads to a better matching of demand and supply[3] and, eventually, greater effectiveness of their services.

At the other end of the spectrum are for-profit commercial organizations. They intend to operate profitably in well-functioning markets. Markets function efficiently when there is a large number of buyers and sellers and

---

[2]   In case of for-profit organizations, it is often about how their customers and brand connect to the cause.

[3]   There is evidence that many not-for-profits indulge in corrupt practices and there is leakage of resources even from their operations. However, for the sake of this analysis, I have assumed that it is an exception and the not-for-profits are not resorting to any illegal means.

both parties have adequate information about the other to make choices. Such conditions create a high degree of competition that incentivizes organizations to become better at what they do and to deliver products and services at a fair price. While actual markets satisfy the above conditions in varying degrees, putting constraints on choices before producers and consumers, for-profit commercial enterprises continue to operate only if they can do so profitably within a certain time horizon. They raise money through debts, which is risky because they will have to pay interest irrespective of their financial performance and through investments by shareholders. While their primary objective is to maximize shareholders' return, the minimum return that they have to provide to the shareholders need to be above the risk-free rate of return, that is, the return the shareholders would have obtained by investing in risk-free instruments, such as government bonds.[4] If they are unable to provide such returns within a defined time window, it is highly likely that that organization will cease to exist.[5]

In between these two extremes, that is, the perpetually loss-making not-for-profits and the commercial for-profit organizations, exist social enterprises with inclusive business models, which have been the focus of this book. They have a revenue model and thus they do not depend on grants or donations in the steady state. Instead, they seek funds as investments like a for-profit organization. However, the key difference is their mission, which is to maximize social impact and not shareholders' return. This implies that while they should not make losses, their returns to their investors are unlikely to be anywhere close to that of for-profit enterprises. Returns to investors may be actually lower than the risk-free rate of return, that is, their investors would make more money if they invested in risk-free assets. Think of investors that we discussed in Chapter 4 on Rang De. The investors were getting a return of only 2 per cent on their investments, which was lower than post-tax interest

---

[4] In financial terms, the returns should be greater than weighted average cost of capital, since the capital invested in the organization is usually a mix of investments and debts.

[5] A for-profit organization can exist for a while even when making losses because investors anticipate that it will make profits eventually, which will more than compensate for all the losses that the organization has incurred.

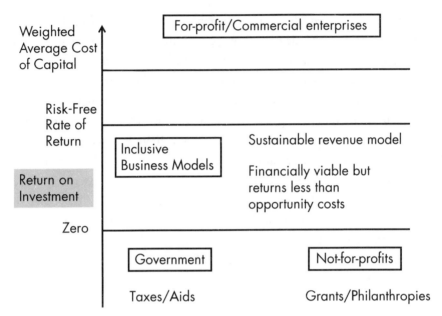

Figure 12.1 Schematic for Mapping Various Organizational Forms

Source: By author.

rates on bank fixed deposits[6] that are relatively risk-free. Despite such low rates of return, investors invest in inclusive businesses because they want to create positive social impact. Their objective is to maximize social impact and not their returns. That is the reason why such investors are called 'impact investors' and their investment 'patient capital'.

The relative position of these four categories of organizations with respect to returns that they can provide is represented in Figure 12.1. The schematic can be useful in guiding social entrepreneurs to decide what form of organization they should create to address the social need that they have chosen. It can also be useful in setting expectations among impact investors about the returns that they can expect if they invest in inclusive businesses. It will communicate

---

6   Interest rates in fixed deposits with banks in India were about 4 per cent in May 2020, when the economy was under severe downturn, while it was around 6 per cent in 2019.

to an investor the message that such organizations are not the best investment options if they want to maximize their financial returns. And finally, it can also be a reckoner for the social enterprises about whether they are remaining focused on their social mission. If a social enterprise starts providing returns to its shareholders that is significantly above the risk-free rate and comparable to returns of for-profit enterprises, it can be a signal to them that they have probably deviated from their social mission and it is time to evaluate their business model to find out if there was need for course correction.

LEARNING FROM INCLUSIVE BUSINESS MODELS

As was discussed above, there is no 'one best way' to deal with the problems of the poor. Different kinds of organizations need to get involved individually and collaboratively to provide products and services that are needed by the underserved. Only then will we be able to pull millions out of poverty in India and other nations facing similar conditions. Even when we look at inclusive business models, there are a variety of ways by which they are addressing the needs of the poor and balancing their other objective of remaining financially viable. In this last section, we synthesize our learning that is mostly based on the cases discussed in the book. Not all inclusive business models are able to address the needs of the poor or create positive impact on their lives. Even though we have not discussed many failed inclusive businesses in this book and, therefore, can be accused of survivorship bias,[7] we have discussed in brief the failure of the microlending industry in India as well as the struggles faced by some of the organizations, such as Vaatsalya and RuralShores, in making their model scalable or financially viable. We now make an effort to identify patterns among the anchor cases in the book to understand what some of the levers may be for creating business models that are both inclusive and financially viable.

---

[7] Survivorship bias happens when one looks only at examples of success and ignores those of failures. This can lead to false attribution of causes for success and correlation being confused as causation.

First, we would like to divide the organizations into two groups, namely those that cater to the 'life needs' of the poor and those that provide them with 'livelihoods'. While these are not always mutually exclusive compartments and there are organizations that are involved in addressing both, in general the principles of meeting these needs adopted by inclusive businesses seem to be different. Organizations that cater to the life needs of the poor sell some products or provide some service to the poor. Five of the organizations discussed in the book fall into this category when we consider their main line of activity. Gyanshala provides education, Vaatsalya healthcare, Rang De credit, SELCO solar lights and LaborNet skill training to the poor. The other five organizations increase income or livelihood opportunities for the poor by directly involving them in some kind of production activity, such as RuralShores and GNFC, or by improving the conditions of their existing occupation so that the poor get more income, as is the case for Hasiru Dala, Reliance's banana sourcing operations and IDE Nepal. There are some organizations that are involved in both. For example, IDE Nepal designs low-cost irrigation tools that enhance the marginal farmer's capabilities. But IDE does not sell these directly to the farmers. Instead, it develops entrepreneurs who sell these products and associated services to the poor farmers, thus enhancing income for both the farmers and the entrepreneurs. Similarly, SELCO creates entrepreneurs who rent solar lights to the poor and if one takes that into account, SELCO should also be considered as catering to the livelihood needs of the poor, like Hasiru Dala or Rural Shores.

ADDRESSING LIFE NEEDS

Let us first look at inclusive business that addresses the life needs of the poor. There, an important consideration should be what kind of need of the poor is being addressed. How has the need been identified and who has articulated the need? This is the reason why we find founders of inclusive businesses that are impactful in the long run to have often spent a long time immersing themselves in the context of their customers before they were able to give a final shape to their products and their services. Conversely, a product or service that is brought from outside without being customized for the context does not survive for long. The time that successful founders spent developing their idea and fine-tuning their business model enable them to understand the real needs of the poor and how, despite all the constraints, such needs can be addressed in a financially sustainable manner.

A good example of this is Harish Hande of SELCO, who argues that very often we confuse *needs* with *desires* and if a business model is created around the latter, it is unlikely to be sustainable. While it is sometimes difficult to distinguish between need and desire, empirical data shows that the poor, like everyone else, are prone to making choices that may be impulsive and seem irrational. However, because of their economic disposition, the cost that they incur for making a wrong choice is significantly more than what is incurred by a person who is financially well-off. As a consequence, it is important for inclusive businesses to be cautious about the nature of the product that they are selling to the poor. One can argue that selling low-cost alcohol[8] to the poor may be financially profitable but does not address the real needs as well as nutrition-fortified yoghurt. Likewise, as discussed in Chapter 4, when microlending organizations in India started to lend to the poor without paying attention to how the money was being used, it resulted in an unsustainable situation for the borrowers and the subsequent collapse of the sector.

It is also necessary to understand how the need was being addressed in the absence of the inclusive business model. Such a comparison will reveal the relative advantage of the product or service that the business intends to sell. If there is no relative advantage, the poor are unlikely to pay for it. Thus, when Vaatsalya opened a hospital in an underserved location, it understood the need to work with local doctors even though many such doctors were not professionally qualified. There was a trust-based relationship that had

---

[8] Spirit maker Diageo innovated on multiple fronts to sell low-cost beer to the poor in Kenya (Wilewska et al. 2012). While this case is a nice example of how innovations are needed across different elements of the value chain to make a product affordable to the poor, it also raises the question whether one needs to be sensitive about the nature of product that should be sold to customers at the bottom of the pyramid. It is possible that by lowering the price of beer, Diageo encouraged greater consumption and attracted erstwhile non-drinkers to drink beer, which may have its attendant health issues.

developed between them and their patients and unless Vaatsalya was able to show a clear difference between their service and those that existed, patients would have continued going to local doctors, making it difficult for Vaatsalya to attract patients and sustain their model.

Finally, inclusive businesses need to keep in mind that needs can evolve, as is suggested by classical literature in organization behaviour. When one's lower order needs, such as food, clothing and shelter are satisfied, one tends to crave for higher order needs, such as social acceptance and recognition. This evolution of needs seems to be creating a challenge for RuralShores, where they realized that many of their employees, having spent a few years with them, started thinking of migrating to cities, being attracted by certain aspects of urban life that they could not enjoy in rural India. This thwarted some of their expansion plans because they were unable to attract and retain employees in their rural centres.

The second important dimension that needs to be addressed is the price of the final product or service. Since the customer is poor, the product or service should not only be offered at the lowest possible price but the outflow of cash from the customer should also be matched with customers' cash inflows. All the cases that were discussed in the book relentlessly focus on cost control. They take out some of the superfluous or not-absolutely-necessary features of the products or services and try to derive economies of scale in every aspect of their design and operations. They also arrange credit for the customers or have flexible payment plans to match customers' income patterns. While the cases describe in detail how each of the organizations reduced their costs, so that the final price to the customer is kept as low as possible, of special interest are Rang De and Gyan Shala. While Gyan Shala fundamentally reengineered the education design and delivery that reduced the final price of their service, Rang De leveraged technology to reduce transaction costs in the credit market, enabling them to provide credit at very low interest rates.

Inclusive businesses often have the pressure to scale. Scale not only provides economies and can thus reduce the final price to the customer but it also creates greater impact. Society would like to see a successful model touch maximum number of lives in a positive manner. That is why leaders of successful inclusive businesses are often weighed down by expectations of scaling. However, closely related to the issue of scale is the extent of customization that is needed by the product or service. Many social entrepreneurs have experienced that products need to be customized to the specific needs of the poor because their contexts differ widely, even within the same geographic region. A product that does not take into consideration such context-specific differences does not solve the challenges that the poor face. Such customization can relate to the product or even to its associated services, such as financing. For example, a street vendor may not need a solar light for an entire day but just for four hours, and unless a renting model is created for him to have the light for those hours, he will not be able to afford it. However, customization requires greater effort on the part of the seller and often creates constraints for scaling. A product that is standardized is more suitable for scaling, but standardization might have the downside of neglecting the real needs of the poor. This was the experience in the micro-lending domain in India, where the pressure of scaling a standardized product led organizations to bypass the time-consuming process of understanding the real needs of the borrower. It is also why we find organizations like Rang De resorting to customization of their loan products as they evolved. Thus, inclusive businesses need to seek a fine balance between scaling that leads to greater positive impact and reduction of costs and the extent of customization that is necessary to address the real need of their customers.

Scaling inclusive businesses become challenging also because of the dispersed nature of these markets. Thus, Simanis (2012) argues that in case of many inclusive businesses, steep distribution costs offset the advantages gained from scale economies, and such businesses need unrealistic volumes and market penetration rates, close to 30 per cent, to break even. Therefore, he suggests that to be financially sustainable, inclusive businesses must seek collaborations or leverage existing distribution infrastructure. While there are not many examples of this in the cases that we discussed, one can view field partners of Rang De as existing distribution channels that it leveraged to reduce their costs of doing business. Likewise, SELCO took the decision of not getting into financial services even though providing credit to their customers was critical for their business. Instead, they leveraged the existing network of regional rural banks to provide credit. GNFC used its own existing distribution network for fertilizers, both to source neem seeds and then to sell neem-based products. Even though such leveraging leads to questions about scaling and long-term sustainability, it enabled GNFC to establish a business model very quickly without incorporating significant costs.

Inclusive businesses need to spend considerable time and effort in building relationships with their potential customers and communities as well as educating them about their products and services. The poor have been at the receiving end for ages and continue to be neglected and exploited. They also do not have access to various sources of information that can be expected of customers from privileged backgrounds. It is, therefore, likely that the poor will have apprehension about unfamiliar products or about unknown organizations, and inclusive businesses need to build trust with them before they can expect the poor to buy their products. Trust-building takes a long time and inclusive businesses achieve these in various ways, all of which are time- and effort-intensive. Thus, LabourNet provided a lot of services to migrant labourers, such as helping them open bank accounts and getting accident insurance that would have convinced the labourers about the welfare intensions of LabourNet, before they would sign up for their skills training programme. Vaatsalya understood the importance of working with local doctors to gain the confidence of the community, while SELCO spent time to understand the real need of its customers and suggested lighting solutions that would minimize the expense of the customers rather than maximize SELCO's revenue.

Finally, to make the product or services affordable to the poor, inclusive businesses seek opportunities for cross-subsidization. None of the anchor cases discussed in the book resort to cross-subsidization, which shows that it is not a principle that can be applied easily. Cross-subsidy in services can work effectively if an inclusive business model can provide the service to both the rich and the poor without raising the prices and impacting the service quality for the rich. These are important because rich customers usually have access to well-functioning competitive markets and, hence, they have the option to buy from someone that provides better quality or lower prices. The best examples of cross-subsidy discussed in the book are those of Narayana Hrudayalaya Heart Hospital and Aravind Eye Hospitals where, because of their large scale of operations, they are able to offer market competitive prices to their rich patients and remain financially sustainable despite subsidizing their poor patients. While we have not discussed in the book any case offering cross-subsidy in products, there are examples elsewhere, such as that of Grameen Danone (Yunus 2007) that sold nutrition-fortified yoghurt in Bangladesh, where customers in urban markets paid more than those in the rural markets, thus subsidizing them. Such price discrimination is only possible provided there is no arbitrage opportunity between these two sets of customers.

ADDRESSING LIVELIHOOD NEEDS

We next discuss our learning from inclusive business models that address the livelihood needs of the poor. One of the best ways of providing employment to the poor is to engage them in activities that are matched to their contexts and skill sets. While some of the organizations discussed in the book created new livelihood opportunities for the poor, all of them ensured that such opportunities were somewhat related to what the poor were already doing, so that it was not very difficult for them to make the transition and get engaged. Thus, RuralShores engaged the youth in transaction processing that was possible with the educational qualifications that the rural youth had and did not venture into English voice-based services,[9] which the youth would have found difficult to handle. Both IDE and Reliance worked with marginal farmers, improving their productivity in farming or guiding them towards new farming opportunities that the farmers could engage in with their existing competencies and knowledge. GNFC created livelihood opportunities through the collection of neem seeds that did not need any new skill to be developed, while HDI worked towards improving income opportunities for existing waste pickers. On the other side of the spectrum, we had Gyan Shala resorting to para-skilling, where the routine part of education delivery was isolated to create employment opportunities that matched the educational

---

[9] A significant number of organizations in the domain of business process outsourcing provide English voice-based services. These organizations take advantage of India's large English-speaking young population who are found in Indian metros and big cities. All such BPO organizations are, therefore, located in large Indian cities and metros.

qualification of young women from the communities who had studied up to twelfth standard.

Training and providing input for best practices was an essential feature of all these examples. While the employment opportunities that were created were familiar and related to what the poor were already doing, all the organizations realized the need to provide substantial input to the employees to improve productivity, enhance quality as well as to develop familiarity with certain novel aspects of their jobs. The most prominent among the examples was RuralShores, who had to familiarize the village youth with norms of professionalism, train them about the information technology interface as well as educate them about quality standards that were expected by their customers. IDE and Reliance worked closely with the farmers to educate them about best practices in farming and use of agricultural tools, while HDI constantly engaged with the waste pickers, teaching them about customer expectations and developing within them a service orientation that is usually lacking among workers in the informal sector.

The second important aspect of involving the poor in the value chain of production is to link them to markets. The poor are usually disaggregated, have limited bargaining power and are often unfamiliar with the dynamics of markets because they do not have access to information at the right time. This is why they depend on multiple intermediaries to bring their products and services to the market. While the intermediaries provide them with information that the producers lack, they also take away a fair share of margins and often turn out to be exploitative. Therefore, inclusive business models that work with the poor often reduce or remove such intermediaries and take upon themselves to link the producers to the market. This is what we witness in the cases of Reliance, GNFC, IDE and RuralShores. In the process, these organizations also assumed a significant part of the operational and business risks. For example, while it was possible to engage the rural youth in remote business processing, RuralShores sought the customers and ensured that there was a steady demand for their business. Likewise, Reliance ensured that the right quantities of bananas that matched the demands of the markets were produced and GNFC sought means of utilizing the neem oil that was generated from the seeds that were collected. Thus, when one involves the poor in the production process that creates livelihood opportunities for them, it becomes important for the businesses to ensure that there is enough demand from the market for such products and services, in the absence of which it will be difficult to sustain such activities. Even when it comes to providing skills training to the poor, as is the case with LabourNet, it is necessary that they are able to generate enough market demand for the work that the labourers were trained to do. Otherwise, better skills that they imparted through training will not translate into higher income. [10]

Many of the inclusive businesses working with farmers improve the efficiency and income of the farmers by reducing intermediaries. While disintermediation is beneficial for the producer, it can have negative consequences as well. For example, many of the intermediaries whom the business replaces may themselves be poor. Not all intermediaries are exploitative and many of them help the producers by aggregation, information dissemination and by providing credit. They might find themselves out of their jobs because of disintermediation. Moreover, in cases such as that of Reliance, where they appoint *hundikaris* as intermediaries, one has to be careful that the new intermediary does not become exploitative. Strategy literature talks about value creation and value capture. [11] In a two-party transaction between a customer and an organization, value creation refers to the difference between a customer's willingness to pay and all costs incurred by the organization, while value capture refers to the difference between the actual price paid by the consumer and all costs incurred by the organization. In a supply chain involving multiple

---

[10] The positive results created by an inclusive business model can be measured at multiple levels, such as output, outcome and impact. Outputs are immediate results of activities conducted by the inclusive organization; outcome refers to the short-term benefits that accrue to the receiver, while impact refers to the long-term benefits. In the case of LabourNet, a labourer acquiring skills through their training is an output; she getting a job because of her enhanced skill can be the outcome and an improved quality of life for her and her family because of her enhanced income will be the impact. For a detailed explanation, look at Stannard-Stockton (2010) or Parsons et al. (2013).

[11] G. Vroom and B. S. Ly (2010), 'Value Creation and Capture', Industry and Background Note, available at https://hbsp.harvard.edu.

players, the amount of value captured by each of the players is the difference between the costs incurred and price realized by each of them. The extent of value capture is dependent on the competitive position or the bargaining power of each of the players. The greater the bargaining power, the more the ability to capture value. Because of various reasons discussed before, poverty is both the cause and consequence of low bargaining power and inclusive businesses often improve the livelihood of the poor by increasing their bargaining power. This enables them to capture greater value. Therefore, while assessing their impact, inclusive businesses need to consider how value is being created and who all are capturing that value. A system is truly inclusive when the share of profits is distributed fairly across various players in the supply chain and none of them is left worse-off unfairly because of the interventions made by the business.

Many of the inclusive business models created entrepreneurs. The best example of this comes from HDI, which did not want to engage the waste pickers as employees because they believed that entrepreneurship went well with the basic nature of waste pickers, who like to be independent and masters of their own fate. To ensure this, HDI provided training to the waste picking franchise owners about management of business and helped them secure contracts with bulk waste generators. Likewise, IDE, which spent considerable effort in developing an ecosystem of livelihood for the marginal farmers, created entrepreneurs who manufactured and distributed irrigation equipment and GNFC created entrepreneurs who acted as intermediaries between the neem seed collectors and the organization. SELCO, even while directly selling solar lights, created entrepreneurs who rented solar lights to consumers who needed them only for a few hours. Entrepreneurship is inherently risky, and some authors have argued that the poor are typically forced to become entrepreneurs because they do not have the option of secured employment.[12] Inclusive businesses may not always have the option of employing the poor and, in such situations, creating entrepreneurs who can serve local markets they are familiar with can be a suitable option. In such cases, inclusive businesses need to shield the entrepreneurs as much as possible from market uncertainties by absorbing some of the operational and business risks.

---

[12]   Scholars have called them 'necessity entrepreneurs' (Caballero 2006) or 'survival entrepreneurs' (Naude 2007).

The poor often lack bargaining power because they do not realize the power of communities. Therefore, some of the inclusive businesses facilitate the creation of communities, so that they can present a united front before other stakeholders, which may be the government, local bureaucrat or a supplier. They educate the community about norms of good governance, so that internal processes are run democratically, free from biases of caste or gender. The best example of this is found in the case of IDE, whose purpose was to empower communities of marginal farmers. Since community-building activities do not generate any revenue, inclusive businesses find it difficult to spend time and resources for it. Thus, among the cases discussed, we find only IDE focusing on community-building because they are structured as a not-for-profit. The other organization that does the same is HDI. But even in their case, most of such activities are done by their sister organization, Hasiru Dala Trust, which, like IDE, is structured as a not-for-profit. This brings us back to the discussion that we had in the first part of this chapter regarding the importance of various organization forms and the limitations of inclusive business models. While building communities is important for producers who are poor, the constraint of achieving financial sustainability will make it difficult for inclusive business models to achieve it, and not-for-profits are in the best position to do so.

The final learning from the cases is about the aspirations of the poor. Very often, when inclusive business models create livelihood opportunities for the poor, be it through employment or entrepreneurship, that is the only choice the poor have. However, as their economic conditions improve, it is possible that their aspirations evolve. At that point in time, they might like to exercise choices. Someone who was handling waste might no longer want to deal with it, but might aspire to go back to his village, own a small plot of land and start farming. Someone else who was working in a rural BPO might want a life in a nearby city where she can work as a primary school teacher. This would present a dilemma for the inclusive business. For the sustenance of the business, it would like to minimize such attrition and retain its top performers. Yet, if it really wants to make a difference to the lives of its employees, it should allow them to exercise their choice and follow their aspirations.

Nobel laureate economist Amartya Sen (1999) describes poverty as deprivation in capability that prevents an individual from living a life of one's choice. Thus, the ultimate objective of any initiative towards removal of poverty should aim to expand the capability of the poor, so that they can choose to lead a life they aspire for. Therefore, inclusive business models, if they want to create the maximum impact, should look beyond the livelihood opportunities that they create and endeavour, as much as possible, to develop the capabilities of their employees that may eventually result in them exercising their choices and leave the organizations. While it will create a challenge for the business, inclusive businesses should be ready to pay that price because only then they would fulfil their mission of poverty removal.

Among our examples, LabourNet is directly involved in imparting skills to poor migrants that increase their choices to some extent. Additionally, we found HDI explicitly articulating this philosophy, whereby they offer to their franchisees the option of moving away from waste management. HDI also hopes that it would not need to exist as an organization after twenty years if they are able to fulfil their objective of significantly improving the economic conditions of the waste pickers as well as bring about a change in the behaviour of individuals and organizations towards generation, segregation and management of waste. That should probably be the objective of every inclusive business model – that they should be able to bring about such fundamental changes in their domains of intervention that the problems of the poor are eliminated and they would no longer need to exist as an organization.

A summary of the synthesis is provided in Table 12.1.

Thus, our idea about how to address the needs of the poor, so that they can come out of the vicious cycle of poverty, has evolved over time. While traditionally, the needs of the poor were met through charities and philanthropic activities, inclusive business models provide them with products or services or involve them directly in production value chains, which increase their income and create livelihood opportunities. Eventually, all such interventions, whether done through charity or by creating a business model, should enable the poor to develop capabilities that would allow them to exercise choice. None of these approaches is inherently superior to another. Each of them must be matched to the context and the specific needs of the poor. For example, several studies indicate that direct cash transfer to the poor is highly effective in reducing poverty and providing poor households with a range of benefits (Lowrey 2018). Neither are these are mutually exclusive. Ideally, all these approaches should complement each other to enable mankind to overcome possibly its toughest problem – that of poverty and inequality.

Table 12.1 Key Learnings from Inclusive Business Models

Inclusive Business Catering to Life Needs	Inclusive Business Catering to Livelihood Needs
Which need of the poor customer is being addressed? Distinguish between need and desire. Will the need evolve?	Engage in labour-intensive activities that are relatively simple to do. Routinize part of existing jobs by separating and standardizing them, provide training, input for best practices.
Reduce cost, arrange for credit, match payouts with income-related cash flows.	Establish market linkages, absorb business and operational risks, ensure adequate demand.
Balance trade-offs between scale and customization.	Create entrepreneurs, develop the ecosystem of complementary services.
Leverage existing infrastructure, collaborate.	Who captures value? Will de-intermediation lead to unemployment problems? Chances of exploitation?
Build trust with individuals and communities, reduce information asymmetry.	Build communities, develop governance capabilities, increase bargaining power.
Evaluate opportunities for cross-subsidization.	Is there an exit path? Do the poor like to be engaged in this profession? Does it match with community ethos?

REFERENCES

Agarwal, S. (2017). 'Government to Expand BPO Subsidy Scheme: RS Prasad.' *Economic Times*, 13 December. Available at https://economictimes. indiatimes.com/news/economy/policy/government-to-expand-bpo-subsidy-scheme-rs-prasad/articleshow/62056019.cms?utm_ source=contentofinterest&utm_medium=text&utm_campaign=cppst (accessed 3 August 2020).

Arakali, H. (2018). 'Hasiru Dala Is Lifting Waste Pickers Up from the Dumps.' *Forbes India*, 30 May. Available at https://www.forbesindia.com/article/ sustainability-special/hasiru-dala-is-lifting-waste-pickers-up-from-the-dumps/50337/1 (accessed 27 May 2020).

Bajpai, Vikas (2014). 'The Challenges Confronting Public Hospitals in India, Their Origins, and Possible Solutions.' *Advances in Public Health* 2014(4): 1–27

Balachandran, M. (2016). 'How an Indian Doctor Built a Billion Dollar Company by Making Heart Surgeries Affordable.' *Quartz India*, 7 January. Available at https://qz.com/india/587550/how-an-indian-doctor-built-a-billion-dollar-company-by-making-heart-surgeries-affordable/ (accessed 28 July 2020).

Banerjee, A. V. and E. Duflo (2011). *Poor Economics.* New York: Public Affairs.

Bhargava, A. (2019). 'How LabourNet Is Bridging the Gap between Employers and Jobless Migrants.' *Business Standard*, 18 May. Available at https://www. business-standard.com/article/companies/how-labournet-is-bridging-the-gap-between-employers-and-jobless-migrants-119051800847_1.html (accessed 6 August 2020).

Caballero, R. (2006). *The Macroeconomics of Specificity and Restructuring.* Cambridge, MA: MIT Press.

Carol, A.B. and K. M. Shabana (2010). 'The Business Case of Corporate Social Responsibility: A Review of Concepts, Research and Practice.' *International Journal of Management Reviews*. Available at https://doi.org/10.1111/j.1468-2370.2009.00275.x (accessed 23 May 2020).

Cafferata, R., G. Abatecola and S. Pogessi (2009). 'Revisiting Stinchcombe's "Liability of Newness": A Systemic Literature Review.' *International Journal of Globalization and Small Business* 3(4): 374–92.

Chakraborty, S. (2018). 'Gayathri Vasudevan's Labour of Love.' *Forbes India*, 22 November. Available at https://www.forbesindia.com/article/leadership-awards-2018/gayathri-vasudevans-labour-of-love/51865/1 (accessed 6 August 2020).

Chandran, P., N. Shekar, M. Abubaker and A. Yadav (2014). 'Informal Waste Workers Contribution Bangalore.' Available at https://hasirudala.in/wp-content/uploads/2016/08/1.-Full-Paper-Chandran-Informal-Waste-Workers-Contribution-in-Bangalore-1.pdf (accessed 2 April 2020).

Chatterjee, B. (2017). 'India Recycles 90% of Its PET Waste, Outperforms Japan, Europe and US: Study.' *Hindustan Times*, 19 February. Available at https://www.hindustantimes.com/mumbai-news/india-recycles-90-of-its-pet-waste-outperforms-japan-europe-and-us-study/story-yqphS1w2 GdlwMYPgPtyb2L.html (accessed 29 July 2020).

Damodaran, H. (2017). 'Empowering through Nimboli: The Story of a Mini-Rural Entrepreneur Laxmiben.' *Indian Express*, 6 July. Available at https://indianexpress.com/article/india/empowering-through-nimboli-4737754/(accessed 4 August 2020).

Das, G. (2019). *Jobonomics: India's Employment Crisis and What the Future Holds*. Gurugram: Hachette India

Das, A. (2017). 'India Relaxes Production Limits for Domestic Urea Producers.' *Independent Commodity International Services*, 28 April. Available at https://www.icis.com/resources/news/2017/04/20/10098742/india-relaxes-production-limits-for-domestic-urea-producers/ (accessed 20 February 2018).

Desmon, S. (2018). 'Beyond Bad Bets: Mosquitos Don't Just Bite at Bedtime.' John Hopkins Center for Communication Programs, 29 October. Available at https://ccp.jhu.edu/2018/10/29/beyond-bed-nets-mosquitoes-malaria/ (accessed 7 February 2019).

Easterly, W., (2007). *The White Man's Burden*. New York: Penguin.

Elkington, J. (2018). '25 Years Ago I Coined the Phrase Triple Bottom Line. Here Is Why It's Time to Rethink It.' *Harvard Business Review*. Available at https://hbr.org/2018/06/25-years-ago-i-coined-the-phrase-triple-bottom-line-heres-why-im-giving-up-on-it (accessed 25 June 2020).

Evans, P. and T. S. Wurster (1997). 'Strategy and the New Economics of Information.' *Harvard Business Review* 75(5): 70–82.

Fernando, N. A. (2006). 'Understanding and Dealing with High Interest Rates on Microcredit.' Available at https://en.wikipedia.org/wiki/Grameen_Bank (accessed 19 May 2020).

Fitzgerald, M. (2010). 'IT Jobs Trickling Down to Rural India.' *Irish Times*, 10 October. Available at https://www.irishtimes.com/news/it-jobs-trickling-down-to-rural-india-1.659471 (accessed 3 August 2020).

Giridharadas, A. (2019). *Winners Take All*. New York: Penguin.

Gupta, U. (2016). 'Neem-Coated Urea: Why Is Narendra Modi Govt Waiting for 5 Years to Make India Self-Sufficient in Fertilisers?' *Financial Express*, 24 November. Available at http://www.financialexpress.com/opinion/neem-coated-urea-why-is-narendra-modi-govt-waiting-for-5-years-to-make-india-self-sufficient-in-fertilisers/454215/ (accessed 20 February 2018).

Gulati, V. (2018). 'Indian "Help Us Green" Wins UN Award for Recycling Temple Waste, Empowering Women.' *First Post*, 12 December. Available at https://www.firstpost.com/tech/science/indian-help-us-green-wins-un-award-for-recycling-temple-waste-empowering-women-5716391.html (accessed 28 July 2020).

Hagiu, Andrei and Julian Wright (2011). 'Multi-Sided Platforms.' *International Journal of Industrial Organization* 43 (November): 162–174.

Harper, M. (2009). *Inclusive Value Chains in India*. Singapore: World Scientific.

Jayashankar, M. (2012). 'Selco's Harish Hande Wants to Spread the Light.' *Forbes India*, 21 January. Available at https://www.forbesindia.com/article/work-in-progress/selcos-harish-hande-wants-to-spread-the-light/32048/1?utm=slidebox (accessed 20 July 2020).

Karnani, A. (2006). 'The Mirage of Marketing to the Bottom of the Pyramid.' *California Management Review* 9(4): 90–111.

Jayakumar P. B. and E. Kumar Sharma (2015). 'Profits in Small Doses.' *Business Today*, 25 October. Available at https://www.businesstoday.in/magazine/

corporate/hospitals-are-now-taking-a-more-calibrated-approach-to-expansion/story/224406.html (accessed 24 July 2020).

Kannothra, C. G., S. Manning and N. Haigh (2018). 'How Hybrids Manage Growth and Social–Business Tensions in Global Supply Chains: The Case of Impact Sourcing.' *Journal of Business Ethics* 148(2): 271–290.

Kazmin, A. (2009). 'A Bright Idea That Helped India's Poor.' *Financial Times*, 25 February. Available at http://vol10.cases.som.yale.edu/sites/default/files/cases/SELCO/a_bright%20idea_that_helped_india.pdf (accessed on 6 August 2020).

Khanna, T. and K. Palepu (2005). 'Strategies that Fit Emerging Markets.' *Harvard Business Review* 83(6): 63–76.

Kellogg, D. E. and W. Nie (1995). 'A Framework for Strategic Service Management.' *Journal of Operations Management* 13(4): 323–37.

Krishna, A. (2007). 'Pathways Out of and into Poverty in 36 Villages in Andhra Pradesh, India.' *World Development* 34(2): 271–88.

Krishna, A. (2007). 'For Reducing Poverty Faster, Target Reasons before People.' *World Development* 35(11): 1947–1960.

Lahiry, S. (2019). 'India's challenges in Waste Management.' *Down To Earth*, 8 May. Available at https://www.downtoearth.org.in/blog/waste/india-s-challenges-in-waste-management-56753 (accessed 28 May 2020).

Lowrey, A. (2018). *Give People Money: How a Universal Basic Income Would End Poverty, Revolutionize Work, and Remake the World.* New York: Crown.

Magnier, M. (2010). 'Indian Outsourcing Firms Find Greener Pastures.' *The Los Angeles Times*, 21 June. Available at https://www.latimes.com/archives/la-xpm-2010-jun-21-la-fg-india-rural-20100622-story.html (accessed 3 August 2020).

Mair, J. and I. Marti (2009). 'Entrepreneurship in and around Institutional Voids: A Case Study from Bangladesh.' *Journal of Business Venturing* 24(5): 419–35.

Majumdar, D. (2018). 'Charting the Rise of Budget Private Schools.' *India Development Review*, 2 May. Available at https://idronline.org/budget-private-schools-education-india/ (accessed 6 August 2020).

Mindtree, (2014). 'I Got Garbage (IGG) - The Technology Platform for Waste Management Is Now Open for Bangalore Citizens.' 17 June. Available at https://www.mindtree.com/news/i-got-garbage-igg-technology-platform

-waste-management-now-open-bangalore-citizens (accessed 20 May 2020).

Murafa, C. (2020). 'The Path to the Covid Recovery Is Paved with Renewable Energy'. *Forbes*, 29 May. Available at https://www.forbes.com/sites/ashoka/2020/05/29/the-path-to-the-covid-recovery-is-paved-with-renewable-energy/#4fbf75af23da (accessed 29 May 2020).

Muralidharan, K., N. Chaudhury and J. Hammer (2011). 'Is There a Doctor in the House? Medical Worker Absence in India.' Department of Economics, Faculty of Arts and Sciences, Harvard University, Working Paper. Available at https://econweb.ucsd.edu/~kamurali/papers/Working%20Papers/Is%20There%20a%20Doctor%20in%20the%20House%20-%2012%20April,%202011.pdf (accessed 26 January 2021).

Nambissan, G. (2012). 'Low-Cost Private Schools for the Poor in India: Some Reflections.' Infrastructure Development Finance Company. Available at http://www.idfc.com/pdf/report/2012/Chapter_8.pdf (accessed 5 June 2020).

Naude, W. A. (2007). 'Peace, Prosperity and Pro-Growth Entrepreneurship.' WIDER Research Paper 2007/2. Helsinki, UNU-WIDER.

Ouchi, W. (1980). 'Markets, Bureaucracies and Clans.' *Administrative Science Quarterly* 25(1): 129–41.

Parsons, J., C. Gokey and M. Thornton (2013). 'Indicators of Inputs, Activities, Outputs, Outcomes and Impacts in Security and Justice Programming.' *DFID Practice Product*. Available at https://assets.publishing.service.gov.uk/government/uploads/system/uploads/attachment_data/file/304626/Indicators.pdf (accessed 15 November 2020).

Polak, P. 2008. *Out of Poverty: What Works when Traditional Approaches Fail.* San Francisco, CA: Berrett-Koehler Publishers.

Porter, M. and M. R. Kramer (2011). 'Creating Shared Value.' *Harvard Business Review* 89(1/2): 62–77.

Prahlad, C. K. (2004). *The Fortune at the Bottom of the Pyramid.* Philadelphia: Wharton School Publishing.

Prahalad, C. K. and G. Hamel (1990). 'The Core Competence of the Corporation.' *Harvard Business Review* 68(3): 79–91.

Plecher, H. (2020). 'Distribution of Gross Domestic Product (GDP) across Economic Sectors in India 2019.' World Bank, 28 July. Available at https://

www.statista.com/statistics/271329/distribution-of-gross-domestic-product -gdp-across-economic-sectors-in-india/ (accessed 30 July 2020).

Ramappa, K. B. and A. V. Manjunatha (2017). 'Impact of Neem Coated Urea on Production, Productivity and Soil Health in India.' Agriculture Development and Rural Transformation Centre Report, Institute for Social and Economic Change, Bengaluru, Karnataka.

Ray, S. (2016). 'Hasiru Dala Is Fighting for the Rights of Bengaluru Waste-Pickers and Turning them into Entrepreneurs.' *Your Story*, 9 August. Available at https://yourstory.com/2016/08/hasiru-dala (accessed on 28 May 2020).

Sachitanand, R. (2017). 'Why Companies like HUL, Patanjali, Dabur Are Taking a Crack at the Market for Ayurvedic and Herbal Products.' *Economic Times*, 15 October. Available at https://economictimes.indiatimes.com/ industry/cons-products/fmcg/why-companies-like-hul-patanjali-dabur-are-taking-a-crack-at-the-market-for-ayurvedic-and-herbal-products/ articleshow/61084207.cms?from=mdr (accessed on 4 August 2020).

Sen, A. (1999). *Development as Freedom.* Oxford: Oxford University Press

Sharma, M. (2019). 'Bengaluru's Waste Chokes Villages on Outskirts.' *Deccan Herald*, 18 August. Available at https://www.deccanherald.com/specials/ insight/bengaluru-s-waste-chokes-villages-on-outskirts-755134.html (accessed 20 July 2020).

Sivaramakrishnan, V. (2009). 'Rural BPO Centres Provide a Ray of Hope for Smaller Towns.' *Live Mint/Wall Street Journal*, 18 June. Available at https:// www.livemint.com/Politics/CMrahH1iLcF7YJeKEagRFL/Rural-BPO-centres-provide-a-ray-of-hope-for-smaller-towns.html (accessed 3 August 2020).

Shukla, M. (2020). *Social Entrepreneurship in India.* New Delhi: Sage Publications.

Simanis, E. (2012). 'Reality Check at the Bottom of the Pyramid.' *Harvard Business Review* 90(6): 120–125.

Smith, W. C. and A. Benavot (2019). 'Improving Accountability in Education: The Importance of Structured Democratic Voice.' *Asia Pacific Education Review* 20(2): 193–205.

Stannard-Stockton, S. (2010). 'Getting Results: Outputs, Outcomes and Impact.' *Stanford Social Innovation Review.* Available at https://ssir.org/articles/ entry/getting_results_outputs_outcomes_impact (accessed 15 June 2020).

Stinchcombe, A. L. (1965). 'Social Structure and Organizations.' In J. March (ed.) *Handbook of Organizations*. Chicago, IL: Rand McNally, 142–93.

Sustainable Jungle (n. d.). 'Selco India: The Art of Sustainable Business and Addressing Social Needs.' *Sustainable Jungle.com*. Available at https://www.sustainablejungle.com/sustainable-tech/selco-india-social-business/ (accessed on 17 March 2020).

Talgeri, K. and S. Singh (2018). 'BPO Industry Adds Lowest Number of Jobs in 7 years: Report.' *Economic Times*, 5 April. Available at https://economictimes.indiatimes.com/tech/ites/bpo-industry-adds-lowest-number-of-jobs-in-7-years/articleshow/63615037.cms?utm_source=contentofinterest&utm_medium=text&utm_campaign=cppst (accessed 2 August 2020).

Thaker, N. (2019). 'Selco Foundation: Using Solar Energy to Foster Entrepreneurship.' *Forbes*, 20 September. Available at https://www.forbesindia.com/article/beyond-suburbia/selco-foundation-using-solar-energy-to-foster-entrepreneurship/55359/1 (accessed 30 July 2020).

TheCityFix Labs India (2019). 'How This Waste Management Company Addresses Challenges in the Sector by Making Entrepreneurs of Waste Pickers.' *Your Story*, 15 March. Available at https://yourstory.com/socialstory/2019/03/hasiru-dala-innovations-waste-pickers-entrepreneurs-bmatxxvdbf/amp (accessed 20 July 2020).

Vaatsalya (2013). 'International Partnership for Innovative Healthcare Delivery.' Available at https://www.innovationsinhealthcare.org/Vaatsalya%20profile%202013.pdf (accessed 20 April 2020).

Vachani, S. and N. Smith (2008). 'Socially Responsible Distribution: Distribution Strategies for Reaching the Bottom of the Pyramid.' *California Management Review* 50(2): 52– 84.

Vitta, S. (2016). 'Can One Company Create Employment Opportunities in Each of India's 500 Districts? Yes, RuralShores Is on Its Way.' *Your Story*, 19 March. Available at https://yourstory.com/2016/03/ruralshores?utm_pageloadtype=scroll (accessed 31 July 2020).

World Health Organization (2019). 'Malaria.' 28 June. Available at https://www.who.int/news-room/facts-in-pictures/detail/malaria (accessed 7 February 2020).

Wilewska, K., C. Oliver, B. Herrera and A. Bajaj (2012). 'Bottoms Up'. *Business Today*. Available at https://www.businesstoday.in/magazine/lbs-case-study/

diageo-success-in-kenya-case-study/story/189547.html#:~:text=The%20 company%20chose%20to%20source,associated%20with%20sourcing%20 from%20afar (accessed 23 June 2020).

Yunus, M. (1999). *Banker to the Poor: Microlending and the Battle against World Poverty.* New York: Public Affairs.

_____. (2007). *Creating a World without Poverty: Social Business and the Future of Capitalism.* New York: Public Affairs.

_____. (2017), *A World of Three Zeroes.* London, England: Scribe Publications.

Zachariah, P. (2009). 'Rethinking Medical Education in India.' *The Hindu,* 9 September. Available at https://www.thehindu.com/opinion/op-ed/ Rethinking-medical-education-in-India/article16880031.ece (accessed 30 April 2020).

INDEX